ETHICS IN PUBLIC SERVICE INTERPRETING

This is the first book to focus solely on ethics in public service interpreting. Four leading researchers from across Europe share their expertise on ethics, the theory behind ethics, types of ethics, codes of ethics, and what it means to be a public service interpreter.

This volume is highly innovative in that it not only provides the reader with a theoretical basis to explain why underlying ethical dilemmas are so common in the field, but it also offers guidelines that are explained and discussed at length and illustrated with examples. Divided into three Parts, this ground-breaking text offers a comprehensive discussion of issues surrounding Public Service Interpreting. Part 1 centres on ethical theories, Part 2 compares and contrasts codes of ethics and includes real-life examples related to ethics, and Part 3 discusses the link between ethics, professional development, and trust.

Ethics in Public Service Interpreting serves as both an explanatory and informative core text for students and as a guide or reference book for interpreter trainees as well as for professional interpreters – and for professionals who need an interpreter's assistance in their own work.

Mary Phelan lectures in translation and public service interpreting at Dublin City University, Ireland, and is the chairperson of the Irish Translators' and Interpreters' Association. Her research relates to the historical provision of court interpreters in Ireland, current interpreter provision in various settings, and associated legislation.

Mette Rudvin completed her PhD in Translation Studies in the UK in 1997 and has been teaching a variety of English and translation and interpreting related subjects at the University of Bologna since 1996; she also set up the first university training course for legal interpreters for minority languages in Italy. She has specialized in Community Interpreting/PSI, a field in which she has published widely, but her areas of research and publication also include interpreting/translation and philosophy, translation and children's literature, ELF, language and game-theory, oral narrative, and Pakistan-studies.

Hanne Skaaden teaches interpreting at Oslo Metropolitan University, Norway. Her research covers first-language attrition and the bilingual migrant, remote interpreting and the process of professionalisation in PSI. She has extensive experience with interpreting in the Norwegian public sector.

Patrick Stefan Kermit has a background in philosophy and theoretical ethics, and has worked in interpreter education for many years. His research encompasses several projects looking into interpreting in the context of the criminal justice system in Norway.

ETHICS IN PUBLIC SERVICE INTERPRETING

Mary Phelan, Mette Rudvin, Hanne Skaaden, Patrick Stefan Kermit

Routledge
Taylor & Francis Group
LONDON AND NEW YORK

First published 2020
by Routledge
2 Park Square, Milton Park, Abingdon, Oxon OX14 4RN

and by Routledge
52 Vanderbilt Avenue, New York, NY 10017

Routledge is an imprint of the Taylor & Francis Group, an informa business

© 2020 Mary Phelan, Mette Rudvin, Hanne Skaaden, Patrick Stefan Kermit

The right of Mary Phelan, Mette Rudvin, Hanne Skaaden, and Patrick Stefan Kermit to be identified as authors of this work has been asserted by them in accordance with sections 77 and 78 of the Copyright, Designs and Patents Act 1988.

All rights reserved. No part of this book may be reprinted or reproduced or utilised in any form or by any electronic, mechanical, or other means, now known or hereafter invented, including photocopying and recording, or in any information storage or retrieval system, without permission in writing from the publishers.

Trademark notice: Product or corporate names may be trademarks or registered trademarks, and are used only for identification and explanation without intent to infringe.

British Library Cataloguing-in-Publication Data
A catalogue record for this book is available from the British Library

Library of Congress Cataloging-in-Publication Data
A catalog record has been requested for this book

ISBN: 978-1-138-88614-8 (hbk)
ISBN: 978-1-138-88615-5 (pbk)
ISBN: 978-1-315-71505-6 (ebk)

Typeset in Bembo and Stone Sans
by Servis Filmsetting Ltd, Stockport, Cheshire

CONTENTS

List of figures   *vii*
List of tables   *viii*

Introduction   1
Patrick Stefan Kermit
   0.1   Ethical theories, interpreters' professional conduct, and the question of how theories, codes of ethics, and actual practices are related   1
   0.2   Theory and practice   2
   0.3   The professional history and development of Norwegian Sign Language interpreters: the pre-professional era   5
   0.4   Ethics and recognition: a tentative conclusion   20
   Note   22
   References   22

Part 1 Situating interpreting ethics in moral philosophy   24
Mette Rudvin
   1.1   Introduction   24
   1.2   Contextualising PSI ethics: history, philosophy, and professional practice   26
   1.3   Ethics in philosophy   27
   1.4   Ethics in moral philosophy: four macro-areas   30
   1.5   The philosophy of ethics: a brief look at the development of some central tenets   37

1.6	The ethics of translation: ethics in Translation Studies	59
1.7	Summing up: the PSI-moral philosophy ethics interface	68
1.8	Conclusion: the existential anguish of choice and decision-making	73
Acknowledgements		74
Notes		74
References		80

Part 2 Codes of ethics 85
Mary Phelan

2.1	Introduction	85
2.2	Historical examples of interpreter ethics	85
2.3	Regulation of professions	86
2.4	Association codes of ethics	87
2.5	Advocacy	111
2.6	Company codes of ethics for interpreters	119
2.7	The Norwegian example	120
2.8	Intercultural mediators	121
2.9	Conclusion	122
2.10	Introduction	122
2.11	Ethics in real-life cases	122
2.12	Conclusion	137
References		138
Websites		142
Cases cited		145

Part 3 Ethics and profession 147
Hanne Skaaden

3.1	Why do we need professional ethics?	148
3.2	What is a profession?	150
3.3	How extensive is the domain for the interpreter's exercise of discretion?	161
3.4	Interpreting as interaction	171
3.5	Ethics, trust and the organisational aspect of professions	181
3.6	Conclusion: ethics, education and professional integrity	193
References		196

Index 202

FIGURES

1.1	PSI loyalty bonds	59
1.2	Interpreting domains: interpreting ethics at the (macro) social level and at the (micro) textual level	62
3.1	An international spectrum of response regarding the organisational aspect of the profession of interpreting in the public sector	182
3.2	The interplay between education (E), practice (P), and research (R)	187
3.3	The interpreter's vantage point	193

TABLES

1.1	Historical periods representing philosophical development: a timeline	38
1.2	Situations that might lead to ethical dilemmas	70
2.1	Characteristics of professions	87
2.2	Establishment of translator and interpreter associations	88
2.3	Code titles	91
2.4	Seven core principles and national organisations	94
2.5	Seven core principles and association codes of ethics	95
2.6	Other issues covered by national codes of ethics	99
2.7	Other issues covered by association codes of ethics	100
3.1	The performative aspect of the process of professionalisation	151
3.2	Factors which impact on the quality of a given interpreting event	191

INTRODUCTION

Patrick Stefan Kermit

0.1 Ethical theories, interpreters' professional conduct, and the question of how theories, codes of ethics, and actual practices are related

If you asked a random person what qualifications are needed in order to be an interpreter, chances are that the answer will be 'an interpreter needs to know the two languages that he or she interprets between'. This is by no means wrong, and for those who work as interpreters and those who study interpreting, knowing one's languages really well is immensely important. In addition, however, an interpreter needs to have both the theoretical and practical skills required for actual interpreting. That is, the interpreter must not only know the two languages in question, but also must master the processes in which interpreting is performed together with, and at the request of, people who do not share a common language.

What might be less obvious to many is that the people who rely on the interpreter's ability to establish their communication become dependent on the interpreter in similar ways as a patient becomes dependent on a health professional, a student on a teacher, or a client on a counsellor. All these dependent states of clientship share the same significant feature: the client is placed in a potentially more vulnerable situation compared to the professional whom the client is facing. Realising this, professionals like the ones described above discuss and develop principles, guidelines and practices meant to secure the clients' integrity and prevent different types of malpractice.

This book presents and discusses professional interpreting and interpreters' professional ethics. This book has been written in order to present research on interpreters' professional conduct and the underlying principles guiding interpreters' different practices. It is divided into three parts.

Part 1 presents different ethical theories throughout the history of philosophy. It explores how these theories have been mobilised in research and texts concerning interpreters, and seeks to identify aspects within the respective theories that are of particular relevance to interpreting and the interpreters' professional ethics.

Part 2 is dedicated to the analysis of existing codes of ethics for interpreters in different countries working under different regulations around the world. This analysis and the comparison of a large number of different codices, and the practices that they guide, reveal both significant similarities as well as differences. One central issue regards the question of whether or not an interpreter may lend any kind of support to a client, that is, in addition to the interpreting itself. This question of advocacy and its limits is important – and probably well known – to all interpreters. Part 2 further looks into the codes of ethics for interpreters who specialise in medical interpreting. A number of empirical examples of documented cases of alleged misconduct or controversial decisions by interpreters are presented and discussed. Section 2.11, entitled 'Ethics in Real-Life Cases', engages in questions regarding themes. such as interpreting quality, the role of the interpreter in specific cases, competency, impartiality, bribery, and neutrality.

Part 3 looks at interpreters' professional conduct and professional practices. It discusses questions regarding best practice, particularly in light of sociological theories about professionalism and the formation of professions. In this section, particular attention is paid to the understanding and scope of concepts, such as *profession*, the *exercise of discretion*, *trust*, and *virtue*. Part 3 illustrates that the interpreter fulfils the *performative aspect* of professional activity, yet, the function's *organizational aspect* of professionalisation – in terms of formal education – is underdeveloped. In conclusion, it is argued that this state of affairs has impact even on the *professional integrity* of those in charge of the interpreted institutional encounter.

0.2 Theory and practice

The three parts of this book discuss: (1) ethical theories and their relevance to questions regarding interpreting; (2) codes of ethics for interpreters; and (3) professional conduct and practices. In each part, theoretical approaches are both presented and contextualised with references to empirical examples and practices among different groups of interpreters.

The relationships between the three topics above are quite complex. For example, ethical theories are normally presented in the form of different ideas about principles, guidelines that can be followed in order to make correct decisions about right and wrong, or suggestions to help us pursue a good life. The people who develop such theories often make claims implying that the principles they suggest are valid independent of time and context. Moreover, ethical theories are often a part of even larger theories concerning matters such as what it is to be human or what we can know for sure.

If one tries to apply such ethical theories directly to general principles that many interpreters agree on, large gaps may appear between what is ethical and what is technical when it comes to interpreting. The question of confidentiality serves as a rough example to clarify this point. Confidentiality is a principle that one will find in most codes of ethics for interpreters. Interpreters are often very strict about confidentiality, signalling to the world at large that, for an interpreter, 'the less said about what we do at work the better'. Confidentiality is, however, seldom counted as a moral principle among people in general. Moral principles are concerned with how you should do the right things, and learning some of these principles is a part of the ordinary upbringing of children. You learn that you shall not steal from others, lie to them, or hurt them in any way. Such principles, well known and dating back to texts like the biblical 10 Commandments, are ethical principles. Confidentiality is not, in itself, such a principle. The reason that it figures highly in interpreters' most common understandings of ethically safe conduct is the general assumption that a lack of confidentiality can result in different kinds of harm to clients. A lack of confidentiality may cause harm, but it may not necessarily do so. Moral principles, however, are often considered to be of a more absolute character, at least those moral principles on which many people base their daily lives. Philosophers who formulate ethical theories generally suggest that their thoughts are valid for all humans, often independent of context. However, different theories about ethics may differ in various ways regarding which deeds are right and which are wrong.

Different arguments about deeds, such as theft and lies, can illustrate some of these fundamental differences between theories: most people agree that stealing and lying are generally wrong and something that should be avoided. But is it wrong to steal in a desperate situation, for example, in order to keep yourself and your family from starvation? In the same fashion, most people regard lying as undesirable. Nevertheless, most of us have told 'white lies' or omitted the truth, and sometimes we have done it for very noble reasons, for example, to spare a person from emotional distress. As will be presented more thoroughly in the following, there are different theories that will defend or reject the idea that stealing is defensible when done in order to save yourself or others. In the same manner, telling a white lie in order to spare someone might be considered ethically right according to one theory, but wrong according to another. The differences between these theories lie, at least in part, in the difference between judging the outcomes of deeds and focusing on their consequences (and here, stealing and lying may cause positive outcomes) verses focusing on a deed's underlying principle and judging it in accordance with that (here, the underlying principles suggest that we must always consider theft and lies to be wrong).

It is implied here that ethical theories, everyday ideas about right and wrong, and the ways in which interpreters find it reasonable to work are not necessarily compatible and are sometimes difficult to unite in a single idea about interpreters' preferred way of carrying out their work. To add even more to this complexity, the concept of 'professional ethics' must also be considered. As a scholarly discipline, theoretical ethics – normally concerned with ethical theories – deals with questions like 'What should I do in order to lead a good life?', 'Which actions are right, as opposed to wrong?' and 'Which moral principles should guide my actions?'.

Professional ethics is centred more around the question 'What does it mean to do a good job, and what should we do in order to promote ethically sound practices in our ranks while at the same time regarding other laws, rules, and regulations that govern our work?'. The questions asked in the context of professional ethics are thus more specifically linked to a professional practice – here interpreting – compared to general ethical theories that tend to aim at making blanket claims that are supposedly valid for everyone.

Professional ethics and questions about good professional conduct are frequently discussed, both in formal contexts such as conferences and workshops on interpreting, but also whenever and wherever interpreters congregate in more informal settings. This is not mysterious in any way. It is simply a part of what belonging to a profession means: interpreters' clients must expect a fairly uniform service in the sense that one interpreter's conduct cannot differ too much from another interpreter's conduct before questions are raised about what the 'right' way of being an interpreter consists of. Thus, interpreters need to talk to each other and ask each other questions like 'What do you usually do when this and that typical situation arises?' or 'How do you manage to avoid dealing with such and such?'. It is, however, important to recognise that the answers to such questions seldom can be given with finality, since such answers themselves depend on a variety of contextual factors. The one factor above all is the opportunity that interpreters have to make decisions for themselves about their daily conduct.

This means that the different sections of this book each grapple with different aspects of what is supposed to be unified in practice. How exactly the different aspects – (1) ethical theories and their relevance to questions regarding interpreting; (2) codes of ethics for interpreters; and (3) professional conduct and practices– should be unified is, however, not an easy question to answer. Interpreters in different contexts may have quite different working conditions and opportunities for making their own decisions about their conduct, so making broad normative statements about how things should be might not be very relevant. In addition, the question about good practice is never a question just about an individual interpreter's practice, but also a question about the conduct of the interpreter profession as a whole.

Instead of trying to come up with general arguments and explanations about how one should try to develop unified practices, the rest of this Introduction is dedicated to the description and analysis of one historical example showing the professional development and the emergence of professional ethics for one particular group of interpreters: Norwegian Sign Language interpreters in the period from the early 1970s to the new millennium. As this might seem strange, some methodological deliberations must first be presented.

0.2.1 A note on methods

There is one quite obvious reason for choosing this case: the author of this Introduction is himself a Norwegian Sign Language interpreter and has been occupied with interpreter education in Norway for a large part of the past 20 years.

Having said this, the case of Norwegian Sign Language interpreters was not chosen because it is believed to be representative of interpreters around the world. On the contrary, it was chosen because it is a quite singular example of very rapid and successful development: from a state of hardly any cohesion or sense of professional communality among Norwegian Sign Language interpreters, to a situation where interpreters today are educated, employed, and paid as Norwegian civil servants, conducting their work within the structure of a national, publicly funded, interpreting service.

Ethics have played an important role influencing the way that this change came about. Thus, by making Norwegian Sign Language interpreters an exemplary case, the aim is to identify some general points concerning the relationship between the three aspects that the different parts of this book deal with. It must also be added that this example is framed in ways that focus on the profession of interpreting and the professional development of interpreters, and not on Deaf[1] rights and history as such. The example is thus offered because of its general relevance to interpreters, regardless of whether they interpret between a spoken and a signed language or two spoken languages.

Though I have tried to describe the recent history of Norwegian Sign Language interpreters as accurately as I can, and in accordance with available sources, I am sure some Norwegian interpreters and Deaf people whose memory stretches back to the times I describe may object to some of my different attempts at making broad statements about the situation's development, as will follow below. I absolutely accept such critiques. One should be careful not to oversimplify history in general, and particularly events in our recent past for which questions about how and why things happened may still be contested. I have written the following historical expositions not in order to claim that this is the only possible way of portraying what happened, but because I want to identify and discuss how different aspects of interpreters' professional ethics are unified in real-life practices. What is of particular significance is that the example suggests that professional ethics and conduct are never just about doing the right things, but also always about taking care of a range of interests, including the interpreters' self-interest.

Methodologically, what I am attempting is thus to mobilise one from several possible narratives about the history of Norwegian Sign Language interpreters in order to engage the narrative as an example in a theoretical discussion about professional ethics. The first topic to hand here concerns the relations between the ethical theories known as utilitarian ethics and deontological ethics. These are thoroughly presented in Part 1, but for the sake of readability, short explanations concerning the key content of these theories are offered here as well.

0.3 The professional history and development of Norwegian sign language interpreters: the pre-professional era

It is no good trying to decide when sign language interpreting began in Norway, but records suggest that signing clergymen or teachers for the Deaf provided some forms of interpreting as far back as the seventeenth century. My interest, however, concerns the later years of what could be coined the 'pre-professional era'. In Norway, this would mean the 1970s. In the beginning of this decennium, sign language interpreters had gradually begun to receive some form of compensation for their services. Hospitals were among the first institutions to decide that interpreters should receive some money in order to be able to purchase food when on long assignments. Later, this reimbursement for expenses also was extended to cover the loss of ordinary income during time spent interpreting at the hospital. As this clearly indicates, no one at that time considered sign language interpreting an activity someone could have as full-time employment. On the contrary, sign language interpreting was seen as a mere charitable and voluntary service. These services were provided by hearing people who knew Norwegian Sign Language. Interpreters in those days were typically children of Deaf adults, but also signing clergy and teachers of the Deaf. Deaf people, when need be, would ask for interpreting as a favour or charity from these interpreters. To sum up the situation, we can establish that the pre-professionalised interpreters:

- lacked formal education as interpreters, though many doubtlessly had brilliant bilingual capacities in Norwegian Sign Language and spoken Norwegian;
- were not recognised at all as a profession or even as someone doing something that could be a full-time occupation;
- did not have any organisation or body either uniting them or representing them (interpreters knew about each other only through Deaf networks);
- did not have a code of ethics or any other externally or internally provided guidelines advising how best to work as an interpreter.

In spite of all these adverse circumstances, interpreting was still carried out between Deaf and hearing people in Norway at an increasing rate in the 1970s. General ideas about disabled people's rights to access and accessibility contributed to promoting the notion that interpreting was something that Deaf people should be entitled to when circumstances demanded it.

One might think that these pre-professional interpreters did not observe any professional principles, but that is hardly correct. Even though they did not have any common standards stated in texts or codes, they obviously provided interpreting and facilitated situations in ways so that interpreting could take place in some form or another. We know quite a lot about these practices, due mostly to the following generation of early professionalised interpreters, who would often – disparagingly – refer to pre-professional practices as those of the 'helper-interpreters'. It must be noted that many of these early professionalised interpreters were talking about their own prior conduct before the 'professional turn' – the phase in which the professionalisation of Norwegian interpreters started to pick up speed. It is, however, important to emphasise that I oppose any denigrating attitudes towards the pre-professional interpreters. All the evidence suggests that they developed rational practices that took into account the interpreters' working conditions at that time, as well as contextual factors, such as the lack of recognition of sign languages as real languages.

Typically, the pre-professional interpreter would see him- or herself as an assisting person who attended encounters between hearing and Deaf people predominately for the sake of the Deaf person. Even though linguists in the early 1960s had already revealed the true nature of signed languages and established beyond doubt that these are as fully fledged and natural as any spoken language (Stokoe 2005), in the 1970s this new understanding and recognition were largely unknown both to the majority of Deaf people and the interpreters in Norway, not to mention the general population. Hence, seeing oneself as someone lending support to a primarily disabled person was an obvious choice for the pre-professional interpreters. These interpreters usually had intimate knowledge of Deaf people: not only about the general state of their affairs – which were often characterised by marginalisation, discrimination and stigmatisation – but they also knew many Deaf individuals in a manner in which the interpreter could assess the Deaf person's needs when he or she had to attend a meeting, for example, with a general practitioner or some public service.

If one were to ask what the pre-professional interpreters did, the answer would be that, first and foremost, that they did what the situation there and then demanded of them. This might seem obvious but given that these interpreters lacked any kind of professional framework, the only thing they could rely on when deciding what a situation demanded was their own judgement. It seems clear that such deliberations on the interpreter's behalf usually considered the question of what the desired outcome of the situation at hand might be. Hence, if a Deaf person brought an interpreter to a job interview, it was self-evident that the interpreter would do his or her best to convey a favourable impression of the applicant and try to enhance the applicant's chances of getting the job.

Another example concerns the establishing of mutual understanding and the avoidance of misunderstandings: if a Deaf person visiting a doctor had trouble understanding the doctor's way of speaking, the interpreter would see it as quite unproblematic to extend the interpretation in an explanatory fashion so that the original message could be reworked with an added explanation so as to be more explicit and understandable. This would work both ways, implying that the interpreter could also explain information to a hearing client if the interpreter deemed it necessary. It must be added that these practices would often be invoked without the interpreter clarifying it for the clients, and that the interpreter often relied on his or her prior knowledge about the Deaf person when he or she decided what level of explication the situation demanded. In other words, the interpreter would see it as natural to take quite a lot of control over the dialogue if he or she felt that it was necessary in order to reach the desired outcome in the situation. This concern for outcomes could also be reflected before and after the actual interpretation took place. For example, if a Deaf person wanted to make sure he or she had correctly understood a letter from a public office where the Deaf person was summoned to a meeting, the interpreter would assist in not only conveying the messages in the letter before the meeting started, but also explaining the content and maybe offering advice about sensible preparations. In the same fashion, after a meeting, the interpreter could discuss what had been said with (normally) the Deaf client, thus offering further clarification and advice in case the Deaf person felt that he or she was not entirely satisfied with his or her understanding of what had actually taken place.

These are but a few roughly sketched examples, but they strive to explain a situation in which an interpreter might try to contribute to the realisation of whatever anticipated outcome a certain situation was established to obtain. This was of course very demanding at times, especially in situations where the question of whether desired outcome would occur was unclear or contested. If a Deaf person, for example, felt that he or she wanted to pour out frustrations and yell at a hearing person, the interpreter could choose to soften or moderate the most explicit language just to avoid embarrassment, thus playing down the element of conflict in the situation. This could be done with the best intentions on the interpreter's behalf, but it still illustrates that taking a lot of control over the communication also means taking on a certain level of responsibility for the situation itself and its outcomes. The tricky thing about this conduct is that it may have spared not only the client, but also the interpreter him or herself from embarrassment. At the same time, this conduct would prevent a client from having his or her honest opinion presented.

It must be repeated that in the 1970s – though the decennium today is presented as quite a progressive one – Deaf people in Norway were a marginalised minority. Norwegian Sign Language was not a recognised language in its own right, and Deaf students in the deaf schools were thus taught only spoken Norwegian. Many Deaf students left school, having achieved only poor results. Very few Deaf people managed to obtain higher education. Most Deaf people had either no education past the age of 16 years, or they had vocational education or training that allowed them to enter the labour market working in trade, crafts, industry or as subordinates in various private or public businesses.

0.3.1 Utilitarian ethics and the pre-professionalised interpreters

The idea that the consequences of our actions decide whether or not they are morally defendable is associated with a philosophy called 'utilitarianism'. This is an ethical theory credited to – in the context of Western philosophy – British philosophers Jeremy Bentham and John Stuart Mill, both liberal thinkers living in nineteenth-century England.

Bentham and Mill were influenced by the tradition of British empiricism, represented by Enlightenment philosophers, such as John Locke and David Hume. A leading idea among the British empiricists was that the world we can access through our senses is our only source of knowledge and understanding. This might not sound like a very radical idea, but at the time it was proposed it represented, among other things, the rejection of the idea that we owe our understanding of the world and of things like right and wrong to a capacity that is ours due to inner faculties that are unique to humans. Such an inner faculty could be seen as the result of divine intervention, and is expressed in the Bible's Genesis where, it says, man was created in God's image. When David Hume, and later Bentham and Mill, suggested that questions of right and wrong are entirely up to humans themselves to decide without regard to faith, this was very radical. Bentham, and later Mill, defended the idea that we are perfectly able, as rational subjects, to distinguish between right and wrong and to decide which is which. Ethics is thus a rational science dedicated to making decisions on moral questions.

To Bentham (2014), the sources of moral judgement must be sought in the empirical world and in what we can sense. He claims that we have two particular sensations to guide our decisions: the senses of pleasure and pain. He also introduces what he calls 'the principle of utility' (hence the name utilitarianism). This principle is based on the claim that all humans routinely calculate the expected outcomes of their actions and the utility of those actions. It is everyday knowledge that some actions promote pleasure, while other actions can cause pain. The utility principle thus implies that we regularly tend to carry out those actions whose utility it is to cause pleasure, and likewise tend to avoid actions causing pain. Bentham did not want to be accused of reducing all moral matters to simply bodily sensations of pain or pleasure, so he emphasised that pain and pleasure can also be seen as key elements in more complex concepts, for example, in the concept of happiness.

Utilitarianism can thus be summed up as the idea that right and wrong have to do with the desired outcomes of different actions. The moral value of actions is decided by the effects that the actions cause. If the effect of an action is someone's suffering, the action is most often – but maybe not always – immoral. If the effect of the action is happiness, then the action is morally appropriate. In cases where the same action causes suffering for some and happiness for others, the action's moral value becomes a question of which consequence is most predominant. If an action causes many people to be happy, and just a few to suffer, it might very well be a morally right action.

Here, it must be noted that utilitarianism refrains from attempting to specify exactly which actions are right and which are wrong, since one and the same type of action can be morally right according to its outcomes in one situation, but morally wrong in another. For example, theft – as already mentioned above – is normally something causing suffering for the bereaved victims, and even the thief is not always assured happiness as a consequence of his or her deed. Nevertheless, if a poor man steals from a rich person in order to save his family from starvation and death, the amount of happiness created by the theft for the family might surpass the rather insignificant suffering of the rich person who hardly registers his or her loss of property.

The other example mentioned above, which most of us can identify with, concerns the act of lying. Lies and deceit normally cause more suffering than pleasure. Nevertheless, most of us have been in situations where we have told white lies or omitted telling the truth. This is normally done with the best of intentions. We might want to avoid awkwardness or to spare someone's feelings, and quite often also spare ourselves trouble. Again, the question of whether or not a lie is permissible, or morally defendable, depends on the outcome of telling the lie.

When Bentham and later Mill published their work, it contributed to the development of the modern liberal understanding of individual freedom and equality. Both Bentham and Mill promoted gender equality, something that very few people did at that time. Mill also argued, on the basis of a utilitarian approach, that everyone should be entitled to freedom of speech and thought (see, for example, Mill 2010).

This liberal impulse is not something we can trace in the history of the pre-professionalised Norwegian Sign Language interpreters. What we clearly can identify is Bentham's principle of utility: the focus on outcomes and the desire to cause more pleasure or satisfaction than pain or dissatisfaction. It must be emphasised that it is doubtful that the pre-professionalised interpreters actively chose utilitarian ways of acting because they had read Bentham or Mill and thought utilitarianism was a really splendid theory. Nevertheless, when an interpreter chooses to go to great lengths in order to obtain a desired outcome of a situation that he or she had interpreted, this can be seen as following a utilitarian moral principle implying that the question of correct, or ethically defensible, professional practice was a question that could only be answered according to the outcomes that the practice contributed to. Above, we have implied that the practices of the pre-professionalised interpreters could take on forms where an interpreter would make rather paternalistic decisions on behalf of his or her clients. By utilitarian reasoning, to deny someone self-determination is normally something that causes suffering. Nevertheless, in the case where two clients are both happy with the outcomes after having been tacitly directed in their conversation by an interpreter, there is no obvious suffering. If the clients are happy and the interpreter satisfied, it is thus hard to suggest that things should have been handled differently. This, however, was exactly what the next generation of interpreters did.

0.3.2 Early stages of professionalisation

The end of the 1970s was marked by one particularly important event for Norwegian Sign Language interpreters. The Norwegian Deaf Association obtained public funding for the first interpreter training courses. These were short courses – in the beginning, only a couple of weeks. The teachers were a few well-known interpreters employed by the Deaf Association, and only students who knew Norwegian Sign Language and already worked as interpreters were admitted.

The establishment of formal education is one key factor that contributes to sparking a succession of important events. In the early 1980s, it was established that a passing grade in the interpreter course would entitle one to become a 'publicly certified' sign language interpreter. In the beginning, this did not mean a lot as the demand for interpreters surpassed that which could be supplied by the few certified ones. Many unqualified interpreters thus carried on as they used to. Before long, however, public funding for interpreters' salaries was being provided by the Norwegian Government, and it soon became a rule that non-certified interpreters could only receive payment if they had obtained a dispensation from the demand for certification.

The Norwegian Government did not merely recognise sign language interpreting as an activity that merited payment. What they recognised, and codified in the National Insurance Act, was Deaf people's *right* to an interpreter, and in order to fulfil this right, funding had to be provided to pay for the interpreting that Deaf people were entitled by right, and law, to access. In the 1980s, this right was limited to only a few and quite specific areas of life, such as education, rehabilitation and health care. By the late 1990s, however, the right to sign language interpreting became virtually unlimited in the sense that Norwegian Deaf people could – and still can – ask for an interpreter for any and all encounters with Norwegian-speaking people.

Obtaining a right to interpretation was the result of years of political struggle, mainly by the Norwegian Deaf Association. Some pre-professional interpreters were also working with the Deaf Association, thus forming an informal alliance between Deaf people and interpreters. The first interpreter courses were, in large part, a result of this cooperation.

The interpreter courses also sparked other significant events. They brought sign language interpreters from all over Norway together for the first time, and before long, these first classes of students and their teachers founded the Norwegian Association for Sign Language Interpreters. The association selected its leaders and tasked them with the responsibility of promoting interpreters' professional interests to politicians and authorities. Thus, systematic work began to obtain better work conditions, more funding for interpreting, better pay rates, longer education, and an organised public sign language interpreting service in Norway. These are all features of what it means to build a profession, something Part 3 of this book sheds further light on.

Already, by the second half of the 1990s and the beginning of the new millennium, the Norwegian sign language interpreters had achieved remarkable things:

- Those wanting to become interpreters now had to complete a three-year undergraduate university course. The first year was predominately dedicated to learning Norwegian Sign Language, and the second and third years trained students in different interpreting techniques as well as professional conduct.
- A national and independent public sign language interpreting service had been established with offices in every one of Norway's (at that time) 19 counties. The head of each office would be a sign language interpreter. There would be an administrative-responsible principal, or even an administrative staff at the larger offices, who handled requests for interpreting, assessed what kind of interpreting was requested, kept timetables to ensure the efficient use of interpreting resources, and – based on the assessment of the assignment at hand – picked the interpreters assumed to be best suited for that particular assignment and briefed them. Finally, depending on the number of Deaf people in each county, there would be a number of interpreters (from just one in the smallest

- county up to nearly 40 in those with the largest Deaf populations) employed as full-time civil servants in tenured positions.
- The national interpreting service would manage to meet the bulk of requests for interpreting. Due to its public funding, it could offer its services free of charge to Deaf people and did so in an efficient and non-bureaucratic manner. Thus, there was never any incentive for a competing private service, and publicly certified interpreters hence had effectively monopolised sign language interpreting in Norway by the mid-1990s. This also meant that all those who previously had worked as interpreters with dispensation had either quit working as interpreters or had obtained certification through education.

Such a rapid development from a state where interpreters were mainly regarded as charitable volunteers to a state where being an interpreter was a recognised profession, is – as far as I know – unprecedented for interpreters. In terms of education, salary and working conditions, interpreters could compare themselves with Norwegian nurses, teachers, physiotherapists or social workers at the end of the 1990s.

A number of factors promoting this development have already been mentioned: Deaf people's publicly recognised right to interpretation is probably the most important factor. The general notion of anti-discrimination and policies that aimed at securing Deaf people equal access to education, work and public services was another important factor. The 1990s were also the decennium in Norway when the linguistic uncovering of sign languages as fully-fledged languages finally became generally recognised in Norway. This did away with ideas about Norwegian Sign Language as a crude communication system inferior to 'real' languages such as spoken Norwegian. Thus, both Deaf people and interpreters could now discard any previous notions of sign language interpreting as something different from interpreting between any two spoken languages.

The alliance between the Deaf Association and the interpreters who wanted to instigate changes proved effective. Interestingly, and not quite intuitively, the setting-up of a public interpreting service meant that all previous formal bonds between the Norwegian Deaf community and the interpreter services were cut. Informally, there was, and still is, a clear sense of an alliance: the work that Deaf people and interpreters have done was not aimed solely at securing jobs for interpreters. On the contrary, the drive and energy that interpreters showed in the 1980s and 1990s were also fuelled by the ambition to contribute to greater social justice and more access and participation for Deaf people. That the Norwegian interpreting service should be independent and public was seen as favourable to both Deaf people and interpreters, compared to a system – which can still be found in several other countries – where the Deaf Association was paid public money to handle demands for interpreters. Some of the rationale for this view of an independent service is linked to another factor not yet touched upon: the newly founded interpreter association quite quickly produced the first codes of ethics for Norwegian sign language interpreters, and this codex would prove to be a very important tool for a young profession striving both for better practises *and* for public recognition as a profession.

0.3.3 *The Norwegian code of ethics for sign language interpreters*

Codes of ethics for interpreters are presented extensively in Part 2 of this book. The very first code of ethics for Norwegian Sign Language interpreters was drawn up in 1983 by the Norwegian Deaf Association in cooperation with the Association for Sign Language Interpreters. After only a couple of years, the interpreters passed their own codex, thus emphasising the above-mentioned severing of formal ties with the Deaf Association. The codex reflected that the interpreters were well aware of the international development in interpreting ethics. It laid down four basic principles that are still in operation to this day (even though the codex has been changed several times), and that can still be found in other codes of ethics for interpreters around the world (Kermit 2007):

The first principle is *confidentiality*. The code lays the same duty of confidentiality on interpreters as that of all other civil servants. These regulations on confidentiality are codified in the Norwegian Public Administration Act, and the code of ethics refer to these regulations.

The second principle is *impartiality*. The interpreter must not – implicitly or explicitly – favour one client above another. All clients depending on the interpreter's services are entitled to equal treatment by the interpreter.

The third principle can be regarded as a further specification of the second principle. It is that *the interpreter has only one task: that of interpreting*. Thus, an interpreter cannot take on other responsibilities when interpreting. For example, the responsibility for clearing up misunderstandings lies outside the interpreter's responsibility.

The fourth principle regards the manner in which the interpreter is supposed to interpret: *the interpreter interprets everything that is uttered in the conversation, without adding or retracting information*. Even though it is a mere topic of philosophical speculation to suggest exactly what this means, as a practical working principle, this is quite straightforward. The interpreter will strive to render your words to the other person in the same form and meaning as when you uttered them.

Summing up these four principles, it is easy to see how they renounce many of the pre-professional practices. Instead of an interpreter who would strive to facilitate things in order to secure desired outcomes, the first codes of ethics promoted and emphasised an idea of the interpreter as simply and solely the pipeline through which utterings stream back and forth between clients whose only need is language translation. This idea about interpreting is today often called the *conduit model*, after the French word for 'pipe' (see, for example, Pöchhacker 2004).

The fundamental idea built into this model is this: most people take care of themselves and their own interests, and they make their own decisions in everyday life while constantly interacting with other people. Simply because a person finds him- or herself interacting with another person through an interpreter, this should not in any way change the obvious and self-evident right to govern one's own life in the same manner as one would otherwise do.

Another slightly different way of saying this would be to maintain that the only relevant barrier to normal communication and interaction between two persons requiring the services of an interpreter is that they have different languages. The interpreter's job is to alleviate this one particular barrier, and only this one, thus enabling the clients to go about their business in exactly the same manner as if they had shared the same language.

The conduit model was already being criticised by researchers in the beginning of the 1990s. Scholars like Cecilia Wadensjö (1992; 1998), Cyntia Roy (1993), and Melanie Metzger (1999) all refuted the idea that the interpreter could reduce his or her services to the point where it would consist only of the single task of translating, like some sort of an advanced translation machine. Instead, they described the interpreter as a participant whose presence influenced the situation and necessitated that the interpreter in one way or another facilitate sensible interpreting taking place.

If the conduit model had many flaws in the eyes of scholars, it was – and still is – highly influential regarding the ways that Norwegian sign language interpreters' codes of ethics have been formulated in the period stretching from the mid-1980s to recently. This is in a way quite understandable, particularly if one considers two important factors.

First, many of the early professionalised interpreters had work experience dating back to the pre-professionalised era. They knew very well the difficulties that could arise in a work situation where there were no set limits to the interpreter's professional responsibility. On the contrary, the interpreter was often put in a situation where he or she took on responsibility for almost everything in an attempt to secure the anticipated outcomes.

Second, in light of the clearer understanding that interpreting is an activity centred around the mediation between two different languages and not an activity where the interpreter first and foremost tries to help one particular client, the conception of this as helpfulness in some ways came into question. The pre-professional interpreters had no doubt strived to improve the lives of Deaf people. The manner in which they had done this, however, could be characterised as quite paternalistic: the interpreter made decisions, particularly on behalf of the Deaf client, and often saw it as natural to do so. Even though this happened at a time where Deaf people were severely marginalised and experienced many difficulties when trying to navigate the hearing society on their own, it does not follow automatically that the interpreters thus should allow themselves to make decisions on behalf of their Deaf clients.

The code of ethics that was orientated towards the conduit model was, hence, not only about restricting and limiting the interpreters' professional responsibilities. It was also very much oriented towards empowering Deaf people. The recognition of sign languages as fully-fledged languages in particular was a turning point through which both Deaf people themselves and interpreters became aware that Deaf people, instead of being identified as primarily hearing impaired, could be seen as members of a linguistic community. When interpreters 'only' interpreted, this was done to emphasise that a Deaf person and a hearing person are fundamentally equal to the interpreter. Having said this, many Deaf people in the early 1990s found the early professionalised interpreters much less accommodating compared to the pre-professionals. Where the latter used to offer assistance, for example, explaining a Norwegian concept or explaining the content of letters where a Deaf person was summoned to a meeting, the early professionalised interpreters instead impressed on their clients that their sole task was to interpret.

0.3.4 Deontological ethics

The idea that the difference between right and wrong actions can be specified in general rules is age-old. The biblical 10 Commandments are an early example of codified rules laying down, for example, that killing, stealing or lying is wrong. This way of reasoning about morals is not too flexible with rule exceptions, because the principles underlying the rules are seen as truths that we are duty-bound to accept.

In the previous section about utilitarianism, it was mentioned how British empiricists suggested that all true knowledge must be derived from what we can sense, and that humans have no innate inner faculties that set them apart from other things in the world. In particular, David Hume's writings on these issues outraged the German philosopher Immanuel Kant. To him, no solid foundation for setting right apart from wrong can be found when our sensations alone are providing guidance. On the contrary, Kant claimed that the ability to distinguish right from wrong is a faculty that sets humans apart from all of Earth's other living creatures.

There is, nonetheless, an important similarity between Kant, the British empiricists, and Bentham and Mill: they all defend the idea that humans are capable of making rational decisions on the difference between right and wrong. Kant, however, rejects the idea that the sensible world is our only source of knowledge. On the contrary, Kant argues that since we are all free, self-determining individuals, each of us have a capacity for reasoning independent of our sensations. The conviction that I am an autonomous, free individual is not something that I can sense. This conviction is something prior ('a priori', Kant 1989) to knowledge derived from the sensible world.

That we are free does not mean that we are allowed to do whatever we see most fitting for the situations we are in, according to Kant. On this, he rejects the utilitarian notion of outcomes that produce happiness or pain. To Kant, calculating the outcomes of our actions is a precarious business, because cause and effect in the sensible world are complex phenomena that we cannot fully oversee or control. It is a daily realisation that things do not always work out the way we planned, and that actions taken in order to do good can turn out to cause harm instead. Thus, to Kant, it is our intentions that decide the moral quality of our actions, not the actions' outcomes.

This might sound quite appealing, but Kant does not suggest that we simply have to rely on what we merely wish to intend by our actions. Since we are free agents capable of rational reasoning, our moral responsibility reaches further: we have a responsibility to rationally consider if the principle (or 'maxim', Kant 1989; 1996) underlying our actions is suited to promoting human autonomy and also works universally as a principle for all autonomous agents.

This might sound complicated, but the argument Kant makes is an argument that many have interpreted to mean that we have to obey universal moral rules in order to be sure that our actions are the right ones. These rules must be based on rational consideration deliberating how we observe our duty to promote moral laws and human autonomy.

Again, the act of lying or not telling the truth, used as an example above, can serve. Even if I recognise that a white lie may have short-term outcomes that might seem good in the moment, I cannot possibly defend the principle (maxim) underlying lying. If I permit myself to lie, I, at the same time, suggest that this should be permissible for all other rational and autonomous subjects. In other words: if I lie, I suggest the universal moral rule that it is right to lie. As a rational subject I can, however, easily reason that such a rule will mean the end of all normal interaction with others. In our daily lives, we depend on the principle that telling the truth and being honest are regarded as right, whereas lying and deceiving are wrong. If the moral distinction between truth and lies is dissolved, so is the possibility of meaningful interaction with others.

It must be added to this example that Kant also emphasises something else: since our capacity for reason is so immense, our moral responsibility in the world is also so serious that we must oblige ourselves to commit to the moral law we lay on ourselves. Thus, to tell the truth and avoid untruth is not something we should do because it suits our temper, but something we should do because it is our moral duty. Kant is quite strict on this point. My moral feelings and any wishes I might have to do good are of no interest to my actions' moral value. It is only when I observe what my moral duty is and act accordingly that my actions are moral.

Summing up this version of deontological ethics (or deontology for short), what is outlined here is a way of moral reasoning based, first, on the principle that what I do, I must rationally be able to want to allow all others to do. It has been pointed out that this could be rephrased as a negative version of what in the biblical context is referred to as the 'golden rule' and is also known from Confucianism: 'so whatever you wish that others would do to you, do also to them' (Matthew 7:12). In Kantian terms, the negative version could be phrased 'whatever you *do not* wish that others would do to you, do also *not* to them'.

Second, we cannot allow ourselves to make excuses and exempt ourselves from the obligation to follow these universal rules that we, deep down, recognise that we want everybody else to commit to. It is in light of this that even white lies become impermissible and immoral, and it is our duty not to succumb to the temptation of lying.

It is debatable whether or not Kant intended that his theoretical views on how we rationally distinguish between right and wrong should be taken literally and turned into working ethical principles in people's everyday life. Kant wanted to refute the utilitarian conception of morality, and he probably both respected and recognised ordinary people's decency and attempts to live good lives. His moral philosophy, nevertheless, has made a huge impact on our modern culture, both for better and for worse. His thoughts on the significance of every person's autonomy have been a key inspiration for modern concepts about human rights and human dignity. (And, interestingly, here Kant's thoughts are not at all at odds with Mill's utilitarian arguments defending the liberal principles of free speech and freedom of thought and faith.) On the other hand, history tells us that Kant's ideas about moral duties can easily be perverted into a general principle suggesting that observing one's 'duty above all' is in itself a moral virtue.

After the Second World War, a number of Nazi leaders and supporters were accused of crimes against humanity. In the trials held at Nuremberg and in Jerusalem in the late 1940s and 1950s, several of these war criminals defended themselves by claiming that they had only acted according to orders from above, and thus had only done their duties. Further, many also expressed the view that doing one's duty was a moral principle in itself. The philosopher Hannah Arendt (1998) discusses this conception of duty and argues that the German people, influenced by Kant and Lutheran Christianity, were vulnerable to this tragic confusion where they could mistake Kant's theoretical idea about a duty to observe the moral law inscribed in all of us for a principle stating that there is no higher moral law than that of obeying one's superiors and doing one's duty accordingly. The tribunal passing sentences in Nuremberg emphasised that everyone is morally and legally responsible for their own actions, no matter if they were commanded to act or not. Obeying an order to do something immoral or illegal does not exempt one from personal responsibility for that action.

0.3.5 Deontology and the early professionalised interpreters

There are several interesting connections between the theoretical ideas about deontological ethics and the development of professionalism and ethical codes of conduct among Norwegian Sign Language interpreters in the 1980s and 1990s. Nevertheless, it must be clearly stated here that there are no indications that the interpreters at this time actually made the conscious choice to adopt a new deontological approach to their professional ethics. Again, as was the case with the pre-professional interpreters, this alignment of actual history with ethical theories is not a reconstruction of events, but the mobilisation of actual events that can serve as examples showing how historic interpreting practices have features that suggest shifts in orientation that resemble differently orientated ethical theories.

It is thus quite easy to observe that the transition from pre-professional to early stages of professionalisation is marked by the writing of an ethical codex stating uniform rules and principles for any sign language interpreter's conduct.

These principles are, it is important to emphasise, not the above-mentioned four rules of professional conduct. These four are merely instrumental rules describing how an interpreter should work. They are not themselves moral principles as such. The deontological moral principles underlying the Norwegian Sign Language interpreters' code of ethics are above all to respect and promote the clients' autonomy. This is a principle very much in line with Kant's thoughts: he formulated the principle that it is impermissible to use another person solely as a means to achieve one's own ends. To use another person to achieve one's own ends might not sound very nice, but in reality, we do this all the time. If I ask a stranger what time it is, I am using this person to get information that I want. If I go shopping, the person at the checkout is someone I encounter in order to pay, not because I take a particular interest in him or her. It is thus Kant's phrase *solely* that is important. We use each other all the time to obtain our own various ends. Treating a person solely as a means to obtain my own ends, is, however, impermissible. Thus, the general politeness expected when you ask someone the time is not only the convention; it is also a way of stating that they recognise you as an autonomous person equal to them. Likewise, paying at the checkout is in itself an act that balances a transaction where mutual benefit is obtained: I get my commodities, the person at the checkout gets my money. In addition, such brief meetings as that at the checkout are also normally accompanied by an exchange of polite niceties, expressing and emphasising the mutual recognition that we are both autonomous individuals.

When the code of ethics for Norwegian Sign Language interpreters emphasise that the interpreter should limit his or her role to those things that concern only interpreting, this can be understood as a way of respecting and promoting the clients' autonomy. The interpreter is not supposed to make decisions on behalf of their clients, or act in any other way that could limit the clients' autonomy. It is important to note that this principle also applies to situations where the interpreter may think that the clients are not acting according to their own best interests. When such situations occur, the difference between following rules and focusing on desired outcomes is quite clear. An interpreter oriented towards deontology must focus on their principles and duty to respect the clients' autonomy, and not focus too much on what the outcomes in the present situation might be.

At the same time, there are some aspects of the history of the early professionalised interpreters that have less to do with ethical principles and theories and more to do with the young profession's self-interest. Among other things, there are also examples implying that some interpreters confused duty with ethics.

0.3.6 Professional ethics and deontology as tools for promoting change and involving new risks

The principle of promoting the clients' autonomy by means of limiting the interpreter's task to those actions purely concerning interpreting was very progressive in the late 1980s. Today, other professions such as nurses and social workers have also cast off more patriarchal models of professional conduct in which the patient or client was subjugated to the professional because the latter 'knew best'.

At the same time, choosing a deontologically orientated code of professional ethics did not serve only the interpreters' clients. To a great extent, this new orientation served the interpreters themselves and their struggle to become a profession. The above-listed remarkable achievements – education, decent salaries, employment as civil servants, a national and independent public sign language interpreting service monopolising sign language interpretation – were not the results of the new ethical code alone, but the ethical code of conduct with its deontological orientation was a considerable factor in bringing about these achievements.

The reason for this major shift has to do with the significant structural difference between utilitarianism and deontology. Utilitarianism suggests that moral reasoning must start with the here and now, and consider what actions are the best possible under the given circumstances. As such, utilitarianism does not challenge the state of things, but rather advises us to make the best of them. In addition, it is the single individual who must decide the appropriate measures to secure the best possible outcomes. Deontology, on the other hand, has a built-in programme for social change because it is less concerned with the state of reality and much more focused on how things *should* be. The moral principles laid down in deontological theory are not based on the here and now, but on a rational idea about what ought to be right. In some sense, acting according to principles out of a sense of duty while at the same time disregarding reality is to demand changes. In addition, deontological reasoning encourages the question of what is right for us as a collective, not only what I as an individual ought to do.

These aspects might interest those who would want to discuss (theoretically) the benefits and weaknesses of utilitarianism versus deontology. From a more practical perspective, I simply want to point out that the adoption of deontologically orientated professional ethics also promoted additional principles that might not be ethical at all. First, deontologically orientated professional ethics promote the idea that the Norwegian Sign Language interpreters should adopt uniform and collective practices, thus making sure that a client could expect the same predictable service independent of which interpreter he or she was assigned. At the same time, in the collegium of interpreters, it is 'one for all and all for one' in the sense that what one does reflects back on all, both for the better and for worse.

Second, it became a goal in its own right to uphold and insist on this uniformity in order to make stronger demands for change and improvements such as better education, better organisation, and more rights. As mentioned above, the Norwegian Sign Language interpreters were very successful in professionalising and achieved great improvements.

Third, there was also a clear demand that all interpreters should be loyal to the demand for uniformity. Such demands are well known historically from the histories of the trade unions or labour unions, and they are not unproblematic because the demand to some extent is a 'do as you are told' (or at least 'do as we all agree') demand. When such demands are made, some might think that obedience to the demand is more important than thinking for oneself. Ethically sound professional conduct, however, presupposes professionals who really think for themselves, and there are depressing examples of how following the code of conduct in an instrumental and unthinking fashion has resulted in malpractice and abuse of the clients whom the code was meant to protect. One such example relates about an elderly Deaf lady who had an appointment at a hospital clinic. The hospital complex was large and rather difficult to navigate, so when the lady met the interpreter in the hospital's foyer, she asked the interpreter if she knew the way to the clinic. The interpreter answered curtly: 'I am your impartial interpreter and I perform no other tasks beside interpreting, so I cannot tell you where we should go.' Even though some might find that this example borders on the outright comical and nonsensical, it is a real-life example from the practice of the early professionalised Norwegian Sign Language interpreters and really happened. There are no reasons to believe that such conduct frequently occurred. Nevertheless, the example shows that Hannah Arendt's warning about the perversion of deontology through confusing duty with what is ethical is relevant.

There is also a fourth point. Interpreting is a complex and many-faceted activity. Both the conduit model and the early codes of ethics like the ones of the Norwegian Sign Language interpreters tend to reduce this complexity and present interpreting as something quite instrumental, and almost machine-like. This reductive conception of interpreting might also have given rise to the dubious idea that the interpreter somehow can be 'invisible', that is, that an interpreter can work in ways so that he or she ceases to be part of the meeting at hand and simply becomes some sort of ghost that takes care of the language barrier. As mentioned above, there is absolutely nothing wrong with the idea of promoting a client's autonomy. On the contrary, this idea is profoundly ethical. However, if such promotion is reduced to observing reductive rules that really do nothing but distance the interpreter, it is unlikely that the resulting practice is ethically defendable.

0.4 Ethics and recognition: a tentative conclusion

Today, the conduit model has been replaced by approaches to interpreting that – to a much higher degree – consider the complexity involved when people try to interact with the assistance of an interpreter. The Norwegian Sign Language interpreters have continued their work to improve and develop their professional practices. Among other things, they revised their code of ethical conduct in the mid-2000s and included a paragraph stating that Norwegian Sign Language interpreters based their practices on the principles of the UN Declaration of Human Rights. Professional conduct is, nevertheless, still very much a question related to confidentiality, impartiality, neutrality and interpreting quality. At the same time, it is also evident that the question of what it means to fulfil the client's right to interpretation has become an issue of great importance. It might seem that the vivid discussions about professional ethics and professional conduct of the 1980s and 1990s have quietened down, and instead we have a more internal discourse about several aspects of how this public service should be developed further. This is a point is its own right: the more established and recognised a profession becomes, the more complex its guidelines and regulations become as well. Thus, for the Norwegian Sign Language interpreters, one cannot today point only to their professional ethics in order to explain their conduct. Ethics and professional ethics are still important, but these are not the only sources influencing practices. This leads us back to the question about the relationships between the three parts of this book: (1) ethical theories and their relevance to questions regarding interpreting; (2) codes of ethics for interpreters; and (3) professional conduct and the process of professionalisation.

I will first sum up some observations we can make from the historic examples above, all related to the relationships between the three parts above, and then move on the question about a structured understanding of the different levels that professionalism and professional ethics can belong to.

The first observation is that the Norwegian Sign Language interpreters had a professional ethics, also in their pre-professional era. When you work as an interpreter, you make a professional and ethical decision whether or not you are backed up by a collegium or by a commonly accepted code of ethical conduct. What kind of ethical conduct you are able to establish is, however, not solely up to the individual interpreter. It was not until the Norwegian Sign Language interpreters had organised themselves and decided to work in a uniform manner that they were able to realise an ontologically oriented practice according to their code of ethical conduct.

The second observation is that the Norwegian Sign Language interpreters did not have to obtain academic knowledge about ethical theories in order to apply the principles described in such theories. This is not problematic, but rather points to the place that ethics has in all our lives. Ethics is not something one acquires by reading ethical theories; it is the other way around. Ethics is a constant element in all human interaction, and ethics is thus something we always already 'have'. Even though many ethical theories are presented in manners suggesting that their authors intend them as new thoughts, ethical theories are also always reflections of human practices already there. What ethical theories can assist in is clarifying one's ethical positions and also critically examining their consistency, or lack thereof. This leads to the third observation.

In the examples above, it is pointed out that both the utilitarian and the deontologically orientated practices had merits. At the same time, they both inspired some practices that we must deem problematic. The utilitarian approach reduced the clients' autonomy, sometimes severely, and the deontological approach gave some interpreters an excuse for a reductive practice where following rules became more important than considering the ethical and professional issues at hand.

The fourth observation regarding the Norwegian Sign Language interpreters' code of ethics is that there is a difference between what the underlying ethical norms are – here, to promote the clients' autonomy – and what are mere technical rules that any interpreter should observe in order to promote the ethical norms. Further, the code serves a range of purposes beside the obvious one of stating guidelines for professional conduct. The code is decided by the profession itself, and, as such, submitting to the code is a prerequisite of being a member of the profession. Hence, the code is also a political tool that the profession can turn outwards or inwards. It can be turned outwards in order to work on improvements and to persuade politicians and civil institutions that they should recognise both the clients' rights to interpretation as well as the interpreters' need for public funding and public recognition. It can be turned inwards in order to correct practices that have been deemed as being out of step with the main established practice (examples of such cases are presented in Part 2).

The fifth observation is the significance of public rights to interpretation, here particularly for the Deaf clients of the Norwegian Sign Language interpreters. The opportunity to start the formation of an organised profession came as a result of public recognition, first, in the form of funding for education and later as a publicly recognised responsibility to fund and run a public sign language interpreting service. Interpreting and interpreting ethics and professional conduct can thus not be regarded in a vacuum. One must consider that interpreters work and live in a given societal context. The Norwegian liberal welfare state has recognised sign language interpreters and provided them with the opportunity to establish and develop as a profession. (Interestingly, interpreters for other languages in Norway have been recognised to a more limited extent.)

The sixth and last observation concerns the solidarity between the Norwegian Sign Language interpreters and their clients. The development of the sign language interpreters' profession is also the result of the interpreters' struggle for increased social justice on behalf of their clients. Initially, 'clients' meant just Deaf people, but as a part of the profession's development came also a more mature understanding that solidarity both with Deaf people and with those whom Deaf people encounter was a means to promote increased social justice. As such, the history of Norwegian Sign Language interpreters is also a story about attempts to make things better.

Note

1   I follow the convention of using capital D in 'Deaf' to signify that I am talking primarily about members of a linguistic community using a sign language, and to a lesser extent about a group of hearing impaired ('deaf' with lowercase 'd') persons (Kermit 2009).

References

Arendt, H. (1998). *Eichmann i Jerusalem: Een Beretning om det Ondes Banalitet*. Oslo: Pax Forlag.
Bentham, J. (2014). An introduction to the principles of morals and legislation. Retrieved from https://ebooks.adelaide.edu.au/b/bentham/jeremy/morals/
Kant, I. (1983). Grunnlegging av moralens metafysikk [Grundlegung zur Metaphysik der Sitten]. In E. Storheim (ed.), *Moral, Politikk og Historie*. Oslo: Universitetsforlaget.
Kant, I. (1989). *Kritik der reinen Vernunft*. Stuttgart: Philipp Reclam jun. GmbH & Co.
Kant, I. (1996). *The Metaphysics of Morals*. Cambridge: Cambridge University Press.

Kermit, P. (2007). Aristotelian ethics and modern professional interpreting. In C. Wadensjö (ed.) *The Critical Link 4: Professionalisation of Interpreting in the Community - Selected Papers from the Fourth International Conference on Interpreting in Legal, Health and Social Service Settings, Stockholm, Sweden, 20–23 May 2004*. Philadelphia, PA: John Benjamins Publishing Company.

Kermit, P. (2009). Deaf or deaf? Questioning alleged antinomies in the bioethical discourses on cochlear implantation and suggesting an alternative approach to d/Deafness. *Scandinavian Journal of Disability Research*, 11(2), 159–174.

Metzger, M. (1999). *Sign Language Interpreting: Deconstructing the Myth of Neutrality*. Washington, DC: Gallaudet University Press.

Mill, J.S. (2010). On liberty. Retrieved from https://books.google.no/books?id=u-X15tBrt2UC&printsec=frontcover&hl=no&source=gbs_ge_summary_r&cad=0#v=onepage&q&f=false

Pöchhacker, F. (2004). *Introducing Interpreting Studies*. London: Routledge.

Roy, C.B. (1993). A sociolinguistic analysis of the interpreter's role in simultaneous talk in interpreted interaction. *Multilingua: Journal of Cross-Cultural and Interlanguage Communication*, 12(4), 341–364.

Stokoe, W.C., Jr. (2005). Sign language structure: an outline of the visual communication systems of the American Deaf. *The Journal of Deaf Studies and Deaf Education*, 10(1), 3–37.

Wadensjö, C. (1992). Interpreting as interaction: on dialogue-interpreting in immigration hearings and medical encounters. PhD dissertation, Linköping University.

Wadensjö, C. (1998). *Interpreting as Interaction*. New York: Longman.

1

SITUATING INTERPRETING ETHICS IN MORAL PHILOSOPHY

Mette Rudvin

1.1 Introduction

1.1.1 Sector-specific interpreting: interpreter agency and ethical challenges[1]

Interpreting has grown and developed significantly as a profession and as an academic discipline in the past few decades. Concomitantly, the discipline of Interpreting Studies (hereafter IS), departing from the exclusive elitist realm of conference interpreting, has branched out into a set of sectorial sub-disciplines – medical interpreting, legal interpreting, interpreting in the education sector, business interpreting, interpreting for the media or for tourism, diplomatic interpreting, etc. This increased segmentation is reflected both in the literature and in the plethora of training programmes specific to each sector. The terminology used to denote the macro-sector of dialogic, face-to-face interpreting in public and private institutions is also somewhat fragmented, although largely referred to as *Public Service Interpreting* (hereafter PSI) and *Community Interpreting* (hereafter CI), whereas *Liaison Interpreting* has lost currency. The issue of professional ethics has received increasing attention in Interpreting and Translation Studies generally, but nowhere more so than in the field of PSI.[2]

This rather fragmented landscape begs the question of whether or not we can speak of a general 'ethics of interpreting', and if so, can we speak of a *collective set of shared ethics* that derives its authority from the consensus of the professional community (i.e. an 'external' Code of Ethics), or does each sector require a specific code? By the same token, are interpreters governed by the rules that apply to the various domains, practices and stakeholders involved? These would be: (1) the *public and private institutions* that require their language services (hospitals, public offices, legal institutions for interpreters, or the client for translators); (2) the *professional associations, companies or cooperatives* they belong to; (3) the *training institution* (if they have received dedicated training). Alternatively, is ethics driven by (4) an *intrinsic, unwritten rule governing language transfer*, or by (5) a *privately-driven 'internal' ethics* by which a single interpreter examines his or her own conscience internally and acts accordingly? Operating with at least these different levels of ethics, the picture is clearly very complex and may lead to situations in which the interpreter is unsure of which ethical level or source he or she should follow, especially if the guidelines or injunctions at the various levels overlap or clash.

The development of IS into increasingly specialised areas of research and practice has had significant implications for the perception of the interpreter's role in the international literature on interpreting. It has brought to the surface and into public debate important issues related to interpreter agency and the degree to which the interpreter is 'visible' and 'proactive' in the interpreting assignment. The debate has led to a bifurcation of schools of thought in the PSI literature represented very broadly by what Sandra Hale (2007) calls the 'mediated approach' vs the 'direct approach'. Where the first approach tends to accept more active engagement by the interpreter, the latter is more cautious regarding the degree to which an interpreter should enter proactively in the interpreting process by providing additional information or otherwise enacting overt alterations. This bifurcation also represents a broader paradigm shift in the humanities (see Rudvin 2006) towards a wider acknowledgement of the reader's (or interpreter's) agency in the communicative event. It has also led to a new set of metaphors reflecting that higher degree of agency and engagement, exemplifying this shift: from a 'pane of glass/conduit' to 'bridge', from 'translator' to 'conversation coordinator', from 'invisible' to 'visible'. Consequently, the code of conduct[3] and ethics that the interpreters abide by also reflect the changing epistemological and methodological framework that guides and governs them.

There is arguably a natural correlation between ethics and PSI practice, motivating the prominence of ethics in PSI literature. The most important reasons for this correlation can be captured in the following features:

- The nature of PSI is highly dialogic, interpersonal and collective, often played out in public and institutional domains of power asymmetry. This power asymmetry may lead to deliberate (or unintentional) abuses of power at the level of language or the para-verbal level.
- The PSI interpreting mode is immediate and requires split-second decision-making; this is obviously also true of conference interpreting, but in PSI settings non-verbal behaviour is an inherent part of the communicative act. Subsequently, communication strategies need to be reflected upon and learned through training beforehand so that they become internalised and to some degree 'automatic'.
- PSI is deeply engaging in human terms because of the face-to-face format that requires immediate and constant interaction with other participants. PSI interpreters must therefore often engage not only with their interlocutors'

propositional and pragmatic intentions but also their affect-driven utterances and behaviour.
- PSI is deeply context-dependent and the settings shift from one institutional and life domain to another, requiring flexibility and adaptation as well as familiarity with the behaviours, norms and terminology of each sector, each with their own particular socio-cultural and institutional constraints.
- PSI is by definition an intercultural activity.[4] This may lead to a highly complex communicative process involving cultural, social and pragmatic features relating to socio-cultural interpersonal relations.

The responsibility for negotiating such complex factors can be a heavy burden on the interpreter and necessitates ethical guidelines to guide and advise, and to help interpreters minimise any potential damage to other interlocutors. The twin aspects of power-asymmetry and vulnerability require special attention and delicacy in order not to cause harm to the foreign-language speakers or to the communities and institutions served by the interpreters.

1.2 Contextualising PSI ethics: history, philosophy, and professional practice

Historically, ethics has been investigated principally in the macro-disciplines of theology and philosophy. In both these domains, ethics has had multiple functions, the most important of which is a 'damage-preventing' function (e.g. 'do not kill', 'do not bear false witness'), but at the same time ethics also functions as an ideal and idealised standard for desirable behaviour ('love thy neighbour', 'give alms'). Both these are normative processes. The broader discipline of philosophy engages with various questions pertaining to life, death, knowledge, language and human behaviour from a more descriptive angle. It is specifically the sub-branch of *moral philosophy* that has had the task of investigating and probing the reasoning and logic behind ethical injunctions, their robustness and validity, and their applicability to any given society. Moral philosophy puts under the microscope both the big questions of life (life, death, afterlife, the environment) as well as the more mundane ones that affect our lives every day and that we often take for granted. Indeed, ethics operates in most areas of institutional life (hospital, courtroom, banks, schools and universities); in science and the organisation of society (genetics, medical technology and cloning, artificial intelligence, farming, rubbish disposal), to social justice, and interpersonal relations. People live their lives guided, often unaware, by many ethical standards and sometimes find themselves trapped in situations without being aware of the circumstances that led them there or how to tackle them. Philosophy helps us untangle and clarify those circumstances and the reasoning behind them so that we can be more aware of how and why human beings behave the way they do. In that way it also helps us to optimise those behaviours in the best interests of individuals and society. Questioning what we take for granted, preconceived notions and 'platitudes', is indeed the stuff of philosophy, as Lewis observes: 'It is the profession of philosophers to question platitudes that others accept without thinking twice' (1969: 1, quoted in Glock, 2003).

As an object of theoretical inquiry (meta-ethics) as well as a guide for human conduct (normative ethics), ethics has been a prime focus of Western moral philosophy at least since the time of the Ancient Greeks.[5] By articulating ideas of 'right', 'good' and 'just', philosophers have had a powerful norm-developing role, strengthening the role and position of philosophy as an arena to suggest problem-solving methods for both individuals and groups of people. The organisation of society into professions (professional groups), and how they affect individuals and the community, also falls squarely within the ambit of ethical reflection. What better channel, then, through which to probe PSI ethics than through the framework of moral philosophy? With very broad brushstrokes Part 1 aims to identify – historically and conceptually – some of the connections between PSI and moral philosophy by tracing a simplified chronological trajectory of the central tenets of moral philosophy and selecting those areas of concern that are most obviously applicable to PSI. By creating a philosophical backdrop against which we can correlate the main ethical tenets of PSI, I hope to provide a fuller picture of the ethics of our profession, an example of how professional practices emerge in a specific historical, cultural and social context. This can be helpful to PSI researchers as they examine ethical tenets and try to formulate guidelines to help interpreters work to the best of their abilities in the service of the community. It can also be helpful to practitioners in order to be more fully conscious and mindful of the ethical decisions they enact, reassured by the knowledge that all professions are governed by ethical injunctions that limit arbitrary choice, and that those same ethical guidelines have developed through millennia in our societies to provide robust answers to difficult questions. In the Introduction to this volume, Kermit has provided some background to the Utilitarian school of philosophy as well as to Immanuel Kant's focus on reason. This Part will provide a panoramic overview of those and other branches of moral philosophy as they pertain to PSI ethics.

1.3 Ethics in philosophy

The broad question of what is right/wrong is encapsulated in Socrates' question of 'how should one live?' and Kant's more specific question 'what is my duty?' (Graham 2011: 50). As such, ethics is a broad, generalised term that defines what is 'good' ('meta-ethics'), embedded in the search for a definition of 'right conduct' (broadly speaking, the conduct that causes the greatest good) and 'the good life' (as in a life worth living, that is satisfying). At the same time, however, it is also the study of how people *ought* to act, and thus seeks a set of rules to help people decide on a course of action ('normative ethics'). Insofar as ethics attempts to formulate a system that determines what is 'good and bad', it is a public system on which there is general agreement in a given society and one which enjoys collective consensus, rather than being 'simply' a private, inner belief. It is precisely this consensus that underpins its robustness and normative efficacy.

The aim of such regulatory practices is to help individuals co-exist efficiently in a group, causing the least possible damage and doing the greatest possible 'good'. As Gordon Graham (2011) discusses, ethics dictates how an individual should behave in their different dimensions of life: in the *private* dimension (family, friends) and in the *public* dimension, as a citizen in a community and as a professional. Thus, ethics reflects both an individual and a collective dimension, private vs public/professional. A system operating in a public collective dimension may do harm, potentially to a large number of people, and therefore it needs to be protected from itself, as it were, precisely to limit that potential damage. Whereas in a private situation an individual has the exclusive ownership of his or her own decision-making, in the public and professional arena that 'ownership' is limited, and the individual also has a responsibility towards the group of which he or she is part. An ethical dilemma may arise precisely when the collective and the private spheres clash, when a potential action or decision based on a private or a cultural norm contravenes the rule of the profession, institution or nation/state. This area is often far from clear-cut and the very distinction public/private, collective/individual is not always easy or possible to establish.[6]

Professions were and are created to serve but also to reflect societies' ways of structuring themselves into organised entities: institutions, economies, kinship formations, religions, etc. These same societies reflect centuries of geo-political development, historical migrations, empire-building and other socio-political activities and continuously undergo diachronic (through time) and synchronic (through the meeting of peoples and cultures) mutations. When we look at philosophical concepts, guidelines and rules captured in the broader umbrella of 'ethics', we see that they are – in part, at least – reflections of intrinsic modes of behaviour that all peoples and professions are led to by historical circumstances as well as by natural inclination. Group-based (social, cultural) dynamics for regulating human behaviour evolve in a given community into specific organisational patterns that require rules and guidelines for good conduct to ensure the survival and viability of the group, be it a family, clan, religious order, political party, nation-state or profession (see e.g. Tomasello 2014). Underlying the specific behavioural guidelines captured in and regulated by each profession, are foundational ethical parameters that apply across professional borders; it is primarily these underlying parameters that have been examined in moral philosophy, often in an attempt to formulate universal or at least general ethical parameters.

A classic example of a moral dilemma often cited in moral philosophy regarding private vs public ethics is that of the soldier (i.e. social and professional ethics) disobeying the order to commit a certain action that will provoke multiple deaths (i.e. private ethics). Or the same soldier having to choose between few deaths and many deaths, or causing the death of one known person versus many unknown people.[7] An example of a PSI dilemma is when an interpreter chooses to break the professional ethic and rule of confidentiality (which is legally binding) or accuracy (professionally binding) for the greater good of the individual or the community.[8]

It is that very *choice*, active and deliberate, that lies at the heart of the human need not only to regulate potentially harmful behaviour but also to provide guidelines or legislation that govern the choice and decisions of individuals and also relieve them of a sense of responsibility that can feel crushing.[9] It is precisely such problems that philosophy as a discipline and religions and mythologies as social practices have attempted to clarify through the ages. By reflecting and clarifying, we can also anticipate dilemmas, and by anticipating them, create awareness and the possibility to reflect upon an action before it occurs, optimally leading to a positive, or, at worst, less harmful, outcome.

While mythologies and religions, by definition, provide hard and fast rules and/or guidelines, philosophy provides an arena in which such existential knots can be debated and discussed in a social forum, what could be defined as an 'intellectual' forum, and one that – unlike religion and mythology – pursues debate solely through the framework of logic, reason or observation. It is thus very much a public arena in which all citizens have a voice in the historical development of that very pursuit of ideas and knowledge. More importantly for this chapter, it is an arena that both reflects and is constitutive of the structural organisation of society, of institutions and professions. It is useful, therefore, to observe and examine our own professional ethical regulations diachronically and synchronically through the framework of philosophy.

Ocone and Ocone provide some suggestions on how to teach ethics in the discipline of engineering ethics in their own discipline – engineering:

> Teaching ethics in engineering is quite different from teaching ethics in philosophy. This is because in philosophy ethics is about analysis – understanding an ethical theory and dispassionately comparing its application to an ethical problem. By contrast, ethics for engineers is about synthesis. Faced with a dilemma, the engineer has to decide on the best course of action. Hence, much like medical ethics, *engineering ethics should be taught in relation to the context in which the ethical dilemma arises*. It can therefore *guide the engineer to make ethical decisions* rather than analysing ethical theories. But ethics in engineering goes beyond the dilemma and the application of ethical principles. Ethics in engineering *implies understanding the social impact of engineering work*. In this respect it is very similar to the way philosophy was seen in the classical ancient world. The disconnection between practice and philosophy is a fairly recent development; classical societies such as the Greeks and Romans attributed great importance to practical behaviour. Hegel defined the ancient Greek world as the era of 'involuntary' ethics where the individuals lived in immediate symbiosis and harmony with their community; only successively, with the advent of theories about individualism, did the link between individual and society weaken. *Nowadays, we tend to identify 'culture' with 'thinking'; classical philosophers did not consider philosophy as a purely intellectual activity – to them it was part and parcel of everyday life. Ethics was not just a concept, but rather an action, that is acting in and for the society.* This is the lesson

that we should keep in mind when teaching engineering: make the students aware of how the technology they will develop will affect people working with it, living near it, consuming its products and so on.

(2012: 1; emphasis added)

A useful take-away point from their brief discussion is that ethics could/should be developed in PSI in a context-sensitive fashion, reflecting on how the ethical parameters of the PSI profession interact with the parameters of parallel institutions (health, legal, etc.) as well as the broader social circumstances and individual people and events. And most importantly, fully understanding its social impact. As an 'action in and for society', ethically-grounded interpreting decisions are bound both by a profession-inherent norm as well as by the impact that decision has on its surroundings.

1.4 Ethics in moral philosophy: four macro-areas[10]

In *Theories of Ethics*, Graham captures the development of focal points in moral philosophy from the Greek philosophers to the present day in broad macro-areas that will here be adopted as a point of departure for analysing PSI ethics (adapted from Graham 2011: 119). Tracing the development of ethics in moral philosophy is clearly an overly ambitious task, and not one suited for a volume such as this. I have chosen to focus on those features of moral philosophy that are most relevant to PSI ethics, not having found a direct connection between moral philosophy, these issues, and interpreting or translating ethics as such. Other branches of philosophy, in particular the philosophy of language and the philosophy of mind, do relate more specifically to language and translation/interpreting related issues, but not directly to PSI ethics. Some ancient Greeks, in particular, the 'atomist' and precursor to aesthetics, Democritus, addressed the (non-)correspondence of word to thing, what we today would call representation or linguistic conventionalism, (Ubaldo 2005 [2000]: 34ff) at the heart of what of any study or practice pertaining to language transfer (see also Berryman 2016). For the purposes of this chapter, however, I have selected only those specific key issues, philosophers and historical periods that are pertinent and central to the PSI-moral philosophy interface to substantiate the claim that the development of professional ethics in modern society originates in a broader notion of what is 'good' and is captured specifically in the discipline of philosophy.[11]

The four macro-areas of moral philosophy[12] that could be said to represent its central tenets are (1) Virtue and 'the Good'; (2) Duty and Responsibility; (3) Consequence of actions and Utility; and (4) Justice and Equality.[13] The three principal interpreting ethics arguably underpinning the core of dialogic interpreting practices – Accuracy, Impartiality and Confidentiality[14]– are, I suggest, in turn reflected in these macro-areas (see Box 1.1).

Very broadly speaking, all categories spring from the first one, or Socrates' search for what is 'good'; indeed, all other branches of moral and political philosophies

BOX 1.1 FOUR MACRO-AREAS OF MORAL PHILOSOPHY

1. Virtue and 'the Good'
2. Duty and Responsibility
3. Consequence of actions and Utility
4. Justice and Equality

could be said to spring from this same search. The first three categories both assert and attempt to circumscribe and define what is, or ought to be, 'good' or beneficial to human beings through one or more of the following (see Graham 2011; Ubaldo 2005 [2000]):

- an external mandate – the gods, God, a supreme being or entity, an ideological principle (especially monotheistic religions, e.g. according to St Augustine);
- identifying, defining and choosing a 'good action' becomes a process of inner reasoning, driven by logic (e.g. according to Kant);
- the importance of emotion and social convention/education (e.g. according to the Romantics);
- human impulses (e.g. according to Schopenhauer).

Moving through a chronological philosophical timeline, the focus of what constitutes 'good' moves from an intrinsic feature defined by the 'thing itself' (as exemplified by the early Greeks) to a process embodied in an individual inner motivation (St Augustine, Luther, Kant, Kierkegaard) to the consequences and functions of a given action (Bentham, but also Kant), captured in categories 1–3. (Note that an external mandate and reasoning are not necessarily mutually exclusive, St Augustine placed great emphasis on both.) Category 4 is relational, governing relationships between individuals and groups.

The fourth principle of Justice and Equality, or social justice, holds that all citizens in any given society are equal before the law and that the law should benefit each citizen equally. That all citizens have equal rights is historically a very recent tenet, but one that has become fundamental to the modern tradition of moral philosophy and – in principle, at least – to most societies in the modern world.[15]

In a normative, prescriptive capacity, this pillar of moral philosophy suggests that, through distributive justice, all citizens should have an equal right to access society's most essential services or 'goods'[16] of health, justice and education, and this is characteristically reflected in key pan-national expressions of law and justice, for example, the United Nations Declaration of Human Rights. This principle is so crucial to most modern democracies that it leads to frequent intense political tension when it comes to legislating and to executing laws dealing with access to public (or private) services (healthcare; justice; primary through tertiary education; welfare benefits; employment). This principle also lies at the heart of the profession of PSI interpreting insofar as it is a community-based service, the very core and *raison d'être* of which is to enable access to fundamental citizen services (health, justice, education, employment, welfare services, etc.) to all members of a society, including those who do not speak the majority language.

The tragic events of the mid-twentieth century caused profound soul-searching among theologians, philosophers, academics and many others, and led to some of the most seminal work in modern moral philosophy by writers such as Hannah Arendt (1906–1975) (see d'Entreves 2016), addressing the overarching existential questions of good and evil. The technological advances of the current millennium, a discussion that Hans Jonas (1955–1976) anticipated (see Franssen *et al*. 2015, for the ethics of technology), are also spawning critical reflections on the essence of human nature with regard to artificial intelligence, the right to life, death and health (medical technology, genetic engineering, artificial intelligence, assisted reproduction, cloning), the right to privacy and the publishing of private information (social media, the internet), and possibly in the near future, the right to truthful information. The environment and ecology and the rights and welfare of animals are also important areas in modern philosophy that deeply affect human ethical behaviour. None of these areas, however, will be addressed here.

1.4.1 Loyalty, honesty and truth-telling: the foundations of the accuracy ethic?

Underlying these four macro-categories is a deeper-level category relating to a notion of honesty, truth-telling and loyalty, in a broad sense of the word. Although *loyalty* as such has not been a primary focus in moral philosophy (indeed, it could be said to be a spin-off or a manifestation of the category of 'virtue'), it responds to deep psychological human drives regulating human relationships, in part based on the notion of keeping promises, a form of contract. It is also an essential component in maintaining a balance in group dynamics (in-group and inter-group) and regulates important professional ethical features, such as impartiality and confidentiality. One aspect that relates to loyalty and the 'contractual' relationship between people is precisely that of honesty and truth-telling as the basis of trust.

This category of values is crucial not just in moral and political philosophy, and indeed in the organisation of any society, but also for translation and interpreting ethics, as will be discussed presently. Successful communication also relates to truth-telling in the sense that communication is feasible only if there is some bottom-line assumption that what someone is saying is true, and a breach of that assumption warrants a reaction or displeasure at some level (disregarding deliberate instances of 'shared dishonesty' in polite lies, irony, humour, protection, etc.). Truth-telling is also at the heart of the 'contract' between speaker/listener and interpreter, both individually and as a profession, and that the speaker/listener must be able to trust the interpreter to convey what he or she is saying. Only by working on this basic assumption will both speaker and listener be able to trust the interpreter.

This underlying category is relevant not only as an ethical value, but as a logical process of reasoning, encapsulated by Kant's work on 'promise-keeping' as a moral obligation.[17] Unless there is an underlying 'contract' between speaker and listener, writer and reader that 'promises' to provide information that is truthful, the very nature of the transactional information event collapses and becomes a logical contradiction, rendering it senseless. Notions of truth, truth-value, honest representation and false information have been amply studied in the philosophy of language (and will no doubt increase exponentially with the advent of the 'fake news' era in the interface between journalism/social media and its impact on politics/-democracy), also from a logico-semantic and pragmatic angle, especially with regards to Gricean pragmatics and to semantics. That is not to say that any spoken or written communication event is truthful in an absolute sense of the word, quite the contrary, but it is the measure against which a listener/reader gauges not just the lack of truth-value but the myriad of discourse strategies related to irony, humour, politeness, face-work, accommodation, hyperbole, etc., playing precisely on a basic, assumed truth value and deliberately flouting standards or maxims. By truth value, I refer, at this point, to a logical process of truthful intention (or lack of it) by speaker/writer, not the objectively quantifiable measure of that content which is by definition filtered through a person's subjective interpretative filter. (This will be discussed further in relation to the paradigm shift in Section 1.6 on Translation Studies.)

Arguably, the core – and indispensable – feature of interpreting, its *sine qua non*, is accuracy (in the full sense of the word), a condition that fulfils the nature of the translation or interpreting act. However illusory it may be in any absolute sense, it embodies the very nature and definition of the process of translation and the profession of interpreting, without which interpreting and translation are rendered senseless. Thus, accuracy is arguably a central (professional) 'good' or 'virtue' as well as being its defining parameter.[18] This should be treated with caution in order not to fall into the essentialist/absolutist paradigm of claiming that interpreting is objective, that it is a mechanical language transfer process with no pragmatic or non-linguistic contingent features, that all clients or users have the same *skopos*, or even that there are not other ethical considerations that may override the ethic of accuracy at a higher level. Accuracy is, I believe, the *telos*, the nature, of interpreting (and translating), but it is not the only ethic to be considered. This will be discussed further in Section 1.5.12 in the discussion on consequentialism.

1.4.2 Beyond Western philosophy?

The four points in Box 1.1 capture a tendency in a broad philosophical tradition represented by Greek, Italian, French, German, Scandinavian, British and, more recently, American scholars but obviously do not represent the entirety of philosophical traditions in the world. It is true that much of the academic literature and research in PSI also comes from these same areas of the world, but that picture is fortunately already changing with much important TS and IS work being done in Asia (especially China and India).[19] Notions from other ethical systems should equally inform international research in PSI, which could profoundly change the landscape and scope of investigation in our discipline and profession.

Other philosophical traditions may advocate values that are different from those represented by twentieth- and twenty-first-century moral philosophy in the Western world (see Chadda and Deb 2013; Goodman 2017; Wong 2017), and by extension reflected in the PSI literature. This is illustrated by societies that honour the fulfilment of an individual's allotted, ascribed social role and where good conduct is measured according to strict social conventions. This also represents the ethical landscape of the ancient Greeks[20] (as represented in the Homeric literature, see MacIntyre 2002: 5), and it can also be found in modern ethical systems of Islamic religion and philosophy where filling a social and religious function and submitting to one's allocated fate in life (by submitting to God) are not just a duty but a virtue.

Obedience may thus sometimes have higher prestige value than independent decision-making as captured in many intercultural models, such as those of Hofstede or Hampden-Turner. Adhering to the will of the group (the family, the clan, one's ancestors, the nation) and behaving in such a way as to save the collective good rather than one's own individual good or face is more prominent in what anthropologists have long classified – if only very broadly – as collectivist rather than individualist approaches to the organisation of society and to the construction of the Self (see e.g. Storr 2019). Other ethics, such as compassion and charity, are key values in the Islamic tradition (represented by alms-giving), and could be seen as parallel to the principle of Justice and Equality, in that it serves to equalise wide socio-economic discrepancies.

Conforming to the needs of the group and respecting its inherent hierarchy rather than promoting the needs of the individual, trigger rather different ethical values. The philosophical traditions of the Indian sub-continent, both in a Hindu and Buddhist representation, generally favour more group-based behavioural values, as does the ancient Chinese philosophical tradition where group harmony is prized.[21] Yet other ethical systems – even more ancient and perhaps universal in a very real sense of the word – are those that foreground Nature and see human life as inscribed in a broader ecological system. Such notions range from ancient animist schools of thought to modern ecological philosophies of Gaia (the Earth) as a self-constituting system into which Man is inscribed as a small and not necessarily indispensable element.[22] The new urgency in the climate crisis will no doubt greatly increase philosophical investigations into Nature (in the sense of planet Earth and what is sometimes referred to as 'wilderness', rather than in the sense of 'the nature of human beings').

1.4.3 'Ethical' and 'moral': words change, notions change, society changes ...

'Ethics' and the related notion of 'morality' are at times used interchangeably in academic literature and in layman's discourse, but the distinction is significant: in very broad terms, we could think of ethics as belonging to a public, collective domain, about which there is at least some degree of consensus in any given social group or community of practice. It is thus a more objective category. Formal codes of conduct or ethics, Graham (2011) reminds us, operate in workplaces or as religious regulatory principles while morals refer to an individual's own principles regarding right and wrong. Thus, 'moral' and 'morality' generally pertain to a more private, personal, inner-oriented and more subjective behavioural and belief domain. Furthermore, the concept of ethics differs from 'morals and morality' because it denotes a *theory* of right action rather than the *practice* of right action; a resulting paradox is that a person can be ethical in their profession, and immoral in their private spheres of life (ibid.). We could thus view 'ethics' as an umbrella term for a guide or code of conduct that regulates, suggests or governs individual people's behaviour towards others.

Another important premise that must be made at this point is that the very use of the terms 'moral', 'good', 'goodness', 'virtue', 'pleasure', 'desire', 'happiness', 'utility', 'satisfaction', etc. is flawed because words themselves are stable containers for non-stable, ephemeral entities (see Box 1.2).

All of these terms, crucial to the development of the tradition of moral philosophy, have travelled in time and space, notably through translation into English from Greek, Latin, German, French, Italian and Danish, to mention only the most frequent. Even words in the same language change substantially over time. In *A Short History of Ethics*, Alasdair MacIntyre also strongly cautions the reader against

---

BOX 1.2 ARETĚ, PHRONĒSIS, TELOS, EUDAIMONIA, ETHOS, MOS

- The Greek word *aretě*, usually translated into English as 'virtue', also suggests 'excellence' or 'in the best possible way' while *phronēsis* means 'practical or moral wisdom'. The natural objective for man, achieved through enacting virtue, is *telos*.
- *Eudaimonia* is often translated into English as 'happiness' although Graham (2011) suggests that 'being in good spirits', or 'well-being' is probably closer to the Greek original.
- Ethics derives from the Greek word *ethos* meaning 'custom' or 'habit' and refers to a code of conduct and behaviour on which a given community has reached consensus.
- Moral derives from the Latin word *mos*, meaning 'custom' (ibid.)

interpreting moral concepts in their language-specific and time-specific formulations, but concludes that

> All of this of course does not entail that traditional moral vocabulary cannot be used. It does entail that we cannot expect to find in our society a single set of moral concepts, a shared interpretation of the vocabulary. Conceptual concept is endemic in our situation because of the depth of our moral conflicts. Each of us therefore has to choose both with whom we wish to be morally bound and by what ends, rules, and virtues we wish to be guided. These are two choices that are inextricably linked.
> (MacIntyre 2002: 259)

Not only do words and concepts change – often drastically – over time and in response to social and cultural changes in the environment in which they are embedded, but these transformations – and the events they represent – are themselves constitutive of change; they are never simple, absolute or neutral. Moral concepts can never be examined apart from their history, MacIntyre notes: 'some philosophers have even written as if moral concepts were a timeless, limited, unchanging, determinate species of concept, necessarily having the same features throughout history ... In fact, of course, moral concepts change as social life changes' (ibid.: 1). Indeed, the very focus of academic philosophy on certain ethical concepts foregrounds those very concepts as key notions in a particular time and society. We could think of a self-constitutive circle similar to the supply-and-demand chain in economics, or again in MacIntyre's words 'Moral concepts are embodied in and are partially constitutive of forms of social life ... philosophical inquiry itself plays a part in changing moral concepts' (ibid.: 2). Such limitations are not trivial, both the meaning of these key notions as they change through time and translation, and the difficulty of pinning them down demand that we problematise any analysis of moral philosophy. In this chapter, I refer to these notions constructed within the semantic field of 'good' in the broadest possible sense as something positive and desirable by most people and on which there is a general consensus in a given social group or society.

It is this very 'situatedness' of concepts (and the words that represent them) that is both problematic and at the same time the core of this chapter: In the same way that moral concepts – indeed, all abstract human concepts – are subject to fluctuation in history (diachronically) and in society/culture (synchronically), the values advocated and the practices played out day by day in our profession reflect a much broader professional and ethical dialogue in society, which itself is unique to that historic and cultural moment in time.

Does this lack of an absolute or universal core feature invalidate any broad analysis of social practices, or lead us to completely relativise and devalue those very practices? It does not, of course. Changes and transformations represent patterns and trends in history over centuries, indeed millennia, many of which represent ways in which human beings have optimised the organisation of social work and interaction (such as in professional contexts).

1.5 The philosophy of ethics: a brief look at the development of some central tenets

Unlike the 'hard sciences' (physics, chemistry, maths, biology) and specialised professions in the humanities (law, theology, economics) where training can be applied directly to exercise professions, philosophy falls in between many areas of study, life, professional affiliation and professional practice. As mentioned, the development of moral philosophy in academic/intellectual life and in professional practice reflects how civil society and ethical behaviour are shaped and understood. The schematic overview of key concepts in moral philosophy as they pertain to PSI necessarily excludes some of the most important discussions, as found in the fertile, provocative and profound discussions of ethics in the post-war period, or the trends that examine recent developments in the sciences and in technology in a world moving towards an increased dependence on bio-technology (genetic engineering, reproductive/cloning technology), automatisation and artificial intelligence. Indeed, the very idea of what it means to be human may soon be questioned and a new understanding of human nature and human interaction may emerge. The ethics of the future may indeed focus on very different areas of concern. One area of concern in modern ethics that combines the darker, primordial side of human nature with modern technology is that of warfare and how wars will be conducted in the future, likely through an increasing use of high-technology non-contact weapons that distance the perpetrator from the victims, allowing the perpetrators not to feel responsible. The ethics involved in using local interpreters in conflict areas, an area of growing concern over the last decade that has been embraced by organisations such as In-Zone and Red-T, belongs to the ethics of human rights and justice, but will not be addressed here.

1.5.1 The development of ethical principles: a brief timeline

The four key philosophical categories mentioned in Box 1.1 can be captured diachronically in three broad macro-categories under the headings of *Virtue Ethics* (initially, the Ancient Greeks), *Deontology* (especially but not only Kant's emphasis on duty) and *Consequentialism* (Teleological ethics). The schematic timelines (Table 1.1 and Box 1.3 on p. xxx) illustrate how key notions of moral philosophy have developed.

1.5.2 The Ancient Greeks and virtue ethics: does being virtuous lead to a good life?

Since humans first became aware of their surroundings, they have reflected on the 'big questions' of life: the place of humans in the universe, the balance of man-nature-the universe, human nature, human knowledge, human behavior and how humans should live their lives. The ancient Greek philosophers addressed these existential problems head on and, as such, are said to be the first moral philosophers

TABLE 1.1 Historical periods representing philosophical development: a timeline

Historical period	Date
Classical Greek period	Seventh–third century BC
Christian era; consolidation of Christian Church from late antiquity	Third century AD
Decline of the Roman Empire, Early Middle Ages; influence of Catholic Church	Late fifth century
Birth and early rise of Islam	632–700
The Reformation	1517(–1648)
The Renaissance	1300s–1600s
The Enlightenment	1685–1815
French Revolution	1789
Romanticism	1790–1850
Industrial Revolution	(first and second) 1712–1915
First World War	1914-1918
Second World War	1939–1945
Digital and technological revolutions	1950s–

in the Western world (see e.g. Fornero 2000; Ubaldo 2005 [2000]; Graham 2011). The Greeks addressed many other areas of what we today call philosophy, encapsulated in the notion of 'virtue' and 'good' or what is beneficial in/for human beings, intrinsically and normatively. These reflections are typically represented by the three founders of classic Greek philosophy, Socrates, Plato and Aristotle. As we shall see below, the focus on virtue has shifted through centuries to other goals and mechanisms, notably deontology and utilitarianism/teleology and applied ethics, schools of thought which were at least to some degree incompatible with the notion of virtue being intrinsic to humankind. A number of important shifts take place following the ancient Greeks, one of which is a departure from the fatalistic view that virtue is ascribed through birth and is intrinsic to the nobility, to one in which virtue and virtuous features can be achieved, regardless of class of birth. Gradually, we see a shift to an approach where 'good' is the result of inner reflection and individual responsibility. Furthermore, the shift from an individual-based worldview to a concern for the aggregate of individuals emerged in the Greek concept of the *polis* as an organisational form that was to influence human organisation around the world. This was fundamental in the successive development of human knowledge and reflection (in philosophy) and in the political and social forms of organisation that were to follow not only in Europe, but also in Asia, inspired by Greek civilisation and philosophy.

1.5.3 'Good'

The terms 'good', 'happy' and 'pleasure' are – at least in their English guise – often conflated, and fall under the umbrella concept of 'a good life', or 'a happy life'.[23] Socrates, Plato and Aristotle were concerned with identifying what is 'good' and what is 'good for someone'; the two latter terms conflate and this was seen to reflect distinctive properties of human nature. Therefore, what is *good* is also *good for* someone because it expresses their deep essential nature as a human being. The quest for an understanding of 'good' was thus also the essence of morality. Virtuous living and the 'right way to live' were enacted through virtues, such as temperance and strength. For Socrates, the pursuit and love of good itself (not actions) are a primary aim, there is a 'transcendent form of good itself', an intrinsic feature of human beings; 'good' is a positive, illuminating force that provides knowledge and virtue (Graham 2011). Good is also encapsulated in the natural balance of the universe. This is a positive cycle in which virtue (*aretĕ* – excellence or virtue) and virtuous behaviour bring about goodness and a good/happy life, well-being or flourishing, as embodied in the term *eudaimonia* (see Box 1.2). *Phronēsis* is a third key feature and suggests practical or moral wisdom. Plato also believed that people act because they pursue what is 'good', albeit never reaching it; the focus shifts towards the action, on 'doing good'. When people 'do wrong', they do so due to a lack of knowledge, wisdom and self-awareness and thus forego virtue and happiness, he believed (see Fornero 2000; Ubaldo 2005 [2000]). Educating and informing are therefore crucial. Aristotle's work constitutes a shift from Plato's search for the one, intrinsically good, entity to a range of things that can be 'good', not necessarily in themselves, but what they are good *for*, they are good *for someone or something* (Graham 2011: 48). For Aristotle, 'goodness' is in the actor, not in the action and therefore we can actively and deliberately choose to be 'good'. Virtue is also tied to the notion of 'reaching excellence' or behaving 'in the best possible way'. Developing and realising his or her or its essence, as a seed realises its essence when it becomes a plant, lead to a state of happiness or fulfilment. This 'good way of living' can be acquired through rationality; thus, choosing rationality is choosing goodness. Our rational 'soul' (which is different from our irrational soul, driven by the senses) can help us to recognise the truth and to control our irrational soul, by controlling our propensity to desire (Ubaldo 2005 [2000]). The underlying aim is to fulfil a *telos*,[24] an end, a discoverable function that is intrinsic to each human or animal or plant; this is almost a biological or ethological (i.e. 'studying behaviour') rather than a moral notion (Graham 2011). Thus, 'good' for Aristotle is not a moral judgement, as in the contemporary sense of the word (ibid.: 50); rather, a 'good life' is one which is engaged and active and attempts to employ the best human characteristics; thus, 'an activity is pleasure-producing if it is valuable' (ibid.: 47). Aristotle, therefore, advocates a balance between intellectual brilliance and good practical sense or wisdom (*phronēsis*) (ibid.: 49). As Ocone and Ocone note above, ethics was considered to be a part of everyday life, an action, acting in and for the society.

Ethics thus becomes the study of 'how one should live' through Aristotle's development of Plato's notion of goodness residing in good actions ('doing good') to '*being* good'.[25] With the onset and spread of Christianity, we see a further development with God being the ultimate source of 'good', and a strong focus on normative ethics, but also a focus on engagement in the community and 'good actions' towards one's fellow human beings, encapsulated in the tenet 'Love thy neighbour as well as, or more than, oneself, thus discouraging excessive self-love. The dictum 'do unto others as you would have others do unto you' epitomises what later became one of the main tenets of utilitarian ethics (ibid.).[26]

1.5.4 The early church

A landmark in Christian moral philosophy is the work of St Augustine of Hippo (354–430), a late convert to the Christian faith, whose focus on intention and motivation further consolidates the above-mentioned shift towards inner reflection. For Augustine, good lies in the intention: 'everything that is done with love is good', so even if an action can seem wrong/sinful from the outside, if it is done with love, it is still a good action (Graham 2011). No external judgement, except that of God, can determine what is wrong or good (i.e. a good action might have been with the wrong intentions). Augustine is not suggesting a myopic and superficial interpretation of the scriptures, nor is he suggesting that rationality should be jettisoned, but rather 'Credo ut intelligam' (I believe so that I may understand) (ibid.). For him, in order to understand the world that surrounds us, we need to have faith, but also to exercise our rationality. The only problem with using our rationality, he argues, is that as humans we are driven by impulses and desires and this means that, even without realising it, we tend to distort our reasoning and to reach the conclusion that is more advantageous for us (a precursor to modern philosophy, as illustrated by Haidt 2012, for example). According to Augustine, to prevent this, we must try to erase ourselves and assume God's point of view.

From Augustine's thesis we notice that even in the Christian world, where God is the source of good, the impact of the Greeks' belief that good can be reached through rationality is still present (see Murphy 2011). There is yet another imprint left by the Greeks in Augustine's philosophy: Plato claims in his theory of knowledge that we possess some truths that we do not learn through experience and through the senses, but that are already in us, a form of innate knowledge. Augustine takes inspiration from Plato and supports the belief that we have a knowledge in us that is not learned, but is the presence of God. Therefore, the pursuit of good is not as difficult as it may seem, because we tend towards it naturally; this protects humans from a socially destructive moral anarchy and absolute egoism. In later eras, this basic assumption of the necessity of good is equally important, but it takes other forms and underpins virtually all individual and public ethical approaches.

Augustine's ideas were largely abandoned in the subsequent evolution of the Christian Church; instead of focusing on conscience, actions became prominent in the Catholic doctrine. Generating church finances through the sale of indulgences (see Murphy 2011) was one of the church's policies that eventually culminated in the Reformation, through the life and work of Martin Luther (1483–1546). During the Medieval period, this shift comes to the fore powerfully, in some respects violently, during the Reformation in the radical departure from Catholic dogma and tradition that Luther represents. With the Reformation, the focus of moral significance was not predominantly in the action itself but shifted to what brought about that action – intention, motivation and reflection, and also duty. Almost a millennium after Augustine, however, but long before the Reformation, Thomas Aquinas (1225–1274) is another landmark in the development of Western philosophical tradition, bringing together Aristotelian and Christian ethical theory in his 'natural law ethics'. He claims that the distinction between right and wrong lies in the very nature of human beings and that 'goodness' and ethical behaviour are intrinsic to human nature (see Finnis 2018). Catholic ethics is deeply influenced by Aquinas's theories and his 'natural theology'.

We see from this brief description that at the heart of the discussion are a few key notions and questions that will follow moral philosophy and professional ethics to the present day: is 'goodness' an external attribute?, is 'goodness' innate in humans?, is an action in itself morally neutral or morally good/bad?, does a good intention justify an action? To these basic notions, later philosophers have also examined issues that impact on what we perceive to be 'good' or ethical. Examples could be: the provision of 'good' on a contractual basis in a win-win agreement between an individual and an organisation; the existential lack of any form of 'good'; and whether or not the beneficial consequences of an action always provide justification for that action (does the end justify the means?). Creating categories and a classification of ethics based on notions of what is 'good' is of course in itself a social construction, both the classification into areas and as semantic terms. Indeed, for the Greeks, 'goodness' was part of a larger, more holistic picture. With advances in evolutionary psychology and behavioural sciences generally, the very classification of an action or approach being good or moral is complex. For example, is good parenting an ethic, or an innate human (and animal) drive, or something else? Nevertheless, these are the classifications and sematic fields that have determined to some degree the development of our ethical behaviour as we know it today, and the notions and terms that constitute our methodological tools in private as well as professional life.

1.5.5 From external rule to internal reflection and personal responsibility

Some key notions have emerged so far to describe how, through the eyes of select philosophers, people and societies believe they should live and behave, and indeed what is the very source and nature of 'good'. Through time, 'good' slowly shifted from an external projection to one that was marked by introverted reflection and motivation, and to what we have come to think of as 'conscience', influenced also by the Christian religion. What is in the individual's 'heart' (thoughts, mind, conscience) becomes as important as the actions.

The Middle Ages thus witnessed a shift where the role and authority of the church gradually decreased and empiricism, science, reason, rationality, logic, objectification were probed in order to provide answers to life's existential questions (Fornero 2000; Ubaldo 2005 [2000]; Boileau 2014). The division of mind and body and the power of the human mind take a central position. Power relations are challenged and upturned. From the medieval conception of an anonymous, unreflective Self following external God-given rules and ecclesiastical authority, a construction of Self emerges where truth and the possibility of an accurate representation of the world (objectivity) can be discussed without appealing to God. We see a shift towards personal responsibility, scientific truth, an objective eye, disengagement with regard to the observable world, and an assumption of control over representations of the world; the Self, rather than the Church, becomes an arbiter of truth (Boileau 2014: 14–18). This eventually leads to a new form of individualism and a new framework of power relations. The lack of an external, transcendent base for truth, the decreasing role of the Church as a source of authority, ontology and moral deliberation – which is replaced by empiricism and reason – increases what Boileau refers to as an 'ontological anxiety' (an 'agonizing human struggle'; ibid.). The belief that science, empiricism, reason and rationality could answer existential questions and fulfil existential human needs led to a new era of human organisation and interaction, and underpins the philosophy of the major thinkers of the sixteenth, seventeenth and eighteenth centuries; even thinkers like Rousseau, who foregrounded the role of nature, advocated rationality and reason, the human mind, over 'dogmatism' (ibid.).

This gradual development of the construction of the Self, analysed and promoted by Descartes, Locke, Hume, Montaigne, Rousseau, Kant and then Hegel and Weber, led to a new social and political organisation of society and to what we know today as the organisation and ethics of professions. Although Montaigne and Rousseau recognise the role of the external, natural world, they also find answers in a subjective, individual 'inner voice', rather than in the dictates of the Church (ibid.). Where Augustine found God in the inner being, Rousseau found unity and goodness and the individual self. It is also against this background of an increasing individualism that a sense of achieved self-hood and a sense of duty and responsibility that we find in modern professions emerge (see Rudvin 2007, on individualism and collectivism in the context of PSI ethics and professionalism). (Box 1.3 presents a schematic timeline illustrating a succession of moral philosophers.)

1.5.6 Deontology and Kant: the rational good and the dutiful good

1.5.6.1 Reason

'The eyes of God can see your thoughts though they are hidden from others.' Two centuries after the Reformation, introspection and responsibility are captured in Immanuel Kant's (1724–1804) focus on duty, individual responsibility and the importance of rational reasoning (Graham 2011; Johnson and Cureton 2018). Consequently, *an action is not in itself good or moral, but made good also by the intention and volition of the actor*. Kant's scientific, scholarly bent led him to seek a rational, logical explanation and grounding for moral behaviour (as Kermit explains in the Introduction to this volume). For Graham,

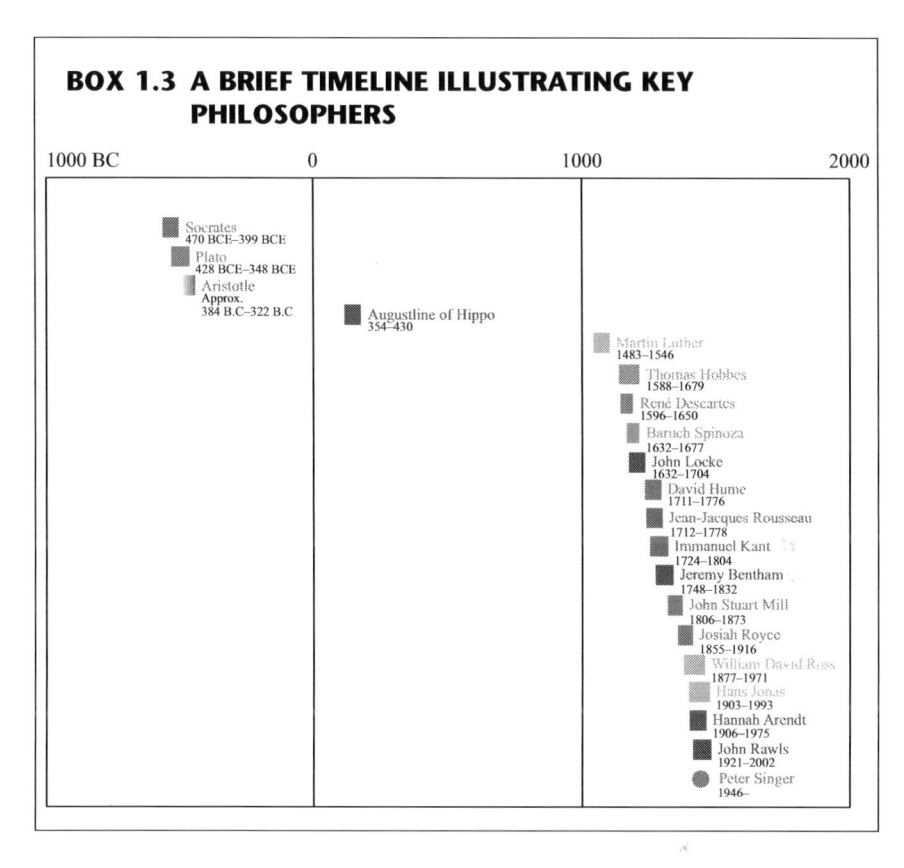

BOX 1.3 A BRIEF TIMELINE ILLUSTRATING KEY PHILOSOPHERS

- Socrates 470 BCE–399 BCE
- Plato 428 BCE–348 BCE
- Aristotle Approx. 384 B.C–322 B.C
- Augustline of Hippo 354–430
- Martin Luther 1483–1546
- Thomas Hobbes 1588–1679
- René Descartes 1596–1650
- Baruch Spinoza 1632–1677
- John Locke 1632–1704
- David Hume 1711–1776
- Jean-Jacques Rousseau 1712–1778
- Immanuel Kant 1724–1804
- Jeremy Bentham 1748–1832
- John Stuart Mill 1806–1873
- Josiah Royce 1855–1916
- William David Ross 1877–1971
- Hans Jonas 1903–1993
- Hannah Arendt 1906–1975
- John Rawls 1921–2002
- Peter Singer 1946–

Kant is among the greatest moral philosophers of all time, and part of his greatness lies in the way he developed and refined the very idea of the moral life precisely in order to provide rational answers to these problems. ... to lay out the fundamental, rational character of moral thought and action.

(2011: 77)

Kant's theory of rational thought and rational, logical proof for moral behaviour is far too complex to address here, but what is important to note, again, is how the focus on individual responsibility through duty is foregrounded as an imperative.[27]

1.5.7 Maxims and imperatives

Kant articulated two universal *maxims*: (1) act only according to that maxim by which you will it to become a universal law; and (2) act in such a way that you treat humanity never simply as a means, but always at the same time, an end. Moral rules, according to Kant, are those which can be rendered *universal* because they are those rules that everyone should wish to abide by, they explain and justify a universal human consciousness and as such provide grounding for collective ethics, suggesting why we should wish to have and follow rules that curtail our freedom.

Kant distinguishes between maxims, which operate at the personal level and do not break any rules, and imperatives, i.e. collective rules the consequences of which also involve other people (an example of this would be: 'I wear whatever I like when I drive' and 'I'm obliged to wear a seatbelt when I'm driving'). This can be divided into hypothetical imperatives that are not based on morality (for example 'if you exceed the speed limit, you will be fined') and categorical imperatives in the following sense: 'I tell myself how I should behave; before acting I ask if my action represents a law that would be useful for everyone'. With a *categorical imperative*, a person acts only 'in such a way that one would want the maxim of one's action to become a universal law', in other words, to assess whether or not the desired or intended action is or is not right, one should consider it becoming a general law (see e.g. MacIntyre 2002; Ubaldo 2005 [2000]; Graham 2011; Johnson and Cureton 2018).

Another question that was important for Kant at the level of intentions vs results was whether or not the person is 'a means or an ends' captured in the question 'am I doing this for my own interests or regardless of my own interests?' An example could be a doctor whose patient has a terminal illness – if the doctor thinks only of himself, he might avoid telling the patient in order to avoid his own discomfort. While, for Luther, humans cannot perform good actions in an absolute sense because they are not able to know all the criteria or foresee all the consequences, for Kant, right/wrong criteria do exist, and they can be arrived at through reasoning, although Kant acknowledged the complexity of such reasoning. Responsibility is shifted firmly on to the individual. An interesting logical shift enacted in Kantian ethics is that personal happiness should not be a focus in itself because it detracts from the universalisability of ethics. Kantian philosophy represented an important epistemological shift towards the perception of the Self and towards a greater sense of individual responsibility, especially in considering the consequences of our actions, i.e. 'what consequences would there be if everyone acted like me?' Friedrich Hegel (1770–1831) was one of the numerous philosophers influenced by Kantian ethics, but his focus was more on results, on the state and on institutions.

1.5.8 *The non-rational: can humans reason their way to knowledge of what is right?*

1.5.8.1 *Empathy and rationality*

But are ethics truly *rational* and negotiated as a result of rational thought and reasoning? An important take-away point from Kant is that one can at least make an *attempt* to understand morality and ethics rationally, that it is not just a given set of rules external to the individual or group, but one that has a profoundly important social function. It is also important to note how even the greatest philosophers, over millennia, have not been able to establish completely rational, objective grounds for ethical behaviour, nor have they done away completely with the idea that there is some objective or general ethical standard, that ethics is not entirely subjective or irrational. As Graham (2011) reminds us, in the last couple of centuries, studies in ethology, sociology, anthropology and socio-biology have attempted to formulate sets of behaviours that are 'good' precisely because they are 'good for' human beings. The deontological approach is food for thought for any profession because it encourages us to reflect on how our behavioural norms and standards, our ethics, have a rational underpinning, and to attempt to articulate what that underpinning is.

The dependency on rationality and reason and the idea that the universe is a rational place was questioned, however, by many subsequent philosophers. This is also challenged by philosophers. Arthur Schopenhauer (1788–1860) advocated a balance between rationality and impulse. 'Inspired by Plato and Kant, both of whom regarded the world as being more amenable to reason', Schopenhauer encourages minimising natural desires 'for the sake of achieving a more tranquil frame of mind and a disposition towards universal beneficence' (Wicks 2017). In Schopenhauer's philosophy, one of the ways to escape suffering (apart from relieving oneself from one's own impulses by containing desire) is to empathise with others. By empathising with someone else we escape our bodies and therefore our suffering (Ubaldo 2005 [2000]). Empathising is thus a first step to moral behaviour. If, for Kant, reason brings us to moral behaviour, and for Schopenhauer humans are driven by impulses and the desire to reason is useless, David Hume (1711–1776) lies somewhere in between. Hume recognises the importance of reason but only because rationality is what we use to achieve what we want, which is decided by our desires. Whether or not behaving ethically or virtuously or having good intentions leads to happiness (at least at a superficial level), is quite another kettle of fish. Kant's ideas were also inspired by Benedict de Spinoza (1632–1677), who set a precedent for a secular analysis of ethics, an 'autonomous' ethics (i.e. 'I create my law') that was independent of an external, heteronomous authority (i.e. 'someone else creates the law').[28]

1.5.9 Justice and equality

Underpinning the evolving focus on ethics in the modern era is the principle that all people are *equal* and have equal possibilities and rights. This came to the fore very powerfully during the Reformation and in the early eighteenth-century philosophers; the practice of slavery, for example, was fiercely challenged and no longer held to be compatible with core moral values of contemporary society. One of the most important consequences of the focus on equality and respect for people is the emergence of general formulations and decrees and declarations of *universal human rights* at the global level.

The increasing focus on responsibility and commitment to public service is reflected across the chronological timeline in Table 1.1 and in Box 1.3. As the organisational models in Western society leave the medieval-feudal era, focus shifts more to individual rights and a more equal distribution of justice evolves. This intellectual and cultural/political evolution of ideas is spurred on by developments in science and technology, indeed, the two domains go hand in hand. The impact of the Industrial Revolution and scientific and technological advances led to a new distribution of resources and access to education and subsequently to positions of social and political power. The notion of responsibility and a commitment to social justice and public service is advocated by an increasing number of philosophers and prominent cultural figures. By the mid-1800s, Max Weber (1864–1920), one of the most prominent thinkers of the post-Industrial Revolution era, and the founder of modern sociology, promotes commitment to public service as an ethic, as do Hans Jonas (1903–1993) in middle of the following century, and John Rawls (1921–2002) in the twenty-first century. These philosophers represent and reflect the mammoth historical and social forces from late medieval times to contemporary times, their ideas developing in response to wars, profound developments in industrial modes of production, and science (especially developments in technology and science in the late twentieth and twenty-first centuries).

New criteria and possibilities were introduced through these changes and through evolving ideas: the possibility of equal rights and distribution of resources could not have been contemplated without the deep changes from agrarian to industrial modes of production, leading to a general levelling of society (and centuries later to an ethical reflection on ecology and on the environment). Wars too, especially the Second World War and a global intellectual attack on Nazi anti-Semitism, led to a wealth of philosophical reflections, e.g. by Arendt and Jonas. As mentioned, the challenges of the new frontiers of science and technology in Information Technology, in genetic engineering, in robotics and Artificial Intelligence, are already leading to a shift in the focus of philosophical reflection. In recent years, even months, a worrying trend is emerging that may jeopardise these very hard-fought and at times hard-won values, in the waves of populism and extreme violent ideologies that may run counter to those very same ideas of justice and equality. Where this will eventually lead remains to be seen in the coming years.

1.5.10 Natural rights and social contract theory: political philosophy[29]

The natural rights theory of Thomas Hobbes (1588–1679) and John Locke (1632–1704) was also of a deontological nature; in their philosophy, humans have absolute, natural, universal rights to life, liberty and property, which are not contingent on actions or on beliefs.[30] This branch of philosophy eventually turned into what today we think of as 'universal human rights' (see Graham 2011). The development of the social contract theory in the political domain by Hobbes, Locke and Jean-Jacques Rousseau (1712–1778) held that people should give up certain individual rights to a government or other authority in order to preserve the social order. Broadly speaking, *contractarian ethics* holds that moral rules are a sort of contract and that a government must provide rights for its citizens. Hobbes, Locke and Rousseau were all concerned with how to legitimise power, primarily through consent. As we have seen, and with a few exceptions, previously power was thought to reside externally in a god (with some exceptions in medieval philosophy, such as Marsilio da Padova (1275–1342) and William of Ockham (1285–1347) (Fornero 2000; Ubaldo 2005 [2000]). The English Civil War (1642–1651) eventually led to many new channels of political thought and social theory. Hobbes' seminal work, *Leviathan* (1651) was in part an answer to the political unrest. As a pessimist, Hobbes claims that man is born selfish, free and rational and that each human tries to defend their own interests, that they are led to becoming 'wolves' and behave aggressively towards each other ('homo homini lupus'). The solution to this potential anarchy and the selfish nature of humans was to activate a contract: our rationality tells us that our very liberty and freedom put us at risk, therefore, we must negotiate and relinquish that freedom and transfer it to the monarch (via the state). That power is thus given by and legitimated through the people, not by and through God; it is therefore irrevocable. For Locke, however, some years later, the situation is a bit different: humans are free, rational and social from birth. In theory, therefore, political power should be redundant, we should be able to organise society through rational thought. However, because we cannot control others' behaviour, an organisation such as a state is needed to activate this control; therefore, we negotiate and transfer our power to a person or body who represents us.[31] This is a temporary contract, however, so if the representative (monarch) is not able to maintain this agreement, he or she can be deposed and replaced. Again, significantly, it is not God who has put the monarch on the throne. This is the forerunner to constitutional monarchy and representational democracy. For Rousseau, humanity is sick and unhappy because people have distanced themselves from nature; they have relinquished their natural characteristics to rationality and civilisation, and this has not brought about a state of happiness. Rousseau's question – 'does civilisation render humans happier?' – should be seen against the backdrop of the wave of colonisation and 'discoveries' of 'primitive peoples' (ergo the myth of the 'noble savage'). Since civilisation cannot be totally jettisoned, rationality must be used constructively to find solutions. Which begs the question – who negotiates the contract? For Rousseau, humans negotiate, relinquishing their liberty to find a more complete and authentic liberty in organised society through the (later controversial) notion of 'general will'.[32] Followers and critics of Rousseau have seen in his work the seeds of both democratic ('we are the state') and totalitarian thought (for example, in Robespierre's presumption of knowing the will of the people), given that 'humanness' is realised through institutions. Hegel both builds on this idea and criticises it, since, in his view, humans find fulfilment through the state, not as individuals (Fornero 2000; Ubaldo 2005 [2000]). Another empirical approach to ethics, but different from Hobbes' natural rights theory, was Hume's descriptive approach; he looked at how we make our moral judgements based on self-interest. Hume argued that humans often act irrationally, and always in self-interest. Thus, not only does he also place 'good' outside the sphere of god/religion or as an intrinsic value of beneficence found in human beings, but he questions human beings' presumed innate ability or tendency to reason and behave rationally. The work of these philosophers illustrates the intense and complex reflections and discussions that underpin the philosophy of politics and social organisation, and underpin our organisation of the professions, and professional ethics, as we know them today.

1.5.11 Justice

Another break with earlier tradition (see Graham 2011: 77ff, quoting Nietzsche) is represented by the idea that being 'poor and meek' is a blessed, not a damned, condition. The focus on justice, equality and caring for all strata of society is one that characterises not just early Christianity but also other world religions, and lays the foundation for one of the pillars of the modern world. As mentioned, justice, equality and the distribution of justice are fundamental parameters that lie at the heart of most modern societies, not just those that are held up as democratic. Even (moderate) dictator-states may have justice and equality, in a wide sense, as ideal goals, although the underlying parameters and the manner in which they are obtained may be different from what we generally think of as democratic. Even in those societies (for example, ancient Rome) where slavery was considered a natural order and violence was glorified, a sense of equality and justice underpinned the system at some level, although it was reserved for privileged citizens and was at the mercy of capricious rulers.

It is quite natural that attention to justice and equal rights falls within the domain of politics. In the nineteenth, twentieth and twenty-first centuries, Weber, Marx and Rawls discuss the ethics of justice as political philosophy, focusing on the distribution of justice and the equal access to economic and social goods (see Wenar 2017). Rawls' social contract – the aim of which is the just distribution of goods – is articulated through a hypothetical theory of 'Justice as Fairness'. This is built on two principles of justice that attempt to reconcile freedom and justice, the first of which is: the 'greatest equal liberty principle'. According to this principle, all members of society should have the greatest amount of liberty possible, but at the same time 'no member shall infringe upon the rights of others' (ibid.). Rawls is concerned with those circumstances that make possible an equal distribution of justice and resources and access to political service; justice must be enabled by circumstances that must be favourable in order to enact justice – requiring, one assumes, public organisation of both circumstances (welfare, support, benefits, etc. to enable health and education) and equal opportunities (access to services, jobs, positions of public service). This lies at the heart of the fundamental PSI ethic of social justice through equal access to public services across language barriers. In *The Secret Barrister*, the anonymous author shows how the UK legal system is based on the fundamental idea of 'fairness' (Anonymous 2017). The UK legal system – as is probably the case with many other legal systems around the world – has miserably failed its users, however, as the principle is not translated into concrete reality. The author shows the complete breakdown in the transition from system/idea to practice. Justice, and the reality of real-world variables, such as organisation, budgets and politics, are often not natural bed-fellows.

1.5.12 Utilitarianism and consequentialism

As explained in the Introduction, with utilitarianism (or more generally consequentialism), philosophers attempt to *measure and quantify what is good* (expressed as 'happiness') through a strictly rational, often very rigid, logical analysis of what is 'good for' ('happiness') the greatest number of people, the well-known 'Greatest Happiness Principle' (GHP). However, as Sinnott-Armstrong (2015) warns:

> These claims are often summarized in the slogan that an act is right if and only if it causes 'the greatest happiness for the greatest number.' This slogan is misleading, however. An act can increase happiness for most (the greatest number of) people but still fail to maximize the net good in the world if the smaller number of people whose happiness is not increased lose much more than the greater number gains. The principle of utility would not allow that kind of sacrifice of the smaller number to the greater number unless the net good overall is increased more than any alternative.

The main proponents of this school of moral philosophy, as described in the Introduction, are the English philosophers Jeremy Bentham (1748–1832) and John Stuart Mill (1806–1873). Unlike the deontological approach, the consequentialist view identifies a good action by evaluating its ultimate consequences, rather than the intention of the agent. Utilitarianism is a branch of the consequentialist approach (also referred to as *teleological ethics*), that focuses on the consequences of an individual's actions. This approach holds that the moral quality of an action is contingent upon its consequences. For example, we have obligations to *help* people because that is the course of action that produces better results than not helping them. It seeks to quantify ethics by suggesting that the most moral or good action is the one that results in the greatest happiness to the greatest number of recipients, the one that produces most 'pleasure'. In other words, the utility is the happiness or pleasure given by an action which will produce greater pleasure than another action. Other forms of *consequentialist philosophy* gauge an action by its consequences, but according to different parameters – for example, hedonism and egoism that measure the validity of consequences according to the pleasure of the actor, or asceticism and altruism that proscribe happiness for others, not for the self. Rule consequentialists, such as Peter Singer (1946–), suggest that moral or good behaviour is achieved by following rules that are chosen exclusively on the basis of their consequences. Arguably, Singer's rather extreme and provocative examples also illustrate the limitations of this approach. Twentieth- and twenty-first-century philosophers, such as Richard Rorty (1931–2007), investigated ethics from a pragmatic point of view, looking at how rules and codes of conduct are selected on the basis of the consequences they lead to and on the basis of their usefulness.

The utilitarian and consequentialist labels are not straightforward, however, and the factors that need to be taken on board when evaluating a consequence are extremely complex. Philosophers have teased out logical nuances of applying consequentialism to ethical decision-making. Sinnott-Armstrong lists some of them:

- *Consequentialism* = whether an act is morally right depends only on consequences (as opposed to the circumstances or the intrinsic nature of the act or anything that happens before the act).
- *Actual consequentialism* = whether an act is morally right depends only on the actual consequences (as opposed to foreseen, foreseeable, intended, or likely consequences).
- *Direct consequentialism* = whether an act is morally right depends only on the consequences of that act itself (as opposed to the consequences of the agent's motive, of a rule or practice that covers other acts of the same kind, and so on).
- *Evaluative consequentialism* = moral rightness depends only on the value of the consequences (as opposed to non-evaluative features of the consequences).
- *Hedonism* = the value of the consequences depends only on the pleasures and pains in the consequences (as opposed to other supposed goods, such as freedom, knowledge, life, and so on).
- *Maximising consequentialism* = moral rightness depends only on which consequences are best (as opposed to merely satisfactory or an improvement over the status quo).
- *Aggregative consequentialism* = which consequences are best is some function of the values of parts of those consequences (as opposed to rankings of whole worlds or sets of consequences).
- *Total consequentialism* = moral rightness depends only on the total net good in the consequences (as opposed to the average net good per person).
- *Universal consequentialism* = moral rightness depends on the consequences for all people or sentient beings (as opposed to only the individual agent, members of the individual's society, present people, or any other limited group).
- *Equal consideration* = in determining moral rightness, benefits to one person matter just as much as similar benefits to any other person (= all who count, count equally).
- *Agent-neutrality* = whether some consequences are better than others does not depend on whether the consequences are evaluated from the perspective of the agent (as opposed to an observer).

Consequentialism is one potentially fruitful way of partially bypassing the thorny essentialist issue of what is the exact nature of accuracy and fidelity in the translation/interpreting process. This strategy applies to interpreting, when there is a conflict between the ethic of accuracy and some other need of the interlocutors or the interpreter him/herself, so that the interpreter is led to omit information, adding/ explaining, intervening, protesting, intervening, etc. If the nature of the interaction is such that the interpreter deems he or she is breaking a higher ethic (interpreting solicitations of violence or hate-discourse, or covert or overt discrimination against one or more interlocutors, or the community), he or she may feel compelled to interrupt the session. It could be as everyday as a religious, social or cultural taboo (for example, sharing bad news such as terminal illness in a culturally inappropriate manner) or realising that the interpreter has access to private information regarding the foreign speaker, or has a positive or negative bias towards him/her. Rather than following the code of ethics slavishly, a useful parameter to follow is precisely that of considering the outcome and specific consequence of the action – who (how many) will the action harm/benefit and by how much? Since such decisions are made instantaneously, training, self-reflection and experience will strengthen the interpreter's ability to come to a decision that safeguards him/herself, the profession and the interlocutors as far as possible. Laurie Swabey (2017) makes this point effectively, stressing the interconnectedness of good decision-making by resorting to critical thinking (reason/rationality), experience (outcome of past decisions), professional standards and individual judgement.

1.5.13 Pluralistic deontology and decision-making

According to Skelton (2012), the American philosopher W. D. Ross (1877–1971) is one of the key figures in the debate on ethics in the nineteenth and twentieth centuries. Ross criticises both Kant and (ideal) utilitarianism for oversimplifying and for the lack of attention to 'the plain man'. Kant's universalisation principle was over-simplified, according to Ross, in that only one motive was foregrounded. Life is rather, he says,

> [a] contest between one element which alone has worth [i.e. the good will] and a multitude of others which have none; the truth is rather that it is a struggle between a multiplicity of desires having various degrees of worth.
>
> *(ibid.)*

He also believed that Kant erred in not allowing for exceptions, that moral rules have 'absolute authority admitting of no exception'. His critique against ideal utilitarianism is that it is wrong to assume that there is a general character which simply makes a right act right in itself. Furthermore,

> in virtue of presupposing that there is only one thing that we ought all things considered to do it distorts our understanding of moral deliberation. For example, when deciding whether to fulfill a promise we think much more of the fact that in the past we have made a promise than of the consequences we might realise by fulfilling it.
>
> *(Skelton 2012)*

Ross seems to be advocating a less polarised approach to ethical decision-making, suggesting that it is simplistic to think in terms of one single possible option when faced with a choice; indeed, he emphasises the complexity of moral life as having a plurality of 'requirements and goods' (hence pluralistic deontology) rather than a single fundamental principle. His much-quoted five (later seven) duties capture parameters that can help guide people as they make difficult choices, and are thus useful to the present discussion; they will be returned to subsequently as a decision-making process that can be applied to PSI. It is important to note that these duties are not equally important, and may also sometimes clash, leading to dilemmas. These five duties are:

1. *fidelity* – to keep our promises;
2. *reparation* – to act to right a previous wrong we have done;
3. *gratitude* – to return services to those from whom we have in the past accepted benefits;
4. *the promotion of a maximum of aggregate good* – more specifically *beneficence* to help other people increase their pleasure and *justice*, to ensure people get what they deserve;
5. *non-maleficence* – not to harm others.

Two other parameters were later added: *self-improvement* and *promise-keeping* (to act according to explicit and implicit promises, including that of telling the truth) (ibid.). On a scale of importance, some of these duties would be of a higher order. The 'duty of non-maleficence is more important than the duty to promote a maximum of aggregate good' (ibid.) and fidelity, reparation, and gratitude 'are in general more weighty than the duty to promote the good ... [resting] on personal relations with others, which generate special rather than general duties' (ibid.). For Ross, the nature of the relationships that we are engaged in, in a promise-keeping capacity ('creditor to debtor, of wife to husband, of child to parent, of friend to friend, of fellow countryman to fellow countryman'), are also different and carry different weight. Duty thus has a 'highly personal character', which is relevant to the discussion on loyalty in Section 1.5.16. This consideration is helpful to our discussion as it relativises the 'universal' codes regarding impartiality, suggesting that the *nature* of the interpreting encounter and the *people involved* in that encounter are important too.

On what basis can a 'good' PSI action be measured and enacted? To answer this question in relation to PSI, we could apply some of Ross's parameters:

- *beneficence*: to help other people communicate and mutually understand an utterance;
- *non-maleficence*: to avoid harming people by mistranslating;
- *justice*: to ensure people get access to services by removing language barriers;
- *self-improvement*: to be adequately competent through training or self-study.

Of the remaining parameters in Ross's model – reparation, gratitude and promise-keeping/truth-telling – the last one applies generally to any professional, but is also implicit in the textual act of language transfer and the primary ethic of accuracy, as mentioned above in relation to loyalty and in relation to Kant's logic of communication,[33] Reparation falls under a legal category of repairing damage done through mistranslation; this could be individual in an interpreting session, or a collective act and responsibility (hospital, court, school, local government, etc.). Gratitude (to people who have benefited us) is more of a general ethic that applies to interpersonal communication in any community group rather than specifically in a professional context. If one were to grade these ethics according to the degree of importance, arguably, non-maleficence would be a baseline ethic, followed by beneficence (which would include truth-telling), self-improvement and reparation.

1.5.14 Existentialism and the freedom of choice

Existentialists (represented principally by Jean-Paul Sartre, 1905–1980) deny the existence of an ethical structure that is external to the human being, rejecting the idea of an intrinsic nature or essence (in an Aristotelian sense); there is no 'existence before essence', there is no preordained essential character (Graham 2011: 60ff). Sartre describes the awareness and knowledge of this human state as 'condemning man to be free'. Choices and decisions must be made individually and independently of universal rules or an objective set of ethical standards. Paradoxically, man is thus 'inescapably free', there is no 'must' or 'cannot' (Sartre 1946, quoted in Graham 2011: 64). According to the existentialists, it is this very responsibility and the loneliness of that knowledge that cause human beings deep anguish, brilliantly captured in the French novelist Albert Camus' work. Graham observes, reassuringly, that 'To say that individuals are free to choose their own values is more naturally interpreted as meaning that they are free to choose *between* pre-existent values' (2011: 76), suggesting perhaps that although we feel 'free' to choose, our thoughts and decisions are always based on thoughts and decisions of others before us. For the Danish philosopher and theologian, Søren Kierkegaard (1813–1855), a countermeasure (or cure) for the anguish of existence and choice, 'the sickness of Death', was faith and religion.

As Graham (2011) remarks, philosophical studies in the twentieth century were marked by a new focus that took on board developments in science and the emerging disciplines of sociology, anthropology and psychology. A general tendency towards *relativism* and a challenging of universal norms is represented by a deep paradigm shift in the Humanities generally; for example, *evolutionary ethics*, holding that ethical practices are evolved ways of behaviour leading to evolutionary success.[34]

1.5.15 Applying ethics to the professions

Ethics is a topic that easily captures the public attention because it relates so powerfully to our everyday actions and thoughts and to our sense of what we are allowed to do and to what we are discouraged from doing. Ethics as an abstract framework and set of rules touches upon the everyday life of all human beings, but it does so in a much more concrete fashion in what is termed 'applied ethics' (Graham 2011), when we apply general ethical rules to specific cases. This is the interface where philosophy, religion, politics and everyday life meet. The most sensitive areas to which ethics are applied are those that touch upon life and death such as abortion and euthanasia but also environmental ethics and equal or civil rights – women's right to vote, divorce, etc. In these cases, we depart from the private and professional domains and enter the public domain of politics and governance (law-making).

One of the main areas of applied ethics is that which relates to the professions, and in particular those professions which make life-changing decisions every day regarding precisely life and death and human/equal rights, namely, medicine and law. Euthanasia and defending criminals being two prototypical dilemmas in the two professions, respectively. As claimed at the beginning of this chapter, those professions are the ones that most urgently need to be protected, and in a sense 'protected from themselves', because they are precisely the ones that can be beneficial but that can do the most damage to the citizens they serve. They are also the professions that most frequently come into contact with interpreters and are thus particularly interesting for our purposes.

The Hippocratic Oath already embodies the deepest ethical value of the medical profession, namely, to practise to the best of one's ability in the best interests of the patient, and to avoid harm. In medical ethics and bioethics, genomics, human engineering and similar areas of bio-technology, moral values and judgements become paramount. These are not only issues such as abortion, euthanasia and stem-cell research, but also more 'mundane' issues such as the sharing of bad news (terminal illness) and informed consent, the cost of life-saving medicines, care for the very old, etc. Some of the core rules of medical ethics that safeguard patients and fit in the macro-areas of ethics described above, are *beneficence* (act in the best interests of the patient), *non-maleficence* (do not harm the patient), *autonomy* (the patient has the right to refuse treatment), *justice* (scarce health resources – who gets treatment?), *dignity* for both patient and practitioner, and *honesty* (truthfulness, respect for informed consent) (see Graham 2011).

The legal profession is at the same time ethically normative, but must also itself abide by a strict regulatory set of ethical guidelines, precisely to limit its potential to do harm as well as ability to enact good. Duties and regulatory norms affect the client-lawyer relationship, respect for client confidence, truthfulness in the information provided, professional independence and many other situations in the course of legal proceedings. Ethical responsibility falls upon the shoulders of all members of the prosecution, or the jury, but obviously in its most profound manifestation in the figure of the arbitrating authority, the judge. The judge is 'protected' from making mistakes in meting out justice by an elaborate legislative code articulated in great detail to avoid gaps and ambiguity. As such, the judge is acting not as a private person but as a representative of a collective body sanctioned by the people.[35] Indeed, one of the deepest differences between a functioning and a non-functioning democracy is the solidity, the efficacy and the honesty of its legal system; a corrupt legal system corrupts the entire fabric of society because while one can always access private medical care, there is no alternative to a collective group-based legal system.

1.5.16 Loyalty: forging alliances, damage potential and making choices

Another philosophical consideration highly relevant to IS is the notion of loyalty. John Kleinig defines loyalty in the following manner:

> Loyalty is usually seen as a virtue, albeit a problematic one. It is constituted centrally by perseverance in an association to which a person has become intrinsically committed as a matter of his or her identity. Its paradigmatic expression is found in friendship, to which loyalty is integral, but many other relationships and associations seek to encourage it as an aspect of affiliation or membership: families expect it, organizations often demand it, and countries do what they can to foster it.
>
> *(2017: 1)*

Loyalty as an ethic, a value and a virtue strikes at the very heart of human social organisation from the smallest (family/friendship) to the largest (nation-state or pan-national)[36] groups, and one which serves the essential function of creating social cohesion and trust, and of providing a system of checks and balances in our relations with other people. It inculcates a sense of responsibility and encourages us to show respect towards other people. It is a value that can cause powerful feelings in people, both positive and negative. When confronted with a clash of loyalties, we are forced to foreground one person, idea or cause rather than another.

Loyalty is both rational and sentimental; rational because it underpins and is constitutive of relation-building and creation of trust, and sentimental because it is perceived as a relationship built on mutual sympathy or affection, kinship bonds, etc. Thus, human sentiment is at the service of an important social-organisational function; the strong feeling we have towards loyalty bonds ensures that we do not desert people easily in self-interest. This serves – in an evolutionary manner – both group cohesion and social organisation per se. The philosopher Josiah Royce (1855–1916) wrote extensively on the issue of loyalty in philosophy, observing that a sense of loyalty comes with identification with a group, and continuity in that identification process. It is through this process that we adopt the standards of that specific group, be it a religion or a profession or a country (see www.lawandbioethics.com). Loyalty touches upon deep psychological processes of identification and belonging, primordial to human beings and functional to the survival and evolution of the species.

Philosophers have long debated whether or not loyalty can only be acknowledged and implemented towards other people, or also if abstract notions and ideas can be the object of loyalty (see Kleinig 2017). In the present discussion I am assuming that people can indeed be loyal to a cause or idea; thus, they can be loyal not only to a professional community of which they are a member loosely or strictly speaking, but also to a standard of professional conduct.

Although loyalty is most often associated with interpersonal relationships, especially friendship, it is a powerful driving factor in an individual's allegiance to their country or their state. Indeed, the principle of loyalty is fundamental to political theory (from the feudal system and monarchies to the modern nation-state – or even pan-national entity – and nationalist ideologies). Treason has been a capital offence in many societies. Loyalty is thus played out at the individual level and at all kinds of collective group levels. It is also played out at a metaphysical level in an individual's relationship with the divine in which ethical dilemmas occur around the world: loyalty (obedience) towards God vs loyalty (support/agreement) towards the nation, state, social group, friends, family, etc.

Can we be loyal to different, discordant people or causes at the same time? Do they exclude each other? Is it natural to have multiple loyalties and be 'members' of different groups to which we are loyal (family, political party, religion, country, etc.) but have conflicting norms? What happens when one of those groups (e.g. religion) demands exclusive loyalty (e.g. non-membership in a political party)? Because of the simple fact that we are members of different socio-cultural groups simultaneously, and these groups may have different needs, objectives and values, competing loyalties are common. The strength of adherence to any specific group will naturally vary, but it is generally strongest vis-à-vis those groups to which we have a deepest sense of identification and commonality.

1.5.17 Loyalty and impartiality: loyalty and the interpreter

In his discussion on political philosophy (see Kim 2017), Max Weber advocates adherence to a few essential traits, namely, *to serve a cause* and *responsibility*. We find these traits in many deontological approaches, but Weber also includes *passion and impartiality*. These two latter traits are often very difficult to combine – passion will often lead precisely to a desire to take sides.[37] Ideally, a politician, through experience and familiarity, is able to maintain a balanced distance. One could argue that it is precisely this balance of passion – which can also be expressed through loyalty – and impartiality that represents the quintessential dilemma between a professional behavioural code and a feeling of loyalty towards an idea, cause or person.

It is indeed in the nature of embracing a cause, of a deep sense of duty and responsibility and the desire to serve the public that impartiality is essential because it enables effective realisation of that duty or service and, more importantly, it safeguards equality and justice and prevents people from taking sides. Such engagement in an idea or cause or religion, however, activates sentiments that may put at risk, as Weber suggests, that very same distance. Impartiality can be challenged by feelings of loyalty towards a person, cause/ideology or institution for a host of reasons, such as alignment at the cultural, ethical, personal level. Furthermore, although taking sides may in some cases seem to be a noble act, it could also be marred by an imperfect access to information and knowledge of possible future consequences. Loyalty would also encapsulate, trigger and actuate the ethic of confidentiality through the need to honour a contractual relationship with both clients and the profession. Crucially, loyalty is based on the ability to create *trust*. The idea of loyalty as a 'psychological contract' is important because it can help shed light on the interpreter's state of mind and the stress that loyalty bonds may activate.

One area of moral philosophy that intersects with the notions of loyalty and impartiality and that is especially relevant to professional domains is that of whistleblowing.[38] The decision to break the confidentiality ethic and inform a service provider, institution or client about events or statements heard or read in a confidential professional setting, be it the firm, the doctor's or lawyer's office, the courtroom, the confessional or an interpreter-mediated event, is often a difficult one that is arrived at after much difficult deliberation and often at a high price – the disapproval of one's colleagues and institution and possible economic or legal sanctions.[39] Confidentiality and impartiality are such important ethics in PSI, as in other professions, precisely because they force us to protect and restrain that very natural sense of loyalty that we might feel towards one or more parties, and jeopardise the objective of the institutional or professional event.

1.5.18 Empathy

Schopenhauer's notion of empathy as the first step to moral behaviour discussed above is interesting in this context because it feeds into an 'ethics of care' that pertains to many professions (especially health and education) and also to PSI, in that it is a correlate to these professions and in its baseline ethic of equal access to services (the principle of justice). Recently, in the wake of the paradigm shift that has marked contemporary IS and TS, empathy has sometimes been championed as a necessary 'competence' or 'skill' that allows an interpreter to better understand the foreign language speaker and to be a better communicator. This may also be a nod to the ethic of care and justice, especially when it plays out in the context of trauma in mental health settings related to domestic violence, torture, refugee issues, etc. It stands in some contrast to the ethic of objectivity and impartiality. No doubt more research will be done in this area in the near future to shed light on whether or not empathy actually increases the quality of language transfer and of communication. A word of caution might be in order here, though, on two accounts: empathy, when not tempered, may skew and problematise and thus impede communication rather than bolstering it and also may also lead to real or perceived partisanship. Empathy is a complex psychological phenomenon, and if the interpreter has not had prior training in this regard, it may quickly lead not just to partisanship and role confusion, but also to vicarious trauma and interpreter burn-out.

1.5.19 Loyalty, rationality and whistleblowing

Vandekerckhove and Commers (2004: 227–228) show how, etymologically, the English word 'loyalty' is connected to terms such as 'faithful, honest, true, steadfast, fidelity, adherence to vows/promises, honest, true, genuine, real, actual, exact', illustrating precisely the key, and problematic, role that loyalty plays as a process, as an attitude and as an emotion (and as a complex combination of these) in the impartiality ethic for the interpreter, at many levels.

They take an innovative perspective on the issue of loyalty, looking at loyalty from a collaborative angle where the loyalty-relationship between organisation/company and employee is a mutual, relational and reciprocal social contract,[40] and where the object of the employee's loyalty is not the company itself, but the company's mission statement. This is interesting because it holds the company responsible, as it were, to be faithful to their original mission statement and protects the employee from any capricious actions taken by the company if the employee were to blow the whistle on them; thus, it dis-incentivises an attack on the whistleblowing employee for self-serving reasons (i.e. for the company), acknowledging that the employee has not actually broken any rules or ethical standards as such.

This is an interesting perspective because it solves, or at least bypasses, the incompatibility problem of extending loyalty to either (not both) parties in a situation where an employee feels it is ethically incumbent upon him/her to blow the whistle. Furthermore, it is a considered decision based on identifiable factors and reasoning, rather than more 'fuzzy' intuitive or affect-driven loyalty concepts:

> The adjective 'rational' in rational loyalty indicates the need for the individual to make a deliberation whether or not her acts are a contribution to the explicit mission, values and goals of the organization she is loyal to. If she finds herself in a situation where organizational behaviour diverts from its explicit mission, goals and values – would demand of her to blow the whistle ... Rational loyalty demands an employee to be loyal to the organization identified in and through the explicit mission statement.
> (Vandekerckhove and Commers 2004: 228)

It demands pro-active decision-making regarding the 'higher good' and a higher level of ethics (society/community beyond the profession and group), as it were.

Such decision-making should be rationalised (through a rational reasoning process, or by way of an internalised process through training and experience, preferably both) and not done 'off the cuff': as Vandekerckove and Commers remark, loyalty refers to a willingness to sacrifice and act for the benefit of something or someone else – in other words, there is a cost involved. Transferring this idea to PSI, we could capture the bonds of loyalty visually in Figure 1.1, where a Bond would act relationally and reciprocally between the Interpreter and Service Provider and between Interpreter and Profession/Text.

The immediate needs of other people involved in the interpreting process, other interlocutors, may also impinge forcefully on an interpreter's loyalty bonds in many ways, ranging from a more general human rights value and desire for fairness, to

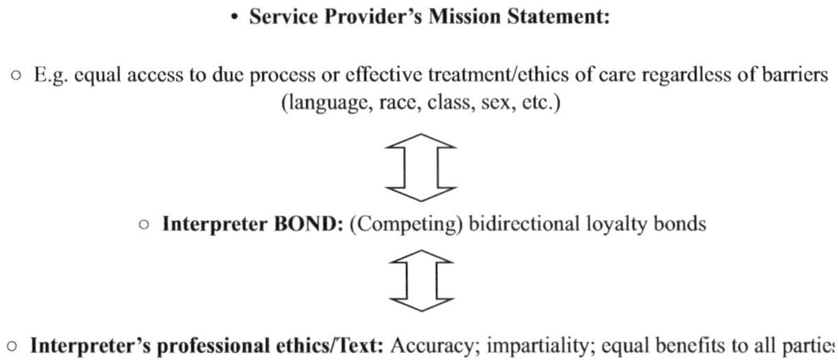

- **Service Provider's Mission Statement:**
  - E.g. equal access to due process or effective treatment/ethics of care regardless of barriers (language, race, class, sex, etc.)

  ⇕

  - **Interpreter BOND:** (Competing) bidirectional loyalty bonds

  ⇕

  - **Interpreter's professional ethics/Text:** Accuracy; impartiality; equal benefits to all parties

FIGURE 1.1 PSI loyalty bonds

practical needs or feelings of empathy or alignment based on in-group characteristics (such as a shared nationality/language/culture, etc.).

This notion of 'rational loyalty' implies that the interpreter would need to consider not so much, or not exclusively, the interactants and people involved in the immediate setting, but rather the Service Provider's mission statement, constructing a bond of loyalty with the mission statement rather than with the actual people involved. This brings the decision-making process to a higher, social level of deliberation (captured in the Camayd-Freixas case discussed in Part 2 in this volume, see also Camayd-Freixas 2008) and may also take away some of the stress involved in the decision-making process, as well as encouraging the interpreter to take a global rather than a more myopic view of each situation. Still, the consideration and decision-making processes are complex, as they need to be weighed against the loyalty bond to the interpreting profession and the text/utterance, as well as all the contingent parameters involved that the interpreter needs to consider in order to reach a balanced decision.

To summarise, loyalty plays out in the dynamic of a trust-based relationship between interpreter and interlocutors at the individual level and as a professional group – to be recognised as a necessary and able vehicle of essential services to the community. This is true of most professions, but what is specific to TI, and even more so to PSI, is the nature of the interpreting or translational act per se that requires a balancing between words and people. For a written text, this loyalty operates arguably at a more abstract level, but in a PSI setting that text is embedded in a very concrete and immediate act and one where the interlocutors are present and may have very specific expectations towards the interpreter.

1.6 The ethics of translation: ethics in Translation Studies

Ethics has long been the object of analysis in IS's sister discipline, Translation Studies (hereafter TS). To gain a fuller understanding of what lies at the heart of the language transfer process and how it relates to broader, philosophical processes, a cursory connection should be made between TS and IS ethics.

1.6.1 The loyalty-equivalence-accuracy conundrum

Throughout history TS has, by its very nature, been concerned with what we could call the 'ethics of loyalty' or 'loyal representation'. Typically formulated either as 'faithfulness' or 'equivalence', we could envision it as 'the categorical imperative' of TS and IS. Although these concepts have rightly been challenged as unrealistic and absolutist imperatives, they nevertheless represent the very heart of the translational process and translational ethics: its very definition, one might say. An important shift in focus has taken place, however, in TS since the 1980s, a shift which has led scholars to turn away from a quasi-exclusive focus on (linguistic) equivalence to a heightened awareness of the social, cultural, ideological and personal features that impact on the translation process and product.[41] The simplistic, reductive and positivist notion of translational equivalence in the early days of TS was no longer tenable, the notion of 'loyalty' to the Source Text (hereafter ST and TT for Source and Target Text respectively) and exclusive authorship and ownership were problematised; new focal points of translation research and scholarship emerged (discussed in Chesterman 2017; Gentzler 1998; Pöchhacker 2004; Pym 2010).

Many attempts have been made to tackle and unravel the dilemma, or 'double-bind', of equivalence, but the real game-changer was Gideon Toury's (1995 [1980]) landmark contribution through his work on norms. His bid to work around what was an unsolvable philosophical problem (the impossibility of perfect equivalence) by defining translational equivalence in terms of what a target culture defines as such led to a whole new descriptive – rather than prescriptive – approach to TS and opened the door to a broader contextualisation – cultural, political, ideological – of the translation process. An example from more recent TS scholarship on ethics and the attempt to define translational equivalence and propose a way out of the maze, in the full knowledge that this must necessarily be a question of degree, is the work of George Floros (2016). He suggests viewing the ST-TT relationship as one of 'mutual survival' where survival is an 'Ur-value' and where each ST and TT unit presumably struggles to exist independently but also in relation to each other. Andrew Chesterman's well-known work integrating the ideas of the philosopher of science Karl Popper into TS (Chesterman 2016; 2017) is one example of the use of philosophy in TS in relation to the ethic of the textual transfer.

A more flexible and fluid approach to both translation and interpreting is largely a result of the paradigm changes that have led to a 'loosening-up' of what constitutes the act of translation, be it written or oral, in line with the postmodern relativist paradigm in the humanities towards social constructivism (see Rudvin 2006). Although this shift was necessary to free the discipline from the shackles of an overly narrow view of equivalence and fidelity as the guiding ethical imperatives, there is also a danger leading to an excessive liberty for the translator or interpreter, allowing for a degree of 'poetic licence' that leaves the ST-TT bond in a sort of limbo, challenging the very notion of what it means to translate. As Floros noted in 2016, ethical relativity can lead to 'ethical anarchy'; simply being aware of this, self-reflexivity is not itself sufficient to resolve ethical issues and there is need for 'minimum level of prescription', he observes. Arguably (see Rudvin 2006), we risk throwing the baby out with the bathwater, as it were, if we lose sight of the nature of the translational process itself.[42] Ethics in TS, as in IS, I would assert, remains intrinsically if paradoxically related to the notions of equivalence, faithfulness and loyalty. Consequently, the shift away from an equivalence focus has also impacted on ethics, problematising the notion of equivalence and challenging the very fundaments of translational ethics.

As TS became further re-contextualised into a broader arena in which contextual impacting parameters (social, cultural, political, ethnic, gendered, etc.) were factored in, the focus also shifted to the function of the target text, its impact on the community in which it took place, and the translator's role in that impact and thus on society at large. Scholars like Tymoczko, Baker and Inghilleri (see Baker 2006; Chesterman 2017; Inghilleri 2012; Pym 2010; Tymoczko 2007) began to investigate the impact of translation and interpreting in non-traditional domains involving conflict and violence where the domain itself evoked a breach of ethics and violations of human rights.

Kruger and Crots' (2014) paper 'Professional and personal ethics in translation: A survey of South African translators' translation strategies and motivations' provides an excellent summary and discussion of the major studies on the ethics of translation – and the different schools of thought in this regard, focusing especially on Chesterman and Anthony Pym, whose work on ethics has been a significant contribution to the TS literature.[43]

Two ethics-related questions that emerge as a result of this shift and in a very direct way are:

- Is the translator responsible for the contents of the text in any way, and, if so, should they refuse to translate a text that is at odds with their personal ethics?
- Is the translator responsible to society for the impact (or lack of impact) of the translated text or utterance? (the 'activist' approach').

Such concerns have led TS a long way from the early days of the textual equivalence of Catford or Newmark (see Chesterman 2017; Gentzler 1993; Pöchhacker 2004; Pym 2010; 2012) to actually looking at the impact of the translator, and of translator ethics, on social practices and whether or not translators should decide to breach textual ethics in the name of a higher order ethic (e.g. involvement vs impartiality in a situation where human rights are being breached).

1.6.2 Impartiality: from Translation Studies to Interpreting Studies

If the intrinsic ST-TT bond is the nucleus of translational ethics at a textual level, it is embedded in other levels or spheres of professional ethics represented in Figure 1.2.[44] The surrounding levels change somewhat from TS to IS, but could be illustrated by 'Textual Ethics' – or the ethics of *representation* – at the nucleus of the circle situated within the domain of 'Interpersonal Ethics' – reflecting the dynamics

62 Mette Rudvin

1. Textual Domain
2. Interpersonal Domain
3. Social – Community Sphere

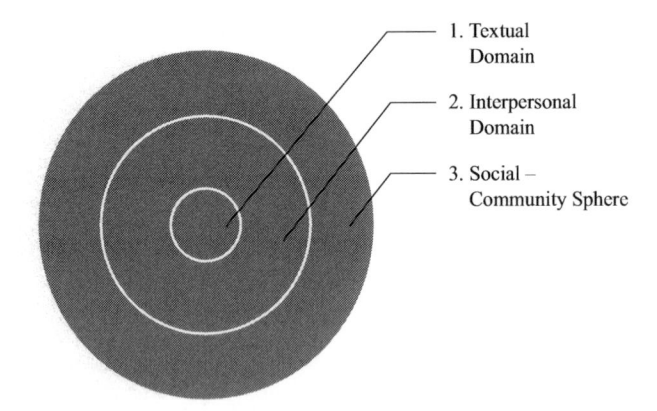

FIGURE 1.2 Interpreting domains: interpreting ethics at the (macro) social level and at the (micro) textual level

between the interlocutors – which is again situated in a broader Social/Community domain involving service to and engagement with the community and the institutions (Justice, Equality, Social Justice).

It might be useful to think of interpreting ethics on two broad 'levels':[45] an *inner-oriented textual level* and an *outer-oriented public level*. The first, the inner circle, relates to a specific duty and responsibility towards the texts/speakers/authors and listeners/readers where quality encapsulates the interpreter's *telos* (or intrinsic characteristic and aim) and lies at the heart of the interpreter's (and translator's) practice. This could be captured in the translator's 'anguish' of finding the balance between respecting ST and TT texts and contexts simultaneously (captured in the notion of fidelity in early TS and IS but also more broadly in the notion of 'loyalty' discussed above). Hale distinguishes between three areas of responsibility (see Hale 2007) at the textual level, which we could envision as a form of social contract: towards the authority of the *text/utterance itself*, to *the author* and the author's intent (insofar as this is possible, there is always a grey area of subjective interpretation of authorial intent) or *the listener* (through a form of dynamic equivalence).

In PSI, textual ethics is largely played out in terms of preferred translation strategies in the interpersonal domain to fit the appropriate (institutional, situational) relationship between interlocutors. This again is situated in and governed by broader social and community norms that may also require reflection on ethics that pertain to social justice and equality. Thus, at the collective level, textual ethics is played out in the middle and outer circle as a *professional ethic* upholding a professional standard, while the social level of a *community ethic* is a more general duty towards community, towards profession, and towards one's clients, creating the conditions through which all members have access to basic community services. We could call this an 'ethics of care' that we also find in other service professions, especially in healthcare or welfare and social services. Justice and equality are also an ethical injunction of loyalty towards the professional community and towards one's clients in a contract-based relationship. As such, the interpreter is an active, engaged contributing citizen, following Aristotle's virtue ethical injunction and aiming to fulfil the consequentialist injunction of bringing about the greatest good for the greatest number of people. At both the internal and external levels, the interpreter is following the deontological injunction of Duty and Responsibility and 'respect for people', be they the authors/speakers-readers/listeners, the profession or the wider community consisting of public institutions and non-majority language users of public institutions.

1.6.3 Translation Studies approaches to ethics

The standards and collective conventions captured in Toury's descriptive norms have made it possible for TS scholars to bypass the ST-TT conundrum; he unravels the dependency of norms on equivalence-based ethics, looking at norms from an external rather than an internal perspective. I would suggest, in line with Schäffner (1999), that norms represent codified, collective, intersubjective standards of practice in a descriptive framework and they become ethics only insofar as they function prescriptively and govern the translator's decisions (into TT). An ethic would thus be closer to what Floros (2016) calls an 'injunction', functioning prescriptively or deontically (see Floros 2011; 2016) and guiding and regulating textual decisions. Chesterman's distinction between specific behavioural values governing norms and interpersonal engagement illustrates this further: 'The value of *clarity* (governing expectancy norms), the value of *truth* (governing the relation norm), the value of *trust* (governing the communication norm) and the value of *understanding* (governing the accountability norm)' (Chesterman 2009: 36ff, cited in Floros 2011). Each of these values could be seen as virtuous behaviour governing a duty or responsibility that the translator has towards the profession/clients, text and any other interlocutors.

1.6.4 Macro-areas of translators' responsibility

Chesterman's (2001) four levels of translation ethics provide a useful classification into utilitarian ethics (focused on the consequences of an action), and contractual ethics (focused on the contractual relationship between the interlocutors), building on the work of moral and political philosophers:[46]

1. an *Ethics of Representation* based on loyalty towards the source text and ethical representation of the Other (*utilitarian ethics*);
2. an *Ethics of Service* focusing on rendering a professional service (*contractual ethics*);
3. an *Ethics of Communication*, the aim of which is to enable communication and cooperation (*utilitarian ethics*);
4. a *Norm-based Ethics* in which norms encode the ethical values held at a particular time in a particular society (based on Toury's work); ethical behaviour therefore means accommodating socially sanctioned norms (*contractual ethics*).

At first sight, if we were to apply these levels to the circles in Figure 1.2, *representation* would belong to the inner – textual – circle, *service* to the outer – social – circle, *communication* to the middle – interpersonal – circle, and *norms* to the outer – social – circle, although we see that certain aspects of norm-based ethics can be placed in the inner circle; overlapping and combinations are possible (as Chesterman concedes, his levels may overlap or indeed clash as they represent different aspects of ethics). In much of his very valuable work, Pym has addressed concrete aspects of professional behaviour and the relationship with the client(s) and editor and the practical and commercial aspects of translation, thus situating translation in the community as a social practice, in the outer circle. Indeed, Pym (2012: 134–163) highlights the value or ethic of optimal intercultural cooperation which generates mutual benefit for all the participants, much like Chesterman's ethics of communication (this would fall into the second and third circles of Figure 1.2).

Does this mean that the translator is accountable for what he or she translates or the impact of the translation product in the community? Although, Pym says, the translator's behaviour may lead to cumulative positive benefits, he argues that 'socio-cultural and [socio-]political effects of translation are not the responsibility of the translator' (quoted in Kruger and Crots 2014).

Responsibility for the broader socio-cultural effects of translation is precisely where schools of thought in TS seem to diverge. Where Chesterman (2017) and Pym (2010; 2012) distinguish between representational and community-driven ethics (our inner and outer circles), scholars like Tymoczko, Inghilleri and Baker (e.g. Baker 2006; Inghilleri 2012; Tymoczko 2007) are reluctant to make such a clear distinction and make a case for the translator's active engagement in society, enacting a 'higher' social and ethical aim of contributing to the improvement of society (especially social justice); Kruger and Crots call this an 'activist approach'.[47] These authors suggest that the translator bears a greater responsibility towards society and not just to the text and its author. They thus situate the professional activity of translation as an intrinsic part of a larger social practice with a clear ethical mandate (of social justice). Loyalty to a higher ethical level, one might say, takes precedence over textual fidelity or loyalty to a professional code of ethics.

1.6.5 Should translators and interpreters be more socially engaged?

Quoting Baker and Tymoczko, Kruger and Crots ask whether a rigid adherence to a code of ethics can actually at times be detrimental to the translator's agency and full empowerment:

> [S]cholars like Baker (2011) and Tymoczko (2007) have argued, the 'neutrality' and 'pragmatism' which are the hallmarks of this professionalism may 'deaden [translators'] ethical sensibilities, thus discouraging their agency and disempowering them in multiple ways' (Tymoczko 2007: 319). A pertinent point suggested by this research, then, is whether professional codes of ethics *ought to* encourage, to a greater degree than they currently do, the role of

personal ethics, and particularly the wider socio-cultural responsibility of the translator. While some scholars (like Chesterman 2001) are likely to disagree with this, others, like Tymoczko (2007), make a compelling case in favour of this approach to translator ethics, suggesting the importance of continued conversation on this matter.

(Kruger and Crots 2014)

Although this effort is laudable and has also led to some very important social projects, the effects of which have been extremely constructive (such as Babel[48]), it could be argued that this falls outside the realm of a translator's – or interpreter's – ethical mandate and falls under the private rather than the professional realm of ethics.

No textual transfer can exist without change or in a linguistic, situational, cultural or ethical vacuum; it is crucial to appreciate the complexity of the process of translation/interpreting highlighted in the works of activist TS scholars and also to acknowledge that translators' and interpreters' actions can negatively affect the community (by accepting translation/interpreting commissions of a non-ethical nature). However, embedding translators' or interpreters' activist ethics into the professional realm may lead to confusion for the individual interpreter/translator, being qualitatively two different categories. Taking a stand in favour of a just cause does not make someone a good translator or interpreter, although it may make them a good person. It is precisely where the layers of textual versus social ethics conflict that the interpreter needs to be aware of which level he or she wishes to foreground – the same complex decision-making process that many other professionals face as they negotiate their private, professional, social, cultural, ideological and financial selves. Whether or not to accept a commission founded on non-ethical content (e.g. translating violent political propaganda, interpreting in a situation involving criminal activity) and thus cause damage to the wider community is an ethical problem shared by many professions, and is not unique to TI.

1.6.6 *Ethics: professional vs personal and external vs internal*

Like most scholars, Chesterman and Pym make a clear distinction between professional and personal ethics, acknowledging, however, that the distinction may sometimes be difficult to maintain, and overlaps will happen. Much like the distinction 'ethics vs morals', personal ethics are often seen to be more subjective and internal than professional ethics, while the latter is a direct product of the specific professional context which can be formulated as a set of obligations in a code. In Kruger and Crots' (2014) words, professional ethics derives its source of authority from an 'external locus of control', namely, the profession. The 'locus of control' in personal ethics, on the other hand, is internal and individual and 'centred on his/her own beliefs' which may involve personal morality and the translator's conception of his/her own role and agency (ibid.) as well as the translator's or interpreter's own subjectivity. Kruger and Crots' study is particularly interesting because it illustrates, through data, how the weight of professional vs personal ethics can impact to different degrees on different translation choices. Training and experience also impact on translation decisions.

> In terms of ethical motivation, both personal and professional ethics exert a strong influence, reiterating the point made by various scholars that it may be difficult to separate personal and professional ethics in translation. The findings of this study suggest that the selection of literal or faithful translation strategies is generally motivated by professional ethics, with the strategy of refusal to translate mostly the consequence of personal ethics. However, this should not be regarded as an absolute correlation … *it appears that the greater adherence to faithful translation that correlates with experience is accompanied by a greater recourse to professional ethics in motivations for translation decisions. It therefore seems as if greater experience corresponds to a greater likelihood of the narrower professional, codified view of ethics being used as a frame of reference for translation decisions.*
> (ibid.: 31; emphasis added)

1.6.7 Faithfulness and responsibility? 'Surface and intrinsic' elements

Kruger and Crots make a useful distinction between 'surface' and 'intrinsic' elements of a text. In their data they found that some translational imperatives were more expendable than others under certain conditions (e.g. omission of crude language, etc.):

> As far as the type of ethical problem is concerned, crude language appears to be one category where there is a comparatively greater willingness to adapt the text, while in the category of potentially inappropriate content, there is a comparatively greater likelihood of translators' refusing to undertake the translation. It appears that there is some distinction between surface and intrinsic elements of a text, with translators viewing surface elements (such as crude language) as more open to adaptation; In the case of text type, it appears that formal, informational texts are less likely to prompt a refusal to translate, and children's literature containing potentially inappropriate material is most likely to provoke this response, but least likely to elicit adaptation as a strategy.
>
> (ibid.)

This finding is interesting because it can also be interpreted in a different manner, namely, how some elements are felt to be more closely related to the personal ethical realm (e.g. crude language, inappropriate context) and less open to compromise and thus more amenable to adaptation. Floros (2011) also shows how his students select ethical strategies of change and adaptation according to the nature of the text. For example, when it came to translating politically sensitive texts with which the students strongly disagreed, they were more inclined to adapt:

Thus, when students are confronted with multiple discourses and morally charged texts where their own responsibility is at stake, they begin to see faithfulness and equivalence in a totally different light. The above problems probably arise from the eagerness of students to understand translation strategies as tantamount to ethical stances – an understanding which represents a tacit rather than conscious level of ethical articulation.

(ibid.)

We could conclude from this that personal ethics, operating at a more 'visceral', spontaneous and intrinsic level, is a powerful factor and a strong filter or obstacle to accuracy. This seems to be logical in that personal ethics is governed by an internal 'barometer', more deeply socialised into the translating subject through a natural life-long socialisation process than professional ethics. New insights into the negotiating process of professional decision-making, such as that offered by Boileau (2014) in the context of dispute mediation, may come from psychoanalytical and philosophical phenomenological (the subject's intentionality) research into the Subject-Object relationship and the projection of the Self/Subject onto dynamics governing the interlocutors.[49] Although the dynamics in a dispute-mediation situation will by definition be conflictual, the triadic dynamics between interlocutors in a PSI situation are in themselves not necessarily conflictual but nevertheless subject to an intense phenomenological and communicative negotiating process.

1.6.8 *The source and target text bond: representation vs falsification*

Some intrinsic bond must by definition exist between ST and TT, and in the highly inter-relational field of PSI, the degree to which this bond holds is partly a matter of loyalty ethics and of the honest representation of the text or utterance, and partly a matter of negotiating the textual and representational bond with the primary speakers. This honest representation is based on the belief (mitigated by numerous factors, but still a baseline belief against which we measure non-truth, lying, fake news, false representation, etc.) that people are not deliberately falsifying facts, or falsifying the target text/utterance's representation of the source text/utterance (see the discussion on Kant and the nature of communication and truth-telling in Section 1.4.1), rendering communication futile.

But do the same ethical levels and features apply to both TS and PSI? Arguably, the stakes are higher in PSI because the content at issue touches upon crucial aspects of people's lives (typically health, justice, education, welfare) but also for the following reasons:

- PSI interaction is less predictable and less easy to control than translation;
- the socio-economic, political and institutional asymmetry is generally high;
- the non-majority language speakers are often less empowered because they lack a given resource at that moment in time (e.g. patients, victims, people seeking benefits, anyone seeking a service from a public institution);

- the interpreter's power is intense in that specific moment if only he or she understands all parties; there is rarely a control mechanism to ascertain what has been rendered.

Consequently, the profession of PSI has had a strong need to encode the interpreter's mandate and the limitations of the interpreter's freedom in order to protect all parties.

The written translator's work – the final product – is open to public or private scrutiny and therefore the internal control mechanism may be stronger in translation than in interpreting. Furthermore, the translator usually has far more time to consider each translation decision than an interpreter. This places fewer logistical and cognitive constraints on the translator than on the interpreter. At the same time, in the immediate context, the interpreting process is more pliable and the interpreter more available to – but at the same time susceptible to – negotiating the textual process and product as well as ethical aspects with the primary speakers, potentially leading to a more open-ended set of strategies or goals than that of a translator.

1.7 Summing up: the PSI-moral philosophy ethics interface

1.7.1 Interpreting ethics

The underlying connection between the principal tenets of moral philosophy and those of the interpreting profession asserted in this chapter is indeed a perfectly natural and logical bond in that all professions reflect their social and intellectual host environment and develop in a specific social trajectory through time. Moral philosophy, as an intellectual investigative practice as well as a behavioural norm-setting practice, can thus be seen as a background against which professional and social practices develop. Consequently, it could be argued that as a 'baseline set' of PSI ethics - accuracy, impartiality and confidentiality - largely transcend sector-specific and mode-specific interpreting forms, but also transcend professional boundaries. Indeed, they successfully capture the four above-mentioned philosophical principles, and would include also the notion of loyalty.

If we look more closely at the tenet of accuracy, it could be described as a 'contract' between:

1. interpreter and client
2. interpreter and source
3. interpreter and text/translation process
4. interpreter and profession.

In this contract, the interpreter has a duty and responsibility towards the text, towards his/her clients and also towards the profession. Impartiality and confidentiality

BOX 1.4 MACRO-CATEGORIES OF PSI AND MORAL PHILOSOPHY

Virtue or 'the Good'	**Accuracy**. Quality of the ST/TT relationship *a virtue*. Inner-oriented textual norm. Respecting *telos*.
Duty and Responsibility	**Accuracy**. Respecting contract with clients. Duty to speakers and listeners. Ethics of Care.
Utility and Consequences	Respecting *skopos*. Examining what is ultimately good and **beneficial for clients**.
Justice and Equality	**Equal access** to services, social justice. **Impartiality and Confidentiality**. Outer-oriented societal norm (duty to society).

actuate the interpreter's alignment and loyalty towards the source (author/speaker), the professional community and institution as well as towards the receiver (reader/listener) in a sense that is not inherent to the interpreting process itself but rather as it 'looks outwards' towards the interlocutors, society and the profession. The connection between the ethical domains of Moral Philosophy and PSI could thus be captured as shown in Box 1.4.

1.7.2 Typologies of interpreting situations

The situations an interpreter might conceivably be faced with are innumerable, but could be roughly classified as shown in Table 1.2.[50]

1.7.3 Interpreting, virtue and 'good': individual vs group ethics

To what degree can we decide what a good life is, quite apart from the complexity of denoting and defining key notions such as 'good', 'virtue', 'moral'? Surely it is a subjective evaluation? Or is it intrinsic to human beings? Does it depend on the environment we live in or does it depend on whether we 'wish to do good' or just 'do/enact good'? These questions are essential to the development of moral philosophy, and some of them are probably unanswerable, at least in an absolute sense. 'Good' is also more difficult to evaluate and discuss at an individual level because an individual's freedom of choice is in theory absolute, as the Existentialists remind us. At a collective level, however, the picture changes quite drastically because as individuals enter into contact with each other they establish certain – normative – behavioural criteria. At this level, rules become explicit, indeed, one could define them as 'instructions decided by the group'. At that precise moment, a decision about which of those behavioural characteristics are good or bad is enacted. It is this level – the group level – that interests us most as interpreters because the group

TABLE 1.2 Situations that might lead to ethical dilemmas

Situation type	Ethical dilemma
Textual	
Information completeness	Interpreting profanities or sexually explicit language; interpreting side-conversations between interlocutors or between interlocutors and the interpreter; interpreting disparaging, critical, insulting comments by either party; (not) correcting one of the parties' mistakes; correcting one's own mistakes; interpreting incoherent or unintelligible discourse[a]
Interpersonal/social	
Interpersonal domain	(Not) providing information, advice, opinions or personal information requested by one of the parties; interpreting affect-governed utterances by either party (emotion, anger, crying, fear, molestation); obnoxious behaviour; offers of gifts[b]; (not) adapting roles on or off duty when meeting interpreting clients
Impartiality/bias	Positive or negative bias when interpreting for a friend or relative or acquaintance; emotional involvement or feelings of sympathy/empathy, disgust or fear due to the nature of the session or the interlocutors involved; having an interest in the outcome of a conflict
Extra knowledge	Knowledge that one or more of the interlocutors is withholding information or lying
Qualifications/competence	Accepting situations which will not allow you to interpret accurately, be it for lack of general or specific language proficiency or for contingent personal reasons (health, fatigue); misrepresenting qualifications[c]
Justice	
Discrimination/illegality	Suspected abuse (child abuse, police brutality); suspected criminal activity
Life/death issues, physical danger	Medication or a medical situation that the service provider is not aware of; a suspect, witness or victim's life is endangered; immediate danger

Notes: The textual category does not necessarily represent true dilemmas where alternatives would be mutually exclusive. The objective to keep in mind here is transparency, that all parties are equally informed. This can be done outside the strict locus of the interpreting activity by informing, explaining or describing to either or both parties what is taking place, for example. For overlapping, incoherent or unintelligible discourse, the interpreter can intervene quite easily to request clarity, explanations or repetition in order to maintain completeness and transparency.

[a] As in Trompenaar and Hampden-Turner's (1997) model of universalist versus particularist roles, where professional and social roles are seen as flexible when the context changes, or continuous as context changes (for example, when socialising with the boss outside the office). See Garzone and Rudvin (2003) for an application to interpreting.

[b] Gift-giving (food, souvenirs, a card or book) can be difficult to avoid because in some cultures it may be perceived as seriously offensive to refuse to accept a gift; indeed, a refusal might jeopardise the person's trust in the interpreter. Gift-giving can be negotiated with the institution beforehand to decide together on an appropriate policy that does not compromise impartiality; gifts can also be left with the institution.

[c] Refusing a commission that an interpreter is not sufficiently qualified to undertake responsibly (for example, due to language proficiency) may sound straightforward enough, but in an emergency situation where no other interpreters are available, it may be difficult. In such a case, this can be made clear to the commissioner of the service so that he or she or the institution can shoulder that responsibility.

as a professional community is what decides and defines those rules either through explicit practices, such as training programmes and codes of ethics, or through a body of acquired professional experience. In a young – and in many countries undefined – profession such as PSI, such exo-normative instructions can be found in the form of explicitly coded ethical parameters (codes of ethics). However, precisely because it is a young profession, these are still largely unexplored. It is precisely for this reason that it is so crucial to render them explicit: what we want them to be (intrinsically), what the consequences of implementing them are (consequentially), and how they are situated in the broader context of society and other professions (duty and social justice).

One of the problems that arises for interpreters, as for other professionals, is when 'what is good for me, privately' is mutually exclusive with 'what is good for someone else' or 'what is good for my group/profession', and this constitutes a prototypical ethical dilemma; ethical dilemmas occur precisely when these needs or desires for what is 'good' clash. This comes to the fore very powerfully in utilitarian approaches to moral philosophy, as we have seen. It was suggested above that what is generally considered 'good' in moral philosophy is that which benefits people, that which increases the well-being of the individual and of the community as a group of individuals, but also one that fulfils its intrinsic nature.

1.7.4 Non-maleficence through self-development: damage control

Interpreting is an action which – albeit indirectly – can cause enormous damage if the power that the interpreter wields is not used with great care and responsibility. Like medical and legal professionals, interpreters can do enormous harm to people's lives by translating incorrectly. The mandate upon them to cause the least harm by interpreting accurately is crucial. One of the main functions of a code of ethics, and ethical standards generally, is precisely to regulate that power and to limit the potential damage. The stakes are often high in the PSI profession as it touches upon the most basic, necessary and often painful (physically or mentally) domains of everyday life.

The danger of ethical mismanagement requires us to carefully consider and evaluate the consequences of interpreting decisions. The responsibility that every interpreter bears upon his or her shoulders may be sorely put to the test when primary (private) and secondary (public) loyalties clash, and this is why interpreters seek to avoid such situations. The enormous power inherent in the interpreting act is held individually, the PSI interpreter does not usually operate in a team where he or she can consult with colleagues and make collective decisions, thus sharing the responsibility and the weight of that responsibility. It is precisely one of the functions of codes of ethics to contain the power the professional has and the damage that might be done through that access to power.

Decisions are usually taken alone, on the spot, and this renders the interpreter all the more vulnerable. In other professions – typically medicine and law – the damage potential is 'direct', but professionals are more easily able to share the responsibility for potential risk through high level training, consulting with colleagues, sophisticated data processing instruments, and also insurance. For interpreters, potential damage – physical, legal or mental – is enacted via the primary service professional. The damage is 'indirectly enacted', but the effects are no less tangible.

In order to protect oneself from (possibly unknowingly) causing harm, it is an ethical injunction to proactively create the conditions in which one can provide an accurate rendition and make the right decisions:

- acquire basic training;
- have an adequate command of the lingua-cultures;
- acquire through continuous self-learning relevant competence in the field-- specific language areas and in new terminology;
- take breaks when the cognitive load on one's memory is too great;
- enact floor management: coordinate turns so that one can hear, process and reformulate all of the information;
- enact repair if one makes a mistake;
- inform the primary service providers if a mistake has jeopardised comprehension.

The aforementioned are all classic interpreting skills that are taught in traditional interpreter courses and are at some point necessary. But as damage control strategies they also have a powerful ethical component, and could be seen in an Aristotelian sense as virtues that enable the interpreter both to maintain the ethic of accuracy and not to cause harm. If other interlocutors are causing harm in a more direct manner, this it is not the interpreter's immediate responsibility. In this case, there is a shift in the level of ethics to the social sphere where the Justice and Equality ethic comes into play and must be decided on a case-by-case basis. This illustrates the core of another important PSI dilemma: if unethical, immoral or illegal actions are being perpetrated – or actions that are harmful to the non-majority language speaker – is it his/her responsibility to report that? To whom does the interpreter owe primary loyalty and allegiance? 'To whom or to what cause does the interpreter owe his or her loyalty? The various strata of our loyalties and responsibilities must be, I would argue, weighed against each other, along with the other two key parameters that have emerged in the course of this discussion: To whom/how many/how much 'good' is being given? and 'How much/to whom is damage being caused?' Obviously, as the consequentialists were well aware, 'good/happiness/pleasure' and 'damage' cannot be mathematically calculated (although many attempts have been made), but each interpreter can weigh each of those parameters against each other in a holistic decision-making process.

Whether or not the PSI interpreter is legally responsible for translation error or damage that is a result of erroneous translation is not entirely clear; in some countries, PS interpreters, especially legal and health interpreters, may take out insurance to protect themselves from unknowingly causing harm. Legally, a core issue here is whether or not an interpreter has acted knowingly, in bad faith, or if the erroneous translation is the result of a mistake. Clearly, if the mistranslation is intentional and does not involve a higher-order ethic of safety or justice, it contravenes all ethical codes. This is one of the reasons why maintaining an ethic of accuracy not only enacts the 'nature' or *telos* of the translation act, but protects the interpreter. If the error is not intentional, it moves into a more 'fuzzy' area when, despite good intentions (and deontologically it is thus an ethical action), the consequences could be devastating.

1.8 Conclusion: the existential anguish of choice and decision-making

Moving away from an isolationist, prescriptive, rule-based professional ethics to a more context-sensitive approach, interpreters might be encouraged to make those decisions alongside the other players in interaction – as teamwork – whenever possible. Ideally, when a dilemma arises decisions should be made engaging with all actors in a transparent fashion through collaborative dialogue. Not all users are familiar with PSI roles and ethics and explaining ethical issues when problems result may be a constructive course of action harnessing all of the resources – pertaining to knowledge, information, expertise and experience – available. Collaboratively, it becomes possible to creatively investigate new options by bringing to the table know-how, information and competencies. Applying the knowledge and solidity of a more general framework of moral philosophy to each specific case (issues pertaining to intrinsic good, virtue, loyalty, consequences, duty to society, etc.) will increase the likelihood of meeting the needs of all players involved and is more likely to lead to a win-win situation and reduce the possibility of harm. Internalising that knowledge and reflective process can be achieved through prior training.

Having established certain general standards of ethical behaviour in interpreting as a code of ethics and having propagated those in the professional community through publication and training, the 'difficult bit' for each individual interpreter in each specific, unique situation is still deciding what to do if and when he or she is faced with a dilemma. Not every situation is traumatic, not every decision requires such tortuous self-reflection; many difficult decisions are enacted in the fraction of a second, intuitively (seemingly) intuitive on the basis of training but also of experience. Interpreter experience gives the professional the weight of earlier cases, of evaluating the outcome of former dilemmas and of their – positive or negative – consequences. Decision-making requires a tripartite thought process in which the individual applies the theory (Aristotle's 'brilliance') acquired through training and experience (evaluating in a splt second recognizable consequences) and the ability to apply those to the unique, specific situation (Aristotle's *phronēsis*). Thus, the interpreter balances the 'good' and potential harm to each party. In doing this, we are applying several ethical processes general to mankind and general to all professions. To this we must add that an interpreter must also consider his/her own private subjective self that necessarily filters all verbal and non-verbal information. A self-awareness of this phenomenological process will, I believe, help the interpreter maintain a necessary distance from the text/utterance that safeguards information processing as well as any emotional investment that could either lead to bias or produce emotional stress.

As Sartre has shown, the anguish of radical freedom underlies the enormous responsibility human beings have on their shoulders as individual agents. For interpreters, choice – especially when faced with an ethical dilemma that can cause harm or where loyalty bonds impact strongly on both reason and emotion –,[51] can indeed be a source of anguish. Floros (2016) also draws attention to that same 'paralyzing effect' of undecidability. Where 'consciousness floats free', but always through 'a seeing subject' (see Graham 2011: 64), the future can and must be fashioned responsibly and dutifully and by making good choices we can curtail existential anguish. We could complete this line of reasoning by concluding that, for interpreters, the anguish of choice is mitigated by referring to a set of standards of professional behaviour, standards that have the weight not only of personal experience behind them, but of a whole professional community and *their* experience as well, an entire body of research and practice. As such, codes and standards are both liberating and reassuring, giving structure (Sartre would say an illusory structure, we might say a 'willing suspension of disbelief' to the absurdity of a structure-less world). It is still up to the individual interpreter's skill and competence and intelligence to weigh those standards against what emerges as an ethical need or mandate in each specific situation.

Acknowledgements

I would like to thank Angelo Bersini, Alda Calanchini-Monti, Anna Bartolomei and Wim Vandekerckove for their valuable comments and suggestions. Any inaccuracies or shortcomings are entirely my responsibility.

Notes

1 The connection between 'Good/Virtue' as a primary ethic in moral philosophy and the principal ethics of PSI was made earlier by the author in: (Rudvin 2015b); in an unpublished presentation at the University of Kirklareli in 2016 and 2018 (available at www.youtube.com/watch?v=7qrtJRufJEg); as a conference paper in Alcalà de Henares in 2017 'Ethics and the Interconnectedness of Moral Philosophy and PSI: What can Moral Philosophy teach the Public Service Interpreter?' at the sixth International Conference on Public Service Interpreting and Translating; and 'The interconnectedness of philosophy and translation. Issues of subjectivity' at the third International Edition Palermo Translation Symposium at the University of Palermo, May 2018.
2 Although the focus in this volume is exclusively on the dialogic form of interpreting and specifically on PSI, many of the aspects illustrated here are also applicable to other forms of interpreting or, indeed, to translation.
3 The term 'Code of Conduct' has become more prevalent in the international literature on interpreting over the last decade, suggesting a less rigid, less prescriptive and more nuanced approach towards the professional role.

4 By 'culture', I mean not only ethnic or national cultures, but all groups that share sufficient behavioural features to self-define as a distinct but fluid, permeable and changing cultural group; examples of non-ethnic cultures are corporate culture, or Deaf culture.
5 The focus of this chapter is limited in that it refers specifically to the Western philosophical tradition, leaving out a significant part of the world's intellectual pool of scholarship and knowledge, for example, the Chinese and Indian philosophical traditions. There are many important distinctions. Richard Shweder (in Haidt 2012) notes how the Western tradition of moral philosophy tends to foreground autonomy as an analytical axiom, whilst the Chinese Confucian tradition would favour relationship-building; furthermore, many traditions, including parts of the Western one, refer to a divine authority as the source of ethical authorship and authority. As Jonathan Haidt (2012) argues, the ethical framework of Deontologists and Utilitarians, such as Kant and Mill, but also most other Western philosophers, is individualistic, rule-based and largely universalist, responding to a society where autonomy and individual rights are highly prized. For Kant, justice and rights are a value in themselves and, for the Utilitarians, the value of these principles lies in their ability to increase individual human welfare. Indeed, Haidt notes, post-religious secular Western thought foregrounds reason, rationality and logic, all highly autonomous cognitive processes. We will see also that the philosophers discussed in this chapter are intensely driven by the need to illustrate and demonstrate theories through reason and logic, typically individualist traits, as Haidt reminds us (ibid.). Indeed, Haidt identifies three major 'clusters' of moral themes, the ethics of 'Autonomy, Community, Divinity', which are not equally represented in the Western, Indian and Chinese traditions. The axiomatic approach to rationality has been questioned, as will be discussed, and has also been an issue in economic theory of rationality and behavioural predictability; interestingly, the notion of rationality has also been challenged by a recent Nobel Prize-winner in Economics, Richard Thaler, in his 'nudge theory'.
6 Plato made the distinction between the private and public sphere in relation to ethics and justice. Is the concept of justice intrinsic to human nature, he asks, and therefore 'private', or is it reflected in and on society, therefore embodying a public dimension? This would entail a shift from a micro-cosmic to a macro-cosmic view of justice (or from inherent to relative). I am grateful to Anna Bartolomei for pointing out this connection.
7 Consider the famous 'trolley problem' experiment in ethics posed by Philippa Foot in 1967 where students were asked to choose between deliberately causing the death of one person or indirectly causing the death of many people by not taking deliberate action and allowing a run-away trolley car to crash.
8 Confidentiality is not in itself a moral or ethical principle, although it (rightly) appears in most PSI codes of ethics. I discuss in this chapter how the PSI tenets of accuracy, impartiality and confidentiality uphold important ethical stakes regarding justice, loyalty and fairness and confidentiality is essential because it creates trust between interlocutors and between institutions and individuals, and because it enables the ethic of non-maleficence, i.e. not causing damage.
9 I refer the reader to Robyn Dean (2016) and Robyn Dean and Robert Pollard's (2011) excellent decision-making framework captured in the demand-control schema and continuum of intervention.
10 My first background readings for this book, providing the bulk of my sources, information and line of argument were Graham (2011) *Theories of Ethics: An Introduction to Moral Philosophy with a Selection of Classic Readings*; MacIntyre (2002) *A Brief History of Ethics*; Tomasello (2014) *A Natural History of Human Morality*; Nuttall (2002) *An Introduction to Philosophy*; Ubaldo (2005 [2000]) *Antologia Illustrata di Filosofia*; and Fornero (2000) *Protagonisti e Testi della Filosofia*. Another valuable source of information was the online *Stanford Encyclopaedia of Philosophy*, a peer-reviewed open-access channel for discussions and studies of the major schools of thought and issues in modern Western philosophy. Since then I have added numerous other sources as supporting material which have informed and given more nuance to my analysis: Craig (2002) *Philosophy:*

A Very Short Introduction; Shand (2003) *Fundamentals of Philosophy*; Warburton (2013 [1992]) *Philosophy: The Basics*; Russell (1945) *History of Western Philosophy*; Blackburn (1999) *Think. A Compelling Introduction to Philosophy*; and Hoffman and Graham (2015) *Introduction to Political Theory*. Kultgen's seminal (1988) *Ethics and Professionalism* has also been consulted. Observations on and conclusions drawn from the material deriving from these sources, where not otherwise specified, are my own.

11 Kermit discusses this point in regard to Aristotelian ethics.

12 Although this is a novel site of investigation, some valuable work has already been done by the co-author of this volume, Kermit (2007), by Dean (2016), Mendoza (2012) and Floros (2011; 2016). It is interesting to note that scientists in the 'hard sciences' also explore the connection between philosophy and the ethics of their own field, such as Ocone and Ocone's brief (2012) discussion on teaching ethics in chemical engineering 'The new engineer and the old philosopher: hedgehog or fox?'. In TS, the tradition is longer, starting with Chesterman's analysis of the ideas of Karl Popper applied to TS (Chesterman 2016) and more recently Floros and Cornelia Zwischenberger, looking specifically at ethics.

13 Values of justice and equality naturally fall into and interface with political philosophy. These categories have been chosen to reflect the main pursuits of moral philosophy as a discipline, but also to provide a grid or filter through which to investigate those same ethical pursuits that are most pertinent to the PSI profession.

14 Hale's (2007) in-depth comparative study of codes of ethics in different countries and different sectors of application reveals that the three main tenets are accuracy, impartiality and confidentiality (often, but not always, in that order). It is these three tenets that I will be regarding in this chapter as fundamental to the ethics of interpreting.

15 This is meant to be a broad statement suggesting principle and intent rather than the actualisation of that intent: the twentieth century was a turmoil of savage breaches of human rights not just in countries the media associate today with dubious human rights policies such as China or Afghanistan, but also colonial policies in Asia, Africa and Australia (the aboriginal genocide lasted into the second half of the last century) and lack of civil liberties in the US. Throughout history, identifying which parties and/or citizens should have access to equal human rights is hotly debated, even today, in issues related to immigration. Nevertheless, disregarding its flawed or incomplete enactment in most societies, the principle of justice and equality (connected also to that of the freedom of speech) remains one of the pillars of modernity and marks the transition from a hierarchical and group-based structure (such as pre-capitalist feudal societies) of social organisation to one in which the individual and his/her rights are foregrounded. A quote from Peter Frankopan's *The Silk Roads: A New History of the World* reminds us that principles of justice also predate the cultural and economic ascent of Western society and the rise of Rome (which was anything but equitable). The Persian king Darius, during the expansion of the Persian Empire in the sixth BC, recommends maintaining an equitable approach towards the newly acquired lands in a trilingual inscription hewn into a cliff in Behistun: 'Keep the country secure, the inscription commands, and look after the people righteously, for justice is the bedrock of the kingdom' (2015: 2). Frankopan's excellent wide-ranging study also illustrates the cross-fertilisation between ideas, religions and philosophies between Eastern and Western empires through colonisation and evangelisation but also through trade and commerce. The scope of that cross-fertilisation of ideas is unfortunately not reflected in this chapter.

16 The countable noun form 'goods', in the economic sense, is at the same time attributive, suggesting something that it is beneficial to human beings. The 'good' imbued in equal access to justice, health and education is also at the heart of the interpreting profession.

17 I am grateful to Angelo Bersini for clarifying this point and illustrating its relevance to interpreting and translating.

18 *How* to achieve accuracy is not something that will be addressed in this volume. Although it has been the subject of TS and IS literature since its inception, its most central and

its most complex feature, it is nevertheless in any absolute sense an impossible mission to accomplish. The complexity of dialogic communication beyond the textual level in a strict sense of the word is so profound that no perfect solution, no true accuracy, can ever be claimed. Apart from complex communication parameters, subjective interpretation of the utterance by each interactant excludes perfect equivalence. This should not stop us from holding it as the objective towards which we strive (see Hale 2007; Rudvin 2002). Ozolins (2016), Angelelli (2004), Wadensjö (1998) and numerous other TS and IS scholars have discussed this aspect from a slightly different angle, namely, that of the (in)visibility and agency of the translator/interpreter and the translator's/interpreter's real, assumed or perceived agency. In order to achieve what might be more loosely called 'successful' communication, other factors also impact the degree to which the interactants fully comprehend each other and the success of the ultimate goal of a PSI encounter (e.g. diagnosis and patient compliance; an application in a refugee hearing; an exhaustive narrative in a police file charge, etc.); transactional features and aims of the communication event also come into the picture.

19 See e.g. the Brill series on Translation and Cross-Cultural Communication Studies in the Asia Pacific (https://brill.com/view/title/32018?qt-qt_product_details-0); Babou *et al.* (2017) on translation in Africa; Trivedi (2007), Dharwadker (1999), Wakabayashi and Kothari (2009), Mukherji (2002) on translation in India.

20 For the ancient Greeks, narrative (tales, epics) was a way of publicly presenting normative ethics and virtues – 'what to do' – as well as a didactic model of applied ethics showing how humans and gods behave, make mistakes, are punished, rewarded, etc.

21 These are extremely broad generalisations because 'Hindu philosophy' or 'Buddhist philosophy' are in themselves umbrella terms for a wealth of different schools of thought. Nevertheless, the countries that have a predominantly Hindu, Buddhist and Confucian religion and/or tradition, generally espouse values and behaviours that foreground the group and conformity to the group both as a value and as a form of social organisation. This does not contrast with the individual spiritual path favoured in Buddhist tradition. See Goodman (2017), Wong (2017) and Chadda and Deb (2013).

22 The degree to which different ethical traditions impact on professional ethics in PSI is an issue that needs to be addressed (see one early attempt in Rudvin 2007) and which may not impact so much on the nature of a 'good' product (as in interpreting *quality* and interpreter *competence*) but may impact deeply on interpersonal relationships and dynamics in the interpreting triad, especially for what concerns impartiality and loyalty to the clients, i.e. 'agency'.

23 Recent studies on socio-biology in connection with ethics, Graham remarks, attempt to look at what is 'good for' human beings in their social and physical environment, and suggest that behaviours we see as 'virtuous' (generosity, bravery, kindness) have evolved as such to protect human lives in social groups, in that we are dependent on other human-beings for survival. 'Accordingly, any plausible account of [human] flourishing will have to take the social and cultural influences into account, as well as the biological and ethological influences. It will be as much anthropological as biological' (Graham 2011: 53).

24 The same word emerges in the classificatory term teleology associated with consequentialism in a more general fashion, as an end – a consequence.

25 This was reflected in what many centuries later in the Protestant Reformation was a landmark shift towards the focus on the intent of an individual's action and direct internal relationship with God (i.e. with the primary source of the rule of ethical conduct) rather than solely the action itself, and the relationship with God (and 'goodness') mediated through other texts, institutions, people and entities (institutional exegeses and the Scriptures in Latin; the Vatican, the clergy, saints, the Virgin Mary, etc. as mediating figures) (see MacIntyre 2002). One of the significant consequences of this shift was an increased sense of personal responsibility through a direct, non-mediated and therefore 'unprotected' relationship with God, a shift that still deeply impacts on behavioural

norms and conduct in typically Catholic versus typically Protestant cultures and their public systems of governance, profession-building, organisation and the concept of ethical conduct. The weight of duty and responsibility in this form of non-mediated communication with the divine has consequences, I would argue, for ethical values and actions.

26 A question that arises from this reflection on 'good for' as a process in which we aim to fulfil certain intrinsic characteristics of human beings is precisely 'what is natural?' (another slippery word, diachronically and synchronically) and if 'natural' can be equated with 'good'. If xenophobia and racism are natural impulses in human beings, that does not mean they are 'good' or commendable, notes Graham (2011: 56). To what extent, then, are we free to act according to our natural characteristics, or to reject them? One of the most important features – cognitive, moral, intellectual – that humans are endowed with is that of choice, and at some level of consciousness we are constantly enacting choice on a continuum from spontaneity ('it felt natural') to deliberation ('I had to think about it a lot, it was a hard decision').

27 I have discussed the issue of rational thought and decision-making in interlingual situations in an earlier paper where economic theories of rational behaviour, especially Game Theory, have been applied to interlingual/intercultural communication and translation (Rudvin 2018).

28 To be autonomous, for Kant, is to act on a law that one gives oneself, a law adequate to one's nature as a free and equal, reasonable and rational person. See Johnson and Cureton (2018).

29 This section is based largely on Graham (2011). Discussions with Angelo Bersini and also Alda Calanchini-Monti helped clarify and flesh out these notions; I am indebted to them both.

30 Exceptionally, Hobbes' philosophy was secular and materialist. Locke encourages tolerance and religious freedom, but does raise the issue of the existence of God, and believes that Christianity is 'reasonable'.

31 I am grateful to Alda Monti-Calanchini for her guidance, observations and resulting vigorous discussions on Kant and on natural law theory and on utilitarianism. I am also grateful to her for pointing out the connection with the myth of the 'noble savage' later in this paragraph.

32 Although we apparently have the liberty to do what we like, it is a partial, superficial and illusory liberty; renouncing an illusory liberty gives us other liberties: through paying taxes, for example, we have access to hospitals and libraries. I am grateful to Alda Calanchini-Monti for this example, and also for the simplified examples of categorical imperatives.

33 Ross's model lends itself well to analyzing professional norms and has been previously used in IS studies by Elizabeth Mendoza (2012).

34 This is also true of Translation and Interpreting Studies, which were deeply influenced by the constructivist paradigms in Cultural Studies, Literature and Linguistics.

35 Although, of course, the decisions are individual and therefore vulnerable, the formulation of a detailed code of ethics thus protects both the citizens as (potential) suspects, witnesses and victims, as well as the judge him/herself.

36 Whether or not a pan-national institution, such as the EU, is capable of engendering the same group-based loyalty ties as the the nation-state, is another question.

37 Related questions would be: is 'passion', in Weber's terminology, a *sine qua non* for a cause, responsibility and duty? Or does it spring from an intrinsic Aristotelian sense of good, or from Kantian service to a higher structural order and idea?

38 The ethics of whistleblowing for interpreters made headlines in the Camayd-Freixas case. See discussion in Section 2.11.6 in Part 2.

39 Interpreters in areas of conflict can be subject to extreme loyalty conflicts: many Afghan interpreters who work for Western troops have been killed or subjected to threats once the troops have left and they have returned to normal civilian life. This is likely due

to the interpreter being seen as changing group loyalties and alignments, betraying the original group bond (and providing access to confidential information) in favour of the foreign power. (See Rudvin's interview with Erik Hertog in Rudvin 2015c.)
40 Loyalty can be seen as a contractual framework, relational contract (ibid.).
41 This is true, as mentioned above, of many disciplines in the humanities. It is especially relevant, however, for those disciplines and professions that embody a dispute-mediating function, even more than a language-mediating function. In *The Myth of Mediation Neutrality*, Kevin Boileau discusses, through a philosophical lens, precisely the impossibility of complete impartiality in a mediating situation.
42 Translation practices in the broader market have changed and will continue to change rapidly as a result of technological development and this will no doubt also remodel the 'intrinsic' aspect of the translational act and translation/interpreting ethics. I refer to more fluid and less univocal textual processes such as localisation-translation, author-editor-translator collaboration, collectively written translations, 'fan translation/subbing/dubbing' or any group and/or anonymous translation process, machine translation processes, etc. The practice of PSI will no doubt be affected by technology in the near future with the advent of remote interpreting, cheaper and simpler Skype-based interpreting or Smart-phones/watches, ear-pieces and/or other devices that provide instant interpreting or interpreting aids, seriously challenging traditional notions of translational agency and (co)authorship. Indeed, AI and other forms of technology could subvert the whole equivalence/loyalty paradigm in the years to come in unpredictable ways.
43 Available at http://spilplus.journals.ac.za (accessed 15 February 2018). One of the interesting conclusions that emerges from the authors' data in this study (which must, as they warn repeatedly, be interpreted with caution and for what it is – the results of a limited data sample) is that translators with more experience were more reluctant to enact changes such as omission with regard to the source text. Professional experience seemed to impact on the selection of translation strategies, 'with greater experience corresponding to a greater preference for faithful translation' (Kruger and Crots 2014). Another point that is relevant to the present discussion is that subjectivity and individual background in ethical motivation are crucial, and this also emerges to some extent in Kruger and Crots' valuable study. This will deeply affect a translator's or an interpreter's handling of an ethically challenging situation and the strategies they choose to adopt.
44 This also reflects Pym's (2012: 76–81) classification of translators' responsibility into three macro areas (responsibility to the content of the text, to the client, and to the profession), and Hale's (2007) areas of responsibility towards Self, Client and Profession.
45 Hale (2007) has a similar very useful distinction, but here I would like to place the focus on the difference between societal processes and products vs textual processes and products in order to highlight the different ethical conundrums that pertain to each domain.
46 Chesterman (2001:139ff, quoted in Kruger and Crots, 2014). For Chesterman, underlying all levels of ethics, is *understanding*, which is 'the highest value for translators; truth, clarity, loyalty, trust – are subordinate to understanding'; it is the 'defining limit of a translator's professional ethics, responsibility, the responsibility of their practice' (Kruger and Crots 2014). I would suggest that understanding could also be seen as a competence that is necessary to enable an ethical translation that aims at a loyal representation. Indeed, Chesterman's argument is convincing: that it is the most important and essential basis, competence or virtue, in that, without it, translation becomes guesswork. Chesterman further proposes a version of virtue ethics applied to translation 'where the most important virtue is the commitment to striving for excellence in translation, to being a good translator'; this is 'combined with other virtues such as fairness, truthfulness, trustworthiness, empathy and determination' (Chesterman 2001:147, quoted in Kruger and Crots 2014). Striving for excellence could also be seen as a goal that incorporates – and is built upon – the other virtues mentioned here.
47 Like these scholars, I believe that language, translation and interpreting are dynamic and fluid processes, and I would question any absolutist concepts of objectivity and

neutrality as found in the prescriptive studies of early TS and IS. I have explored the problematic nature of objectivity/neutrality/impartiality in Translation and later in Interpreting in a number of conference papers from 1994 onwards, for example: 'The concept of "performance" in oral narrative: a point of departure for translation studies?' at the 1st International Congress on Translation and Interpreting: Present Trends at the University of Las Palmas (1994); 'Challenging the "neutrality maxim": an interactional approach to community interpreting' at Interpreting in the 21st Century. Challenges and Opportunities. 1st Forlì Conference on Interpreting Studies at the University of Bologna (2000); and 'The many faces of "neutrality" and "equivalence": community interpreting in Italy. Issues in interaction and participation' at the conference Third International EST-Congress, Copenhagen (2001).

48 Situating oneself individually, as a professional, in a broader social-activist position is a perfectly acceptable, indeed laudable, position to take, but consensus cannot be acquired by the group as a whole; therefore, it remains within the realm of personal ethics. Parts of the group can take a stance as a professional group (as AIIC has done with In-Zone, Médicins sans Frontières, or numerous other professional groups), but that still does not make those ethics 'professional' in a general sense.

49 The subjectivity of translation as a cultural and cognitive process is explored in a forthcoming publication.

50 See Cartwright (1999) for a broad range of interpreting dilemmas.

51 Allegiance and loyalty may be towards one's immediate cultural or ethnic compatriots, although this is of course not always the case as an interpreter will often interpret for people of different culture/ethnic background. Nevertheless, this bond is at the heart of frequent ethical dilemmas striking not only at the heart of an interpreter's professional identity and function, but his or her deepest loyalties.

References

Angelelli, C.V. (2004). *Re-visiting the Role of the Interpreter: A Study of Conference, Court and Medical Interpreters in Canada, Mexico and the United States*. Amsterdam: John Benjamins Publishing Company.

Anonymous. (2018). *The Secret Barrister: Stories of the Law and How It's Broken*. London: Macmillan.

Babou, C.A., Oyali, U., Ndong, L. and Seye, M. (2017). Perspectives on translation studies in Africa. Bayreuth African Studies Working Papers, 17. Available at: https://epub.uni-bayreuth.de/3350/1/Perspectives%20on%20translation%20%20studies%20in%20Africa.pdf. (accessed March 2019).

Baker, M. (2006). *Translation and Conflict: A Narrative Account*. London: Routledge.

Baker, M. (2011). *In Other Words: A Coursebook on Translation*. London: Routledge.

Berryman, S. (2016). Democritus. In *The Stanford Encyclopedia of Philosophy* (Winter 2016 Edition). Available at: https://plato.stanford.edu/entries/democritus/ (accessed March 2019).

Blackburn, S. (1999). *Think: A Compelling Introduction to Philosophy*. Oxford: Oxford University Press.

Boileau, K. (2014). *The Myth of Mediation Neutrality: The Psychoanalytic, Phenomenological, and Linguistic-Structural Approach to Mediation*. Missoula: EPIS Press.

Camayd-Freixas, E. (2008). Statement of Dr. Erik Camayd-Freixas Federally Certified Interpreter, at the U.S. District Court for the Northern District of Iowa Regarding a Hearing on 'The Arrest, Prosecution, and Conviction of 297 Undocumented Workers in Postville, Iowa, from May 12 to 22, 2008'. Available at: https://judiciary.house.gov/_files/hearings/pdf/Camayd-Freixas080724.pdf (accessed October 2018).

Cartwright, B.E. (1999). *Encounters with Reality: 1,001 Interpreter Scenarios*. Alexandria, VA: RID Press.
Chadda, R.K and Deb, K.S. (2013). Indian family systems, collectivistic society and psychotherapy. *Indian Journal of Psychiatry*, 55(2), 299–309.
Chesterman, A. (2001). Proposal for a Hieronymic oath. In A. Pym (ed.) *The Translator: Studies In Intercultural Communication*. Special issue: *The Return to Ethics*, 7(2), 139–154.
Chesterman, A. (2016). *Memes of Translation: The Spread of Ideas in Translation Theory*. Amsterdam: John Benjamins Publishing Company.
Chesterman, A. (2017). *Reflections on Translation Theory: Selected Papers 1993–2014*. Amsterdam: John Benjamins Publishing Company.
Craig, E. (2002). *Philosophy: A Very Short Introduction*. Oxford: Oxford University Press.
Dean, R. (2016). An idol of the mind: barriers to justice reasoning in sign language interpreters. Paper presented at the conference CL8, Critical Links/A New Generation, Heriot Watt University, Edinburgh.
Dean, R. and Pollard R. (2011). Context-based ethical reasoning in interpreting. a demand control schema perspective. *The Interpreter and Translator Trainer*, 5(1), 155–182.
D'Entreves, M.P. (2016). Hannah Arendt. In *The Stanford Encyclopedia of Philosophy*. Available at: https://plato.stanford.edu/archives/win2016/entries/arendt/ (accessed October 2018).
Dharwadker, V. (1999). A.K. Ramanujan's theory and practice of translation. In S. Bassnett and H. Trivedi (eds), *Post-colonial Translation: Theory and Practice* (pp. 114–140). New York: Routledge.
Finnis, J. (2018). Aquinas' moral, political, and legal philosophy. In *The Stanford Encyclopedia of Philosophy*. Available at: https://plato.stanford.edu/archives/sum2018/entries/aquinas-moral-political/ (accessed October 2018).
Floros, G. (2011). 'Ethics-less' theories and 'ethical' practices: on ethical relativity in translation. *The Interpreter and Translator Trainer*, 5(1), 65–92. Available at: https://www.tandfonline.com/doi/abs/10.1080/13556509.2011.10798812 (accessed October 2018).
Floros, G. (2016). The ethics of mutual survival: which 'side(s)' to do justice to?' Paper presented at the international conference TRANSINT2016 Translation and Interpreting: Convergence, Contact, Interaction, University of Trieste, Italy.
Fornero, G. (2000). *Protagonisti e Testi della Filosofia*, vol. D/2. Varese: Paravia.
Frankopan, P. (2015). *The Silk Roads: A New History of the World*. London: Bloomsbury.
Franssen, M., Lokhorst, G. and van de Poel, I. (2015). Philosophy of technology. In *The Stanford Encyclopedia of Philosophy*. Available at: https://plato.stanford.edu/archives/fall2015/entries/technology/ (accessed October 2018).
Garzone, G. and Rudvin, M. (2003). *Domain-specific English and Language Mediation in Professional and Institutional Settings*. Milan: Arcipelago.
Gentzler, E. (1993). *Contemporary Translation Theories*. London: Routledge.
Glock, H. (2003). *Quine and Davidson on Language, Thought and Reality*. Cambridge: Cambridge University Press.
Goodman, C. (2017). Ethics in Indian and Tibetan Buddhism. In *The Stanford Encyclopedia of Philosophy*. Available at: https://plato.stanford.edu/archives/spr2017/entries/ethics-indian-buddhism/ (accessed October 2018).
Graham, G. (2011). *Theories of Ethics: An Introduction to Moral Philosophy with a Selection of Classic Readings*. London: Routledge.
Haidt, J. (2012). *The Righteous Mind: Why Good People Are Divided by Politics and Religion*. London: Penguin Books.

Hale, S. (2007). *Community Interpreting*. Basingstoke: Palgrave Macmillan.
Hoffman, J. and Graham, P. (2015). *Introduction to Political Theory*. London: Routledge.
Inghilleri, M. (2012). *Interpreting Justice: Ethics, Politics and Language*. London: Routledge.
Johnson, R. and Cureton, A. (2018). Kant's moral philosophy. In *The Stanford Encyclopedia of Philosophy*. Available at: https://plato.stanford.edu/archives/fall2017/entries/kant-moral/ (accessed October 2018).
Kermit, P. (2007). Aristotelian ethics and modern professional interpreting. In C. Wadensjö, B. E. Dimitrova and A-L Nilsson (eds), *The Critical Link 4: Professionalisation of Interpreting in the Community. Selected Papers from the Fourth International Conference on Interpreting in Legal, Health and Social Service Settings* (pp. 241–249). Amsterdam: John Benjamins Publishing Company.
Kim, S.H. (2017). Max Weber. In *The Stanford Encyclopedia of Philosophy*. Available at: https://plato.stanford.edu/archives/win2017/entries/weber/ (accessed October 2018).
Kleinig, J. (2017). Loyalty. In *The Stanford Encyclopedia of Philosophy*. Available at: http://plato.stanford.edu/archives/fall2013/entries/loyalty/ (accessed October 2018).
Kothari, R. (2006). *Translating India: The Cultural Politics of English*. Delhi: Foundation.
Kruger, H. and Crots, E. (2014). Professional and personal ethics in translation: a survey of South African translators' strategies and motivations. In *Stellenbosch Papers in Linguistics*, 43, 147–181. Available at: https://www.ajol.info/index.php/splp/article/viewFile/111744/101509 (accessed October 2018).
Kultgen, J. (1988). *Ethics and Professionalism*. Philadelphia, PA: University of Pennsylvania Press.
MacIntyre, A. (2002 [1967]). *A Short History of Ethics*. London: Routledge.
Mendoza, E. (2012). Thinking through ethics: the processes of ethical decision making by novice and expert American sign language interpreters. *International Journal of Interpreter Education*, 4(1), 58–72. Available at: www.cit-asl.org/new/thinking-through-ethics/ (accessed October 2018).
Mukherji, S. (2002). Personal commitment: the craft not sullen art of translation. In B. N. Rukmini (ed.), *Translation, Text and Theory: The Paradigm of India* (pp. 25–34). New Delhi: Sage Publications.
Murphy, M. (2011). The natural law tradition in ethics. In *The Stanford Encyclopedia of Philosophy* Available at: https://plato.stanford.edu/archives/win2011/entries/natural-law-ethics/ (accessed October 2018).
Nuttall, J. (2002). *An Introduction to Philosophy*. Malden, MA: Polity Press.
Ocone, R. and Ocone C. (2012). The new engineer and the old philosopher: hedgehog or fox? *Tcetoday*, 52–53. Available at www.tcetoday.com
Ozolins, U. (2016). The myth of myth of invisibility? *Interpreting*, 18(2), 273–284.
Pöchhacker, F. (2004). *Introducing Interpreting Studies*. London: Routledge.
Pym, A. (2010). *Exploring Translation Theories*. London: Routledge.
Pym, A. (2012). *On Translator Ethics: Principles for Mediation between Cultures*. Amsterdam: John Benjamin's Publishing Company.
Rudvin, M. (2002). How neutral is 'neutral'? Issues in interaction and participation in community interpreting. In G. Garzone and M. Viezzi (eds), *Perspectives on Interpreting* (pp. 217–233). Bologna: Clueb.
Rudvin, M. (2006). The cultural turn in community interpreting: a brief analysis of epistemological developments in Community Interpreting literature in the light of paradigm changes in the humanities. *Linguistica Antverpiensia*, New Series (Special Edition, edited by E. Hertog and B. van der Veer, 'Taking stock: research and methodology in community interpreting') 5, 21–41.

Rudvin, M: (2007). Socio-cultural constraints and the public service interpreter: the impact of individualism vs. collective group identity on interpreting strategies and performance on notions of 'professionalism'. *Interpreting*, 9(1), 47–69.

Rudvin, M. (2015a). The interpreting profession. In H. Mikkelson and R. Jourdenais (eds), *The Routledge Handbook of Interpreting* (pp. 432–446). London: Routledge.

Rudvin, M. (2015b). Etica, filosofia e mediazione linguistica. dall'etica della filosofia al codice deontologico della mediazione linguistica. *Lingue Linguaggi*, 16, 393–412. Available at: http://siba-ese.unisalento.it/index.php/linguelinguaggi/article/view/15553 (accessed October 2018).

Rudvin, M. (2015c). Interpreting for justice: Erik Hertog interviewed by Mette Rudvin. *Cultus*, 8, 126–142. Available at: www.cultusjournal.com/files/Archives/Rudvin_Hertog_Cultus_8.pdf. (accessed December 2018).

Rudvin, M. (2018). Mediated multilingual interactions. suggestions for a game theoretic framework. *Cultus*, Special Issue 10(2), 19–56. Available at: www.cultusjournal.com/files/Archives/Cultus_10_2_-Rudvin-Mette.pdf (accessed October 2018).

Russell, B. (1945). *The History of Western Philosophy*. New York: Simon & Schuster.

Schäffner, C. (ed.) (1999). *Translation and Norms*. Clevedon: Multilingual Matters.

Shand, J. (ed.) (2003). *Fundamentals of Philosophy*. London: Routledge.

Sinnott-Armstrong, W. (2015). Consequentialism. In *The Stanford Encyclopedia of Philosophy*. Available at: https://plato.stanford.edu/archives/win2015/entries/consequentialism/ (accessed October 2018).

Skelton, A. (2012). William David Ross. In *The Stanford Encyclopedia of Philosophy*. Available at: https://plato.stanford.edu/archives/sum2012/entries/william-david-ross/ (accessed October 2018).

Storr, W. (2019). The controlling force. *New Philosopher: Being Human: All About Us*, 23(1), 94–97.

Swabey, L. (2017). Ethical dilemmas in medical interpreting: an analysis of authentic scenarios. Workshop presented at Alcalà de Henares at the Sixth International Conference on Public Service Interpreting and Translating (PSIT6), University of Alcalà de Henares, Spain.

Tomasello, M. (1999). *The Cultural Origins of Human Cognition*. London: Harvard University Press.

Tomasello, M. (2014). *A Natural History of Human Thinking*. London: Harvard University Press.

Toury, G. (1995 [1980]). *Descriptive Translation Studies – and Beyond*. Rev. edn. Amsterdam: John Benjamins Publishing Company.

Trivedi, H. (2007). Translating culture vs. cultural translation. In P. St. Pierre and P. C. Kar (eds), *Translation: Reflections, Refractions, Transformations* (pp. 277–285). Amsterdam: John Benjamins Publishing Company.

Trompenaars, F. and Hampden-Turner, C. (1997). *Riding the Waves of Culture: Understanding Diversity in Global Business*. London: Nicholas Brealy.

Tymoczko, M. (2007). *Enlarging Translation, Empowering Translators*. Manchester: St. Jerome Publishing.

Ubaldo, N. (2005 [2000]). *Antologia Illustrata di Filosofia*. Florence: Giunti.

Vandekerckhove, W. and Commers, M.S.R. (2004). Whistleblowing and rational loyalty. *Journal of Business Ethics* 53(1–2), 225–233.

Wadensjö, C. (1998). *Interpreting as Interaction*. London: Longman.

Wakabayashi, J. and Kothari, R. (2009). *Decentering Translation Studies: India and Beyond* Amsterdam: John Benjamins Publishing Company.

Warburton, N. (2013 [1992]). *Philosophy: The Basics*. London: Routledge.
Wenar, L. (2017). John Rawls. In *The Stanford Encyclopedia of Philosophy*. Available at: https://plato.stanford.edu/archives/spr2017/entries/rawls/. (accessed October 2018).
Wicks, R. (2017). Arthur Schopenhauer. In *The Stanford Encyclopedia of Philosophy*. Available at: https://plato.stanford.edu/archives/sum2017/entries/schopenhauer/ (accessed October 2018).
Wong, D. (2017). Chinese ethics. In *The Stanford Encyclopedia of Philosophy*. Available at: https://plato.stanford.edu/archives/spr2017/entries/ethics-chinese/ (accessed October 2018).
Zwischenberger, C. (2016). Ethics in the spotlight – and its impact on the future evolution of the translational professions. Paper presented at the conference TRANSINT2016 Translation and Interpreting: Convergence, Contact, Interaction, University of Trieste, Italy.

2
CODES OF ETHICS

Mary Phelan

2.1 Introduction

Part 2 is divided into two sections and in this first section we will focus on commonalities and divergences in codes of ethics, comparing how 20 different associations deal with core ethical principles. Company codes of ethics, which are important in countries where interpreter provision is outsourced, are also considered.

2.2 Historical examples of interpreter ethics

The interpreter's role, and what exactly is permissible or not, have been an acknowledged issue for centuries. For example, trustworthiness and confidentiality were key for Julius Caesar when he bypassed his usual interpreters and asked trusted friends to take on their role (Mairs 2011: 74). Over the course of a century, from 1529 to 1630, the Spanish passed a series of laws detailing that court interpreters in the colonies should be 'skilled and qualified' and treated with respect. Court interpreters were expected to be impartial, to interpret everything that was said, to attend court hearings and prison visits, not to accept gifts or payments, and not to discuss or advise on legal matters (Giambruno 2008). These laws detailing the behaviour expected of court interpreters were in effect a code of ethics.

A high level of awareness of interpreter norms was demonstrated during the eleven-week trial of Queen Caroline of Brunswick at the House of Lords in London in 1820, where interpreters for Italian, German and French were employed. George IV wanted a divorce, and, as adultery was the only ground for divorce at the time and neither party would admit adultery, the solution found was for the House of Lords to pass a bill of pains and penalties, which meant that the Queen was effectively put on trial, charged with adultery. Her interpreter was instructed 'to interfere if he found any difference between the German and English meanings of the questions and answer' rendered by the other interpreter. The Lord Chancellor 'directed the interpreter to use the same form of words, as to number and person, as the witness in translating her replies'. Similarly, Earl Morton requested that counsel address the witness rather than the interpreter, use 'did you' instead of 'did she', and use the first person singular when giving the answers. When the interpreter commented that the witness kept repeating the same words, he was told 'let us have the translation of them'. On one occasion, the interpreter admitted to the court that he did not understand an expression (*Freeman's Journal*, 29 August 1820). When a peer complained about the incoherence and incorrectness of a translation, the interpreter explained that 'the witness would persist in talking while he was translating, and he could not hear and speak too' (*Freeman's Journal*, 11 September 1820). The issues covered – whether to use third person through the interpreter or to speak directly to a witness and the use of the first person I when interpreting what the witness said, the difficulty of interpreting when a witness kept talking, what the interpreter should do if he did not understand an expression – are all live issues for modern-day interpreters.

While court interpreting has existed for centuries, nowadays interpreters are needed in many new settings (medical, immigration, international protection, social welfare, housing, employment law) to ensure that people can access services in an equitable, meaningful and respectful manner. While there is agreement on the role of the legal interpreter, there is ongoing discussion and controversy about the role, and in particular the role boundaries, of interpreters working in medical and some other settings.

2.3 Regulation of professions

Codes of ethics are traditionally most associated with professions, particularly those of doctors and lawyers. However, nowadays there are codes of ethics, often self-regulating ones, for companies, organisations, social workers, librarians, engineers, journalists and many others. In order to protect the public, regulation and legislative frameworks have extended to teachers, architects and healthcare professionals, resulting in a clear career path that includes taking specified courses, obtaining specific qualifications and in some cases also passing professional examinations. Where there is regulation, membership of a regulatory body becomes obligatory and members agree to adhere to a code of ethics and may face disciplinary procedures for infringements. Continuing professional development also usually becomes obligatory. In addition, regulatory bodies may be involved in accrediting training programmes and ensuring that all professionals have the required qualifications and expertise to exercise a particular profession.

What are the characteristics of a profession? Table 2.1 contains ten characteristics, very few of which currently apply to public service interpreting or even to more established court interpreting, in any jurisdiction. Take a moment to consider how many apply to public service interpreting in your country. Even if you are

TABLE 2.1 Characteristics of professions

Characteristics of professions	Yes	No
University undergraduate degree in relevant area		
University postgraduate degree in relevant area		
Internship/apprenticeship/traineeship (usually one or two years)		
Professional examinations organised by a professional body (in addition to qualifications)		
Compulsory membership of a regulatory or professional body		
Accreditation of training programmes by the regulatory or professional body		
Code of ethics and code of conduct or practice		
Compulsory attendance at continuing professional development courses		
Disciplinary/fitness to practise procedures		
Statutory regulation		

based in a country with a system of interpreter training and provision, it is unlikely that you will respond 'yes' to all ten points.

By contrast, translation and interpreting tend to be unregulated; where there is no legislative framework to protect the title, anyone can call themselves a translator or an interpreter. In many countries, public service interpreting is far from being a profession and factors, such as lack of accredited training courses, lack of understanding of the importance of standards, and in some cases job insecurity and low remuneration, militate against professionalisation. Elsewhere, there may only be examinations or a certification system, without any accompanying training course. In some ways, public service interpreting can still be considered a young profession and perhaps regulation is a question of time. In the interim, one action that can be taken comparatively easily, and has been taken by many associations, is to develop codes of ethics.

2.4 Association codes of ethics

From the point of view of associations, codes of ethics are very desirable on a number of levels, in particular, to professionalise the sector and to act as a signal that interpreters belong to a profession and, by extension, behave in an appropriate, professional manner. Codes of ethics fulfil a practical function of providing an ethical framework that outlines the principles that apply to interpreters and the professional standards expected of them and to which they may be held accountable. They encourage interpreters to consider ethical issues and how best to respond when they arise. More detailed codes of conduct and codes of practice provide guidance and examples on how to implement ethical principles. Codes encourage association members and, as they are freely available on the internet, even non-member interpreters, who take the time to read them, to behave ethically. Codes are also useful to those who work with interpreters and wish to find out more about what to expect of interpreters although access to this information is restricted to those who can read the language in which a code is written; the person who does not speak the majority language may have very different expectations.

In addition, codes of ethics are essential to the development of trust with all parties (see Skaaden, Part 3 in this volume). However, all too often, interpreter codes are an attempt at self-regulation in an unregulated environment; membership of an association may not be obligatory and if a code is breached, the association may not have any real power to impose sanctions. Codes alone are insufficient; there needs to be training for interpreters where they have an opportunity to discuss the implications of ethical principles and to explore possible scenarios and the effects of different approaches with trainers and colleagues, preferably in the context of accredited training which can allow them to reflect on the boundaries around their role but ideally in the context of ongoing support throughout their careers.

Associations of translators and interpreters were founded as early as 1910 and continued to be founded over the following decades, particularly after the Second World War and again in the 1980s. Some of the associations listed in Table 2.2 may have resulted from mergers of existing associations or indeed from a split in an association or a desire for a more specialised or a regional grouping.

There has been an ongoing difficulty in that, when some association codes of ethics were originally written, there were few or no training courses for translators

TABLE 2.2 Establishment of translator and interpreter associations

Date	Acronym	Association	Country
1910	IoL	Institute of Linguists	UK
1913	STF	Association of Government Authorized Translators in Norway	Norway
1920	ÖVGD	Austrian Association of Certified Court Interpreters	Austria
1945	AIT	Association d'Interprètes et de Traducteurs	Switzerland
1947	SFT	Société Française des Traducteurs	France
1950	AITI	Associazione Italiana Traduttori e Interpreti	Italy
1953	AIIC	International Association of Conference Interpreters	
1954	Universitas	Österreichischer Dolmetscherverband Universitas	Austria
1955	SKTL	Finnish Association of Translators and Interpreters	Finland
1955	BDÜ	Bundesverband der Dolmetscher und Übersetzer	Germany
1955	CBTI-BKVT	Belgian Chamber of Translators and Interpreters	Belgium
1956	STIC (now CTTIC)	Society of Translators and Interpreters of Canada Since 1970: Canadian Translators, Terminologists and Interpreters Council	Canada
1959	ATA	American Translators Association	USA
1963	PEM	Panhellenic Association of Translators	Greece
1974	APCI	Association of Police and Court Interpreters	UK
1978	NAJIT	National Association of Judiciary Interpreters and Translators	USA
1979	KAJ	Translation Industry Professionals	Finland

TABLE 2.2 (Continued)

Date	Acronym	Association	Country
1979	ATIA	Association of Translators and Interpreters of Alberta	Canada
1980	ITA	Israel Translators Association	Israel
1982	AATI	Asociación Argentina de Traductores e Intérpretes	Argentina
1982	TAC	Translators Association of China	China
1985	JAT	Japan Association of Translators	Japan
1985	NZSTI	New Zealand Society of Translators and Interpreters	New Zealand
1986	ITA	Irish Translators' Association	Ireland
1986	UNETICA	Union Nationale des Experts Traducteurs près les Cours d'Appel	France
1986	ITI	Institute of Translation and Interpreting	UK
1986	MMIA/IMIA	Massachusetts/International Medical Interpreters Association	USA
1987	AUSIT	Australian Institute of Interpreters and Translators	Australia
1990	ADATI	Association of Danish Authorized Translators and Interpreters	Denmark
1990	TEPIS	Polish Society of Sworn and Specialized Translators	Poland
1994	NRPSI	National Register of Public Service Interpreters	UK
1996	AIT	Association of Interpreters and Translators	Bulgaria
1996	KSTCR	Chamber of Court Appointed Interpreters and Translators of the Czech Republic	Czech Republic
2003	ASETRAD	Asociación Española de Traductores Correctores e Intérpretes	Spain
2004	NTF	Norwegian Association of Interpreters	Norway
2004	PEEMPIP	Panhellenic Association of Professional Translators Graduates of the Ionian University	Greece
2005	SAPT	Slovak Association of Translators and Interpreters	Slovakia
2006	APTIJ	Asociación Profesional de Traductores e Intérpretes Judiciales y Jurados	Spain
2009	SITA	Scottish Interpreters and Translators Association	Scotland
2009	IAPTI	International Association of Professional Translators and Interpreters	
2010	USST	Association of Sworn Court Interpreters	Croatia
2011	ALTI	Association Luxembourgeoise des Traducteurs et Interprètes	Luxembourg
2011	Rättstolkarna	Swedish Association of Court Interpreters	Sweden
2014	BBVT-UPTIA	Union Professionnelle des Traducteurs et Interprètes Assermentés	Belgium
2014	DPTS	Association of Translators and Interpreters of Slovenia	Slovenia
2015	APTRAD	Portuguese Association of Translators and Interpreters	Portugal
2016	EXPERTIJ	Experts et Traducteurs Interprètes Judicaires	France

and interpreters who were largely self-taught. Over time, universities introduced undergraduate and postgraduate courses focusing mainly on translation and conference interpreting and offering a limited array of languages. However, public service interpreting, with its new demands in relation to settings and languages, posed particular difficulties in creating new courses and at the time of writing, very few universities offer programmes for public service interpreters. As it can be difficult for public service interpreters to obtain a qualification, they may find themselves ineligible to join national associations unless there is an option to take an examination or provide evidence of substantial experience.

An early example of an association code of ethics is that of AIIC, the International Association of Conference Interpreters, which adopted a code of ethics in 1957 (Boéri 2015: 32); we are not aware of any earlier code drawn up by an association. Since then, the number of codes has multiplied. Indeed, an intriguing aspect of the world of translation studies is the large number of codes devised by international, regional, national and local associations of interpreters, by courts, immigration services, and by companies contracted to provide interpreters. For example, in 2004, Bancroft located 145 documents from 25 countries (2005: v). This raises questions: is such a large number of codes necessary? Should codes of ethics be broad and cover all possible settings, or is there a need for specific codes for specialised settings?

A variety of words are used to describe association codes of ethics. In Table 2.3, of a total of 20 codes, 10 use the word 'ethics' while nine use 'conduct' and two codes use both. The word 'practice' is used in three codes. The word 'professional' is used in 12 code titles, to distinguish those who (hopefully) hold professional qualifications from others who are using their knowledge of languages to gain employment but who do not hold qualifications in interpreting.

However, the choice of 'code of ethics', 'code of conduct' and 'code of practice' is not always thought through. For example, the International Association of Professional Translators and Interpreters' (IAPTI) code of ethics is a list of duties and does not contain any ethical principles. At this point it would be useful to consider dictionary definitions of the three types of code:

> A *code of ethics* is an agreement on ethical standards for a profession.
> A *code of conduct* is an agreement on rules of behaviour for a group or organisation.
> A *code of practice* is a set of written rules which explains how people working in a particular profession should behave.
>
> *(Collins English Dictionary)*

The key difference is that while codes of ethics focus on ethical standards or principles, both codes of conduct and codes of practice focus on behaviour, although codes of practice appear in the definition to be more linked to professions than codes of conduct. An example of clear usage of terms is the AUSIT code, which begins with a code of ethics which then serves as the basis for a code of conduct;

TABLE 2.3 Code titles

Title of association	Title of code
• American Translators Association (ATA)	Code of *Ethics and Professional Practice*
• International Association of Professional Translators and Interpreters (IAPTI)	Code of *Ethics*
• International Medical Interpreters Association (IMIA)	Code of *Ethics*
• Spanish Professional Association of Court and Sworn Interpreters and Translators (APTIJ)	Code of *Ethics*
• European Legal Interpreters and Translators Association (EULITA)	Code of *Professional Ethics*
• National Association of Judiciary Interpreters and Translators (NAJIT)	Code of *Ethics* and *Professional Responsibilities*
• Australian Institute of Interpreters and Translators (AUSIT)	Code of *Ethics* and Code of *Conduct*
• Spanish association of translators, editors and interpreters (ASETRAD)	Code of *Professional Conduct*
• Federal Association of Interpreters and Translators (BDÜ)	Code of *Professional Conduct*
• Institute of Translation and Interpreting (ITI)	Code of *Professional Conduct*
• National Register of Public Service Interpreters (NRPSI)	Code of *Professional Conduct*
• Société française/ Sydicat français des Traducteurs (SFT)	Code of *Professional Conduct*
• Washington State Department of Social and Health Services	
• Associazione Italiana Traduttori e Interpreti (AITI)	Code of Professional *Ethics* and *Conduct*
• Association of Police and Court Interpreters (APCI)	Code of Practice
• Massachusetts Court System	Code of *Professional Conduct* for Court Interpreters of the Trial Court
• California Healthcare Interpreters Association (CHIA)	California Standards for Healthcare Interpreters
• U.S. Federal Courts	Standards for Performance and *Professional* Responsibility for Contract Court Interpreters
• Judicial Council of California	*Professional* Standards and *Ethics* for California Court Interpreters
• National Council on Interpreting in Health Care (NCIHC)	A National Code of *Ethics* for Interpreters in Health Care National Standards of Practice for Interpreters in Health Care

the code of ethics sets out the ethical principles while the code of conduct details expectations regarding interpreters' expected behaviour in the light of each ethical principle.

The term 'standards' is defined as a 'code of good conduct for an individual or group' (*Merriam-Webster Dictionary*) but there does not seem to be any consensus on the content of standards because the term is used in the United States for what are in reality very different documents. For example, the NCIHC National Standards of Practice for Interpreters in Health Care and the Professional Standards and Ethics for California Court Interpreters (Judicial Council of California) are in essence codes of conduct attempting to standardise interpreter behaviour. Standards of Performance is the name given to a two-page document by the US Federal Courts which is basically a code of ethics. Meanwhile, the California Healthcare Interpreters Association's (CHIA) Standards consist of a lengthy document which digresses into issues such as research on language barriers and health outcomes. Finally, the International Medical Interpreters Association's (IMIA) Medical Interpreting Standards of Practice uses Likert scales to document and assess how interpreters apply ethical principles in practice. The purpose of the document is four-fold, as it is designed: (1) to provide guidance in the development of training programmes; (2) to act as an evaluation tool for training and self-assessment; (3) to act as preparation for healthcare providers to work with interpreters; and (4) to be a foundation for the IMIA certification examination. Clearly, this multipurpose document was designed to compensate for a shortage of training opportunities for both interpreters and healthcare providers.

While many codes of ethics apply to both translators and interpreters, in some, there is no specific mention of the work of interpreters (FIT Translator's Charter 1963, 1994; Société Française des Traducteurs 2016). Most codes detail ethical principles applicable to both translators and interpreters, while some deal first with common areas of concern to both groups and then with issues specific to translators and those specific to interpreters (AUSIT). A small number of codes are for public service interpreters only (National Register of Public Service Interpreters, Institute of Translation and Interpreting, Norwegian Interpreters' Code), for police and court interpreters only (Association of Police and Court Interpreters, National Association of Judiciary Interpreters and Translators), or for medical interpreters only (National Council on Interpreting in Health Care, International Medical Interpreters Association, California Healthcare Interpreters Association).

There is a great deal of variation in the length of codes: they vary from one page in the case of Société Française des Traducteurs (SFT 2016), to seven pages in the case of the National Register of Public Service Interpreters (NRPSI 2016a), and 15 for the Australian Institute of Interpreters and Translators (AUSIT 2012). In general, the trend is for codes for interpreters, like codes for other professions and indeed occupations, to increase in length and include more examples and guidance.

Most codes of ethics are semi-anonymous; we know that they have been prepared by associations or other bodies but we do not know who exactly was involved. There is some evidence of change on this front. For example, ten members of the California Healthcare Interpreting Association Standards and Certification Committee, including Claudia Angelelli (see Angelelli 2006), were involved in developing the California Healthcare Interpreting Standards (2002). Similarly, the manual entitled *Professional Standards and Ethics for California Court Interpreters* (Judicial Council of California 2013) acknowledges the contribution of seven individuals. The AUSIT code (2012) begins with the names of six members of the working group along with those of two consultants (see Ozolins 2014). The European Legal Interpreters and Translators Association (EULITA) (2013) code includes a useful recommendation that 'specific Codes of Best Practices should be drafted by the respective judicial administrations in cooperation with the representatives of legal interpreters and translators working for them'. Two French associations, UNETICA (Union Nationale des Experts Traducteurs Interprètes près les Cours d'Appel) and EXPERTIJ (Experts et Traducteurs Interprètes Judicaires), do not have their own code and instead refer their members to the EULITA code.

2.4.1 Core ethical principles of association codes

While one might expect all codes of ethics for interpreters to be fairly similar, in reality, as will be demonstrated here, they are quite diverse and do not always cover what could be considered key principles. In 1994, Schweda-Nicholson (1994: 82) listed the points covered by seven codes as:

1. The interpreter's overall role
2. Competence and required skills
3. Impartiality
4. Completeness and accuracy
5. Conflicts of interest and ground for disqualification
6. Confidentiality
7. Continuing professional development (CPD).

Skaaden (2013) has suggested that principles 3 and 4 are core principles because impartiality and, in particular, completeness and accuracy, differentiate the work of interpreters from that of other professions. She suggests that the other principles hinge on these two core principles. Tables 2.4 and 2.5 focus on 20 codes of ethics of international, regional and national associations that were available in English and whether or not they cover Schweda-Nicholson's seven principles. It should be noted that the amount of information on each point varies greatly from one sentence in some codes to half a page or more in others. How do the codes define the seven principles for interpreters? Do they approach them in a similar manner? Are there any differences?

In Tables 2.4 and 2.5, just two of the 20 codes, those of AUSIT and the CHIA California Standards, cover all of Schweda-Nicholson's seven principles and two

TABLE 2.4 Seven core principles and national organisations

	AITI[1] (2013)	ASETRAD[2] (n.d.)	ATA[3] (2010)	AUSIT[4] (2012)	BDÜ[5] (2014)	EULITA[6] (2013)	IAPTI[7] (n.d.)	ITI[8] (2013)	SFT[9] (2016)	SITA[10] (n.d.)
Role	✓			✓		✓				
Competence	✓	✓	✓	✓	✓	✓	✓	✓	✓	✓
Impartiality	✓		✓	✓	✓	✓		✓		✓
Completeness/accuracy			✓	✓		✓		✓	✓	✓
Conflict of interest	✓			✓	✓	✓	✓	✓		
Confidentiality	✓	✓	✓	✓	✓	✓	✓	✓	✓	✓
CPD	✓		✓	✓	✓			✓	✓	

[1] Associazione Italiana Traduttori e Interpreti (Italy) Code of Professional Ethics and Conduct
[2] Asociación de Traductores, Correctores e Intérpretes (Spain) Code of Professional Conduct
[3] American Translators Association Code of Ethics and Professional Practice
[4] Australian Institute of Interpreters and Translators Code of Ethics and Code of Conduct
[5] BDÜ Bundesverband der Dolmetscher und Übersetzer/ Federal Association of Interpreters and Translators (Germany) Code of Professional Conduct
[6] European Legal Interpreters and Translators Association Code of Professional Ethics
[7] International Association of Professional Translators and Interpreters Code of Ethics
[8] Institute for Translation and Interpreting (UK) Code of Professional Conduct
[9] Syndicat français/Société française des traducteurs (France) Code of Professional Conduct
[10] Scottish Interpreters & Translators Association Code of Conduct for Individual Members

TABLE 2.5 Seven core principles and association codes of ethics

	APCI[1] (n.d.)	APTIJ[2] (2010)	CHIA[3] (2002)	IMIA[4] (2006)	NAJIT[5] (n.d)	NCIHC[6] (2004)	NRPSI[7] (2016)	ATIA[8] (2015)	SKTL[9] (2016)	ÖVGD[10] (2017)
Role			✓		✓	✓				
Competence	✓		✓	✓			✓	✓	✓	
Impartiality	✓	✓	✓	✓	✓	✓	✓	✓	✓	✓
Completeness/ accuracy	✓	✓	✓		✓	✓	✓	✓	✓	
Conflict of interest	✓	✓	✓		✓		✓		✓	
Confidentiality	✓	✓	✓	✓	✓	✓	✓	✓	✓	✓
CPD	✓	✓	✓	✓	✓	✓			✓	

[1] Association of Police and Court Interpreters (UK) Code of Practice
[2] Asociación Profesional de Traductores e Intérpretes Judiciales y Jurados/Spanish Professional Association of Court and Sworn Interpreters and Translators Code of Ethics
[3] California Healthcare Interpreters Association California Standards for Healthcare Interpreters
[4] International Medical Interpreters Association Code of Ethics
[5] National Association of Judiciary Interpreters and Translators (NAJIT) (USA) Code of Ethics and Professional Responsibilities
[6] National Council on Interpreting in Health Care (NCIHC) (USA) A National Code of Ethics for Interpreters in Health Care
[7] National Register of Public Service Interpreters (NRPSI) (UK) Code of Professional Conduct
[8] Association of Translators and Interpreters of Alberta, Canada Code of Ethics and Supplemental Code for community, conference, court and medical interpreters
[9] Finnish Association of Translators and Interpreters Code of Ethics
[10] Austrian Association of Certified Court Interpreters Code of Ethics

codes (ASETRAD and IAPTI) cover a mere two principles. These findings echo those of Hale (2007) who compared 16 codes from nine countries, focusing on the three principles of confidentiality, accuracy and impartiality. Somewhat surprisingly, Hale found that these three principles were not included in all the selected codes; confidentiality appeared in just over 80 per cent, accuracy in 75 per cent and impartiality in just under 70 per cent (2007: 108).

Role, function, task or duty is mentioned by 7 or 35 per cent of the codes in tables 2.4 and 2.5. For EULITA, legal interpreters 'play an essential *role* in all efforts to ensure the equality of citizens in justice-related communications'. For AUSIT, interpreters 'play an important *role* in facilitating parties who do not share a common language to communicate effectively with each other'. For NAJIT, their *function* is 'to remove the language barrier to the extent possible'. For AITI, the *task* of interpreters is to 'ensure oral communication between speakers of different languages'. For the Massachusetts Trial Court,

> A court interpreter is the communication facilitator for the parties involved in a proceeding, and, as such, plays a vital *role* in the protection of the rights of LEP (Limited English Proficiency) and DHH (Deaf or Hard of Hearing) individuals engaged as parties and witnesses in legal proceedings in the Trial Court.

Contract court interpreters in the US Federal Courts are 'officers of the court with the specific *duty* and responsibility of interpreting between English and the language specified'.

Competence is mentioned in 14 or 70 per cent of the codes. In the EULITA code it relates to (1) interpreting techniques; (2) knowledge of language and subject matter and adequate preparation time; and (3) improving interpreting skills and knowledge. The AUSIT code emphasises that interpreters 'only undertake work they are competent to perform, in the languages for which they are professionally qualified through training and credentials'. The American Translators Association code states that 'Professional translators and interpreters decline assignments that are beyond their expertise or capacity.' The National Register of Public Service Interpreters Code of Professional Conduct provides that:

> The *competence* to carry out a particular assignment shall include: a sufficiently advanced and idiomatic command of the languages concerned, with awareness of dialects and other linguistic variations that may be relevant to a particular commission of work; the particular specialist skills required; and, where appropriate, an adequate level of awareness of relevant cultural and political realities in relation to the country or countries concerned.
>
> *(2016 unpaginated)*

Impartiality is mentioned in 17 or 85 per cent of the codes. For example, the NRPSI code explains impartiality as:

Practitioners shall at all times act impartially and shall not act in any way that might result in prejudice or preference on grounds of religion or belief, race, politics, gender, age, sexual orientation or disability otherwise than as obliged in order to faithfully translate, interpret or otherwise transfer meaning.

The National Association of Judiciary Interpreters and Translators code advises interpreters to avoid 'unnecessary contact with the parties' and links impartiality with conflicts of interest.

Completeness/accuracy is addressed by 14 or 70 per cent of the codes. The NAJIT provision is quite detailed:

Source language speech should be faithfully rendered into the target language by conserving all the elements of the original message while accommodating the syntactic and semantic patterns of the target language. The rendition should sound natural in the target language, and there should be no distortion of the original message through addition or omission, explanation or paraphrasing. All hedges, false starts and repetitions should be conveyed; also, English words mixed into the other language should be retained, as should culturally bound terms which have no direct equivalent in English, or which may have more than one meaning. The register, style and tone of the source language should be conserved. Guessing should be avoided. Court interpreters who do not hear or understand what a speaker has said should seek clarification. Interpreter errors should be corrected for the record as soon as possible.

Conflict of interest is covered by 11 codes or 55 per cent with the Institute of Translation and Interpreting code providing a useful example:

Members' personal, private, religious, political or financial interests should not conflict with their duties and obligations to their clients. Should such a conflict arise it should be declared to the client and if the conflict is unacceptable or cannot be resolved, the member should withdraw from the contract having regard to their contractual obligations.

(2013: 3)

Confidentiality features in all 20 or 100 per cent of the codes in question with the ITI defining it as follows: 'Members shall maintain complete confidentiality at all times and treat any information that may come to them in the course of their work as privileged information, not to be communicated to any third party without prior written authority.'

However, confidentiality may not apply where disclosure is required by law (AUSIT, NRPSI, ITI). The ATA has a useful provision that allows interpreters to discuss issues with colleagues, while respecting confidentiality: 'When consulting with colleagues, the translator or interpreter must give enough context to show what the problem is while limiting and disguising information so that no confidential information is disclosed.'

Continuing professional development or CPD appears in 13 or 65 per cent of the codes, often in the form of lifelong learning by the interpreter, as in the case of NAJIT: 'Court interpreters and translators shall strive to maintain and improve their interpreting and translation skills and knowledge.'

The ITI includes a requirement to attend continuing professional development courses:

> For as long as they continue in practice, members and, in the case of corporate members, their translator and interpreter employees, are required to undertake continuing professional development as appropriate, in order to continue to offer the highest possible standards of work by maintaining and updating their language skills, subject knowledge or any other skills or knowledge necessary for the work.

It is worth mentioning that of the codes examined, only one, that of AUSIT, addresses the use of technology for interpreting:

> Interpreters familiarise themselves with the increasing use of technology for interpreting, including telephone, video and internet interpreting, and diverse recording/transmitting devices. Interpreters who engage in interpreting using these technologies prepare themselves by understanding the purposes of their use and the way in which communication is shaped by these technologies. Institutions, agencies and clients who use these technologies are encouraged to develop protocols and brief interpreters on their use and on any particular requirements they may have.

2.4.2 Other issues covered in codes of ethics

A surprising result from an extended comparison of the codes was the inclusion of other aspects of interpreter behaviour that one might not necessarily expect to feature in codes of ethics or codes of conduct. The information in Tables 2.6 and 2.7 is drawn from the codes of ethics of the same 20 associations as covered in Tables 2.4 and 2.5, but the focus is on 13 supplementary points contained therein. On the positive side, it is clear that codes are evolving and addressing local issues that are of importance to associations and their members. However, the fact that national associations have decided that these issues need to be spelt out in their codes suggests that unsavoury practices are not uncommon. It seems that as associations become aware of poor practice through complaints or media coverage, they introduce new elements to their codes in an attempt to influence interpreter behaviour. However, in some cases, this approach results in codes where the focus is on bad rather than good practice.

TABLE 2.6 Other issues covered by national codes of ethics

	AITI (2013)	APTIJ (2010)	ASETRAD (n.d.)	ATA (2010)	AUSIT (2012)	BDÜ (2014)	EULITA (2013)	LAPTI (n.d.)	ITI (2013)	SFT (2016)	SITA (n.d.)
Taxes	✓		✓							✓	
Remuneration	✓	✓	✓	✓		✓		✓		✓	
Acceptance of gifts		✓			✓				✓		
Advertising	✓		✓			✓			✓	✓	
Credentials		✓	✓	✓	✓	✓					
Illegal activities	✓								✓		
Criminal record											
Bribery and Corruption									✓		
Client poaching	✓								✓		
Criticism of colleagues	✓					✓					
Subcontracting of work						✓		✓	✓		✓
Public comment									✓		
Sanctions	✓					✓			✓		

Notes: for acronyms, see notes to Table 2.4.

TABLE 2.7 Other issues covered by association codes of ethics

	APCI (n.d.)	APTIJ (2010)	CHIA (2002)	IMIA (2006)	NAJIT (n.d.)	NCIHC (2013)	NRPSI (2016)	ATIA (2015)	SKTL (2016)	ÖVGD (2017)
Taxes										
Remuneration								✓		✓
Acceptance of gifts										
Advertising	✓							✓		✓
Credentials					✓			✓		
Illegal activities							✓			
Criminal record							✓			
Bribery and corruption										
Client poaching										
Criticism of colleagues								✓		
Subcontracting of work	✓						✓			✓
Public comment										
Sanctions	✓			✓			✓	✓		✓

Note: for acronyms, see notes to Table 2.5.

Dealing with each of the 13 points individually, the first point relates to taxes which are a concern for three associations or 15 per cent of the 20 codes examined. AITI in Italy, ASETRAD in Spain and SFT in France, include a provision that members must act in accordance with the law and in particular in relation to social welfare and tax obligations. While, strictly speaking, it may not be the business of associations to police these matters, they may be concerned about potential reputational damage if members do not pay taxes.

Remuneration is included in 45 per cent of the codes but from different points of view. For example, the code of APTIJ, the Spanish sworn interpreters' association, mentions fees in the context of impartiality: 'Fees received from one of the parties to the suit shall have no influence in the way they carry out their work.' The American Translators Association code provides that interpreters can negotiate fees 'that realistically reflect their experience, skills, and quality of service'. Fair remuneration, something that relates to interpreters' self-interest, is an issue for five associations, four in Europe and one international. The Italian AITI code provides that 'Translators and interpreters shall refrain from providing their services in exchange for remuneration that is not commensurate with the quality of their work.' Similarly, in Spain, the ASETRAD Code of Professional Conduct states that translators and interpreters have the right to: 'Remuneration that enables them to practise their profession efficiently and with dignity, in equivalent conditions to members of other professions holding similar qualifications.'

In Germany, the BDÜ code provides that: 'Remuneration charged by a BDÜ member must always be adequate. BDÜ members may not undercut proper remuneration in an unethical manner. However, members are permitted to consider the client's income and financial circumstances when agreeing to remuneration.'

The IAPTI code recommends that interpreters 'Not favor unfair competition by offering or accepting fees below those generally considered to be proper and fair in the market where they practice their profession' (see also Part 3 in this volume and the role of professionalisation).

Three codes or 15 per cent mention gifts, with the Spanish sworn interpreters' association, APTIJ, prohibiting all gifts while AUSIT permits 'typical small gifts in specific cultural contexts' and the Institute of Translation and Interpreting allows for 'small gifts and advantages in the normal course of business'.

Advertising is included in eight codes or 40 per cent. The BDÜ expects members to refrain from 'misleading or subjective, comparative advertising'. The Institute of Translation and Interpreting code states that promotional material should be 'legal, decent, honest and truthful'. The Association of Police and Court Interpreters code provides that

> Members shall not publicise their services in any manner which may reasonably be regarded as being in bad taste. Publicity must not be inaccurate or misleading in any way and should be discreet. Members shall not publicise their services to the Police.

The topic of credentials appears in seven codes or 35 per cent, all of which make similar points. BDÜ members are to refrain from 'excessive claims about their services offered, qualifications or professional experience'. Members of the Spanish association ASETRAD 'shall not claim to hold qualifications they do not possess'. American Translators Association members 'represent our qualifications, capabilities and responsibilities honestly'. AUSIT practitioners 'always represent their credentials honestly.' According to the National Association of Judiciary Interpreters and Translators code: 'Court interpreters and translators shall accurately represent their certifications, accreditations, training and pertinent experience.'

Illegal activities are covered in three codes or 15 per cent. The Institute of Translation and Interpreting code provides that members 'shall not accept work that they believe may further any illegal or criminal activity, concerning which they shall have a duty of disclosure to the proper authorities'. Similarly, the National Register of Public Service Interpreters code states that 'Practitioners shall not accept or carry out work which they believe might render them liable to prosecution for criminal behavior, which might incur civil liability or which contravenes the United Nations Universal Declaration of Human Rights.' The Italian AITI code provides that 'Translators and interpreters must not carry out assignments that could, in all likelihood, involve them in illegal activities.'

Just one code (5 per cent), that of the National Register of Public Service Interpreters, mentions criminal records of interpreters: 'Practitioners have a duty to report, without delay, any unspent conviction ... or caution received in either the UK or overseas to NRPSI.'

While it might seem unnecessary to tell members not to give or take bribes and not to act corruptly, to behave honestly, another UK association, the Institute of Translation and Interpreting, is the only one to include corruption and bribery explicitly in its code:

> Acting Corruptly – The Institute shall regard members as acting corruptly if they give or offer a gift or advantage to someone with the intention of persuading them to act against their professional obligations and/or the interests of those to whom they owe a duty (such as a client). Members who request and/or accept and act on such an incentive shall be regarded as acting corruptly.
>
> A Bribe – An incentive to act against one's professional obligations or duty to others is a bribe. [...]No member shall accept remuneration from any party that could be construed as a bribe.

Poaching of clients is mentioned by two associations (10 per cent), the Institute of Translation and Interpreting and Italian AITI. The code of the former provides that 'Members must not deliberately approach another member's client with a view to obtaining work from that client' while that the latter includes an article on non-solicitation of clients in the context of team work.

Two codes (10 per cent) cover criticism of colleagues. The BDÜ code provides that members 'shall refrain from commenting on the performance of colleagues. Criticism of faulty work should be put forward objectively and constructively' while the Italian AITI code states that 'Translators and interpreters must refrain from expressing in public or to clients opinions that could damage the professional reputation of a colleague. Any technical opinions or assessments must be expressed in a balanced, objective manner.'

Subcontracting of work is an issue in six codes (30 per cent) with approaches varying considerably between the different associations. The Association of Police and Court Interpreters only allows members to recommend a colleague if requested to do so 'and in an emergency' and members 'shall not receive any payment from another Member'. The National Register of Public Service Interpreters permits subcontracting, subject to the person having 'the necessary competence' and being subject to a code of professional conduct. The Scottish Interpreters and Translators Association allows subcontracting but not 'without prior consent of the Principal' (the Principal is defined as any organisation, body or individual from whom a member accepts work). The Institute of Translation and Interpreting allows for subcontracting, providing it is in conformance with their code. The BDÜ also allows for subcontracting on condition that subcontractors have the necessary abilities and skills but does not allow members who commission subcontractors to 'withhold an inappropriate percentage of the fee agreed upon with the client as compensation for referring/placing work.' The IAPTI code provides that all members shall:

> in the event of hiring another translator or interpreter as an employee or independent collaborator, guarantee that person proper contract conditions and fair pay, in accordance with the work carried out, and, moreover, respect the conditions agreed to and fully abide by them.

The topic of public comment is included in one code (5 per cent). The Institute of Translation and Interpreting allows for public comment in the context of media and public statements:

> In making public statements and in their contacts with the media, members must bear in mind that, if they have been identified as members of the Institute, their statements may be interpreted as representing the view of the Institute or of the profession; they shall therefore respond accordingly with dignity and professionalism.

Sanctions or disciplinary procedures are covered by eight codes of ethics (40 per cent). Codes are essentially meaningless if there are no repercussions for serious breaches. Regulated professions have disciplinary procedures or provisions for fitness to practise inquiries to deal with complaints and for the purpose of regulation. Details of the outcome of cases may be made available on the regulatory bodies' websites and in the media. However, in the case of interpreter codes, it seems that only two organisations, the National Register of Public Service Interpreting and the American Translators Association, make public the names of members who are found to have infringed the code. The former code is backed up by the very detailed 16-page National Register Disciplinary Framework and Procedures (National Register of Public Service Interpreting 2016). The organisation has a Professional Conduct Committee and a Disciplinary Committee, and members have the right to appeal to a Disciplinary Appeals Committee. There is an online complaint form and information on disciplinary outcomes is regularly published on their website. Where members are suspended or expelled, their names are included online. The Chartered Institute of Linguists has very similar processes for disciplinary procedures (2013) but does not publish names. The American Translators Association has a Policy on Ethics Procedures (2013) and an ethics complaint form on its website and publishes the names of sanctioned corporate and individual members online. The Committee of the Association of Police and Court Interpreters in the UK 'has the power to remove any Member whose conduct renders him in the opinion of the Committee unfit to remain a Member of the Association'. While the AUSIT Board of Professional Conduct is primarily concerned with providing support and guidance to members, it can investigate disputes, grievances and breaches of the AUSIT Code of Ethics. The Board 'provides rigorously considered, evidence-based written opinions' and has the power to expel members (AUSIT website). The American Translators Association Policy on Ethics Procedures details procedures to deal with violations of their Code of Ethics; the possible sanctions being public censure, suspension of membership or expulsion. Grounds for sanctions include:

1. Conviction of a felony or other crime of moral turpitude under federal or state law in a matter related to the practice of, or qualifications for, professional activity.
2. Gross negligence or willful misconduct in the performance of professional services or other unethical or unprofessional conduct based on demonstrable and serious violations of the Code.
3. Fraud or misrepresentation in the application for or maintenance of ATA membership, professional certification, or other professional recognition or credential.

In the case of the Scottish Interpreters and Translators Association (SITA), either the association committee or a panel appointed by the committee can investigate and, if necessary, remove a member's name from the list of members if there is an allegation of misconduct or dishonourable behaviour. The Italian (AITI) Code of Professional Ethics and Conduct (2013) opens with the topic of sanctions. If a member breaches the code, the appropriate sanction could be 'a warning, a censure, exclusion or expulsion'. The International Medical Interpreters Association Ethical Committee can review complaints and if members do not abide by their code, they may lose 'certification and good standing with the organization'.

The Code of Practice of the Association of Police and Court Interpreters (APCI) includes some very specific points about what interpreters shall not do:

12. A Member shall not visit a detained person in prison for professional reasons unaccompanied by a legal representative, a probation officer or other appropriate official.
13. Members shall not go to a witness' home or meet a witness elsewhere at the request of a police officer or anyone else to take a statement or for any other purpose unless accompanied by an officer in charge of the case or other police officer.
14. Members shall at no time use their own transport to convey witnesses or defendants even if requested to do so by the Principal [a person or body from whom an interpreter receives work].

Social media, and in particular, criticism of colleagues thereon, is another aspect that has not been tackled although this point overlaps with such issues as criticism of colleagues and confidentiality covered above. In 2011, the Heads of Interpreting Services of international organisations and institutions (HINTS) issued a declaration on social media outlining their concerns about the reputation of the conference interpreting profession:

> Sharing negative professional experiences in public, expressing disrespectful views on colleagues, employers, meeting participants or even posting meeting documents, all damage the status of our profession, which is not only based on the quality of the interpreters' work, but also on their discretion and confidentiality.
>
> *(AIIC 2012)*

Perhaps this is something that will be considered for future codes of ethics for interpreters.

2.4.3 More specific guidance

Some codes go into greater detail on potentially grey areas, for the benefit of interpreters, for the benefit of those working with interpreters, or for both parties. For example, the National Register of Public Service Interpreting (NRPSI) Code of Professional Conduct (2016) makes explicit when exactly the interpreter can intervene:

5.12 Practitioners shall not interrupt, pause or intervene except:
    5.12.1   to ask for clarification;
    5.12.2   to point out that one party may not have understood something which the interpreter has good reason to believe has been assumed by the other party;

5.12.3 to alert the parties to a possible missed cultural reference or inference; or

5.12.4 to signal a condition or factor which might impair the interpreting process (such as inadequate seating, poor sight-lines or audibility, inadequate breaks, etc.).

A potentially controversial situation is what interpreters should do if they believe that a speaker is lying. Many service providers would be very pleased to be provided with this information but as interpreters are impartial, it is not part of their remit to oblige. If an interpreter did offer information spontaneously or in response to a question, this would be unfair in comparison to an equivalent scenario where no interpreter was involved. The AUSIT code advises that 'If obvious untruths are uttered, interpreters convey these accurately in the same manner as presented.'

Untrained interpreters often fall into the trap of speaking to one party without explaining to the other party what they are talking about. This leaves the other party feeling excluded and wondering what is happening. It may also give the interlocutors a very poor impression of the interpreter. The AUSIT code recommends that 'Interpreters keep the participants informed of any side comments made by any of the parties or of their attempts to engage the interpreter in a private or any other conversation.' Another issue regularly raised by interpreters is what they should do if they have to wait with a client in a waiting room. The AUSIT code recommends that: 'Interpreters take care that conversations that may arise during periods of waiting remain courteous but do not become personal, and that information divulged in the course of such conversations also remains confidential.'

While it can be very useful for interpreters to have a brief chat with a client before an assignment to ensure they speak the same language and can communicate, with some clients it may be difficult to avoid the conversation becoming more personal. Hale's advice to interpreters to avoid being left on their own with clients is another way of avoiding potential problems (2007: 130).

Moving away from association codes and on to a detailed code aimed exclusively at court interpreters, the Massachusetts Code of Professional Conduct for Court Interpreters of the Trial Court recommends that interpreters 'shall maintain a low profile' and 'be as unobtrusive as possible'. According to this code, interpreters are expected to know where microphones are located to ensure that what they say is captured on electronic recording. An important item is case preparation which can really make a difference to the quality of interpreting during a trial, but something that can be difficult to access in some courts:

6 a) Each court interpreter shall prepare for the case, whenever possible, and particularly with respect to lengthy and complex criminal and civil trials, by reviewing the case material, including the charges, police or other reports, complaints or indictments, transcript of interviews, motions, or any

Codes of ethics **107**

other documentation to be used in the case, particularly if counsel plans to quote directly from them. Such requests shall be made to the attorney processing the case with the awareness and consent of both parties. The information is to be used solely for the technical preparation of the court interpreter.

When the court interpreter meets the non-English speaker for the first time, they are to 'interview' them and explain their role, with the approval of counsel. This places considerable responsibility on the interpreter and signals a lack of understanding about the nature of the interpreter's task. Court interpreters are expected to explain the following points:

- The interpreter will translate any statements or comments at all times.
- If the non-English speaker has any questions they should be directed to counsel or the court rather than to the interpreter.
- To explain interpreting techniques and that they will interpret everything that is said and that the non-English speaker should wait until the interpreter has finished interpreting a question before answering.
- If the non-English speaker has any questions, they must direct same to their lawyer or to the court, not to the interpreter.
- The interpreter is expected to familiarise him or herself with the way the non-English person speaks (or signs), their cultural background and their proficiency in their native language.
- The non-English speaker should not maintain eye contact with the interpreter unless it is a sign language interpreter.

According to the Massachusetts code, if interpreters encounter a 'word, phrase or concept' which they do not understand, they are expected to inform the court or consult a dictionary. Following on from this is a point that comes down to the interpreter's professional judgement:

> b) Whenever the court counsel utilises a word, phrase, or concept which the court interpreter finds may confuse the non-English speaker, particularly when a concept has no cultural equivalent in the non-English speaker's language or when it may prove ambiguous in translation, the interpreter shall so inform the court.

In some courts it can be very difficult to hear what is being said. The Massachusetts code deals with this point as follows:

> If interpreters cannot hear what is being said for whatever reason, they are expected to inform the court. Interpreters are expected to correct errors for the record once they realise they have been made. This may necessitate a bench conference with the judge and lawyers.

The code also covers the contentious issue of interpreter errors spotted by other people in court. This point is directed at the court rather than at individual interpreters.

> b) Whenever an alleged error is perceived by someone other than the court interpreter, that person should, if testimony is still being taken from the stand, bring the allegation to the attention of the court. If the error occurs in a jury trial, the allegation should not be brought to the attention of the jury. A sidebar should be requested so that the matter may be brought to the attention of the court. At that time the court will determine first whether the issue surrounding the allegedly inaccurate interpretation is substantial enough to warrant correction. If the court agrees that the error could be prejudicial, then the court shall hear evidence as to what the correct interpretation should be from information submitted by both counsels, from the court interpreter (who is already an expert witness), and from any other experts selected by the judge. The judge shall make a final determination in view of the evidence as to the correct interpretation. If the determination is different from the original interpretation, then the court shall amend the record accordingly and so instruct the jury, if necessary.

Another problem that occurs quite commonly is when, for example, a person with limited English proficiency mixes some English with their own language. If this happens, court interpreters are expected to repeat those words in English for the record. If the person switches completely to English, then the interpreter 'will stand back so that the parties are aware of the English response and await the court's direction'.

In the case of objections, the code stipulates that 'the court interpreter shall interpret everything that was said up to the objection and instruct the witness by hand gesture not to speak until the court has ruled on the objection'. If interpreting becomes difficult for any reason, interpreters are expected to inform lawyers and/ or the court. If a speaker makes a mistake, interpreters are not supposed to correct the mistake. The code also recommends that if a case is expected to involve more than two hours of 'continuous simultaneous interpretation', two court interpreters should be employed.

The inclusion of very specific information is no doubt particularly helpful in the court context where judges and legal professionals may not have any training about how to proceed in certain situations when working with an interpreter. Rather than lose time on discussing how best to proceed, decision-makers can refer to a code.

2.4.4 Criticisms of association codes

Clearly, codes alone do not guarantee that all interpreters will take the time to read, reflect on and implement ethical principles. No matter how many examples they contain, codes can never act as a substitute for discussion of and reflection on ethical situations that arise, could arise, or have arisen in interpreters' work. As there may be no obligation on interpreters to join a professional association and many do not have access to training, practising public service interpreters may not necessarily be familiar with any code of ethics.

Pöllabauer, in her conclusion to a critical discourse analysis of interpreted asylum hearings in Austria, where interpreters shortened and paraphrased what was said, provided explanations and attempted to save their own and others' face, suggests that 'traditional codes of ethics may only be valid on paper' (2004: 175). While the exact qualifications of the interpreters included in this study are unclear, Pöllabauer explains that they were either conference interpreters or non-professional interpreters. How realistic is it to expect interpreters who have not undergone training to abide by a code of ethics? Conference interpreter training focuses on conveying the message which may not be the most appropriate approach in asylum hearings.

Mayoral Asensio (2011) recommends that association codes of ethics for translators and interpreters be abolished on the grounds that they are anachronistic, do not correspond to real life, are impossible to comply with, are inflexible, do not respect the translator or interpreter's free will and are what he calls sectarian, i.e., he believes that they contain an implicit provision that translators and interpreters must adhere to left-wing ideology, something that, unfortunately, he does not clarify. His proposed solution is for all translators and interpreters to sign a confidentiality agreement and a contract for each assignment. By singling out confidentiality, he seems to be implying that other aspects, such as impartiality and accuracy are unimportant. Would anyone suggest that codes of ethics for doctors are anachronistic and they should simply sign a non-disclosure agreement to ensure that they respect confidentiality? Of course not. It is quite obvious that such codes are important to protect patients and doctors.

There have also been criticisms of codes of ethics from a number of scholars who object to what they perceive as rigidity in the codes and who use words such as 'positivist', 'outdated', 'conservative', 'prescriptive' and a clash with 'morally responsible action'. For example, Rudvin focuses on the needs of institutions rather than of those who do not speak a majority language:

> I foresee a future in which interpreter roles are no longer defined by strictly positivist, out-dated and conservative Codes of Ethics that do not account for institutional- cross-cultural, sociological- and ideological concerns, not to mention budget, but one in which interpreters are more globally empowered and one in which the competencies of the interpreter will better match the needs of the institutions.
>
> *(2006: 38–39)*

Inghilleri, whose research centres on interpreting in court, asylum cases and war zones, suggests that: 'Interpreters must be permitted to exercise their agency to voice their concerns, to make what they deem to be the right ethical choice in the moment, even if their professional duty suggests otherwise' (2012: 48). She goes on to argue that:

> In interpreting contexts where an interpreter does not perceive a public deliberative procedure to be operating in the interest of justice, he or she may experience a professional conflict and moral uncertainty. In these situations, existing codes of ethics offer little guidance for morally responsible action. This suggests that alternative ethical models are required which view conflict, uncertainty, and injustice as an inevitable condition of discourse rather than a temporary state of affairs that can be resolved in rational, discursive activity through communicative reason.
>
> *(ibid.: 49)*

Inghilleri has also criticised the 'impartial interpretation of utterances' because it 'allows interpreters who act impartially to remain morally blameless, without responsibility for the outcome of the interaction, regardless of whether it results in an individual being wrongly imprisoned or set free, deported or granted asylum, tortured or even killed' (ibid.: 49–50). Surely these matters are the responsibility of the judge, the lawyer or the international protection officer rather than of the interpreter? Why should the interpreter be to blame for doing their job and interpreting what is said? Would a person who needed an interpreter be better supported and therefore in a more favourable position than someone who spoke the relevant language? That does not seem just or equitable.

Similar concerns are raised by Angelelli, whose research focuses mainly on interpreting in healthcare, and who has criticised codes of ethics a number of times, arguing consistently that they do not reflect what happens in real-life situations:

> Current prescriptivism does not allow professional associations to address the complexity of the role of the interpreter as it unfolds fully in practice. All principles laid down in codes of ethics or standards of practice should be empirically grounded and tested, rather than prescribed or assumed.
>
> *(Angelelli 2008: 159)*

Prescriptivism is an inevitable and inherent element of codes of ethics for all professions and it is not just something 'current'. The difficulty with Angelelli's stance is that a great deal of empirical research on medical interpreting in particular focuses on untrained, untested interpreters, some of whom are expected to carry out other work as well as acting as interpreters. The medical staff with whom they work may not have undergone any training in how to work with an interpreter and may ask interpreters to take on other tasks. Is it really desirable to base a code of ethics on what could be considered poor practice? Would this be considered acceptable in any other field? Just as it would clearly be undesirable for a code of ethics for teachers to be based solely on research on the work of untrained teachers, so is it undesirable to base a code of ethics for interpreters on the work of untrained interpreters.

In fact, as will be demonstrated in this chapter, research *has* influenced codes of ethics, a prime example being the codes of three medical interpreter associations in the United States, all of which were based on research. It is interesting that all three codes allow for advocacy, something eschewed by other associations worldwide. The notion of basing the codes on research sounds very positive, but if the research is based on poor practice that has developed over time, then perhaps it is simply a way of entrenching that poor practice.

In other codes, provisions have been introduced to cater for local circumstances and to tackle instances of poor practice. Many codes are updated over time and indeed the undated American Translators Association (ATA) Code of Ethics and Professional Practice Commentary makes a virtue of this approach:

> This commentary is intended to be a living document, providing in-depth explanation and examples that reflect our common experiences. We envision a framework where members will contribute examples over time of the code in practice to enable a deeper understanding of the effects of our behavior on ourselves, each other, and the industry as a whole.

2.5 Advocacy

Advocacy is probably the most controversial issue in public service interpreting and one ridden with confusion due to differing understandings of the term. Advocates usually work for the interests of a group and often do so in public. Synonyms for advocacy include 'championing for', 'pleading for' and 'campaigning for'. Wadensjö describes interpreter advocacy as 'actively supporting, defending and pleading for' a client (1998: 6). For Inghilleri, advocacy can even equate to 'clarifications or repair of misunderstandings due to clashes of culture or language' (2012: 7), something that practising interpreters would consider essential to ensure that communication can take place.

If interpreters respect impartiality, then, logically, advocacy is out of the question. We have seen that 17 (85 per cent) of the 20 codes in Table 2.5 include impartiality. Similarly, the ISO 13611 guidelines for community interpreters state that they should 'restrict their role to community interpreting without offering opinions or advice (even when requested to do so) or acting as an advocate'. Of the 20 codes examined above, two (10 per cent) – AUSIT and the Finnish Association – do not allow advocacy under any circumstances. The AUSIT code has come out very strongly against advocacy:

> 6.1 Interpreters and translators do not, in the course of their interpreting or translation duties, assume other roles such as offering advocacy, guidance or advice. Even where such other tasks are mandated (e.g. by specific

institutional requirements for employees), practitioners insist that a clear demarcation is agreed on by all parties between interpreting and translating and other tasks.

The Finnish Association stipulates that: 'The interpreter shall not act as an assistant or advocate for those being interpreted and shall not be obliged to discharge any duties other than interpreting during the assignment.'

The Washington State Department of Social and Health Services DSHS Code of Professional Ethics does not mention 'advocacy' specifically. However, it stipulates that interpreters must not:

1. Counsel, refer, give advice, or express personal opinions to the individuals for whom they are interpreting/translating.
2. Engage in activities with clients that are not directly related to providing interpreting and/or translating services.
3. Have unsupervised access to clients, including but not limited to phoning clients directly, other than at the request of a DSHS employee;
4. Market their services to clients, including but not limited to, arranging services or appointments for clients in order to create business for themselves, or
5. Transport clients for any business, including social services or medical appointments.

However, three medical interpreter associations based in the United States, the International Medical Interpreting Association (IMIA), the National Council on Interpreting in Health Care (NCIHC) and the California Healthcare Interpreters Association (CHIA), have taken a different approach allowing for advocacy in certain circumstances. All three have codes that mention impartiality, but somewhat confusingly, also mention advocacy, which appears contradictory – how can an interpreter be simultaneously impartial and act as an advocate for a patient? A further point of confusion is that the three associations differ greatly in what they mean by advocacy. While the IMIA Medical Interpreting Standards of Practice (1995) are silent on the topic of advocacy, the topic does appear in the IMIA Code of Ethics (2006) albeit with caveats: 'Interpreters will engage in patient advocacy and in the intercultural mediation role of explaining cultural differences/practices to health care providers and patients only when appropriate and necessary for communication purposes, using professional judgment.'

However, according to a separate document, the *IMIA Guide on Medical Interpreter Ethical Conduct* (Hernandez-Iverson 2010), what is meant by advocacy is patient education, for example, informing patients that they have a right to an interpreter, explaining that they do not have to pay the interpreter, providing information on how to request an interpreter and in relation to face-to-face and telephone interpreters in a particular hospital.

The NCIHC has two relevant documents, namely, the National Code of Ethics (2004) and the National Standards of Practice for Interpreters in Health Care

(2005). The former is a 23-page document which commences with nine points followed by extensive discussion. Their point on advocacy is:

> When the patient's health, well-being, or dignity is at risk, the interpreter may be justified in acting as an advocate. Advocacy is understood as an action taken on behalf of an individual that goes beyond facilitating communication, with the intention of supporting good health outcomes. Advocacy must only be undertaken after careful and thoughtful analysis of the situation and if other less intrusive actions have not resolved the problem.
>
> *(2004: 3)*

While the provision on advocacy is carefully worded and seems quite limited, it does appear to give *carte blanche* to healthcare interpreters to act as advocates 'with the intention of supporting good health outcomes'. According to the NCIHC website, their National Standards of Practice for Interpreters in Health Care (2005) were developed over a two-year period during which focus groups met and surveys were carried out of hundreds of 'working health care interpreters' across the United States. The Standards were 'derived from well-established practices in California and Massachusetts' (Beal, n.d.). The Standards acknowledge that advocacy involves a departure from an impartial role (2005: 11) and explain that the purpose of advocacy is 'To prevent harm to parties that the interpreter serves' (ibid.: 10), i.e., to patients. Two examples of advocacy are provided, the first being: 'The interpreter may speak out to protect an individual from serious harm. For example, an interpreter may intervene on behalf of a patient with a life-threatening allergy, if the condition has been overlooked' (ibid.: 10). A life-threatening allergy could arise due to food, insect venom, latex, medication or indeed antibiotics. In their decision-making process on which antibiotic to prescribe, prescribing doctors typically ask patients if they are allergic to penicillin or any other antibiotics. Is the interpreter really to act as a safety net who is expected to recall this level of detail? Also, what about the doctor's responsibility here? Who is the medical professional – the doctor or the interpreter? The second example is somewhat different: 'The interpreter may advocate on behalf of a party or group to correct mistreatment or abuse. For example, an interpreter may alert his or her supervisor to patterns of disrespect towards patients' (ibid.: 10). The second example given is a whistleblower role, where the interpreter reports patterns of disrespect towards patients. Where interpreter provision is outsourced to a company, it may be more difficult for the interpreter to locate the appropriate person to contact.

The third association is the California Healthcare Interpreting Association (CHIA) whose detailed 84-page California Healthcare Interpreting Standards (2002) are based 'on both research and practice described in the current literature of the various academic fields, as well as healthcare interpreter training literature' (ibid.: 9). The Standards acknowledge that interpreters may have other duties and responsibilities including 'helping patients with directions, escorting patients to different locations, and informing patients of operating hours' (ibid.: 40). They distinguish four possible interpreter roles: (1) as *message converter*, the interpreter interprets what is said; (2) as *message clarifier*, the interpreter watches out for possible misunderstandings and attempts to find solutions; (3) as *cultural clarifier*, the interpreter watches out for misunderstandings caused by cultural differences. The fourth, optional, interpreter role is where the interpreter acts as a patient advocate:

> In this role, interpreters actively support change in the interest of patient health and well-being. Interpreters require a clear rationale for the need to advocate on behalf of patients, and we suggest the use of the ethical decision-making process to facilitate this decision.
>
> *(ibid.: 14)*

The CHIA six-step ethical decision-making process is as follows (2002: 55):

1. Ask questions to determine whether there is a problem.
2. Identify and clearly state the problem, considering the ethical principles that may apply and ranking them in applicability.
3. Clarify personal values as they relate to the problem.
4. Consider alternative actions, including benefits and risks.
5. Decide to carry out the action chosen.
6. Evaluate the outcome and consider what might be done differently next time.

Advocacy is defined in Appendix D of the CHIA Standards as 'an action taken by an interpreter intended to further the interests of, or rectify a problem encountered by one of the parties, to the interpreting session, usually the patient' (ibid.: 65). The Standards supply the reasons behind this approach. They cite the difficulties experienced by patients with limited English in accessing care, making appointments and understanding prescriptions and suggest that interpreters are the only people who can ensure that such patients can access healthcare. They acknowledge that this approach has potential risks and recommend that before intervening, interpreters carefully consider the following four questions (ibid.: 45):

- What changes are required to meet the needs of the patient?
- What options exist for the patient?
- Who can potentially carry out the positive changes?
- Is the patient in agreement with this course of action?

It is questionable if even an experienced medical interpreter would be in a position to answer these questions. For example, would the interpreter be cognisant of all possible options for a patient? The fourth question would involve the interpreter explaining the options to the patient and attempting to obtain agreement.

To sum up, advocacy means different things to the three different organisations. For the IMIA, advocacy is patient education, while, for the NCIHC and CHIA, it is about the patient's good health outcomes/well-being. For the NCIHC, advocacy is 'action taken on behalf of an individual that goes beyond facilitating communication with the intention of supporting good health outcomes', and, for the CHIA, its purpose is to 'support change in the interest of patient health and well-being'. The examples given in the different codes are quite disparate. Is the interpreter really qualified to make a judgement call on how to support good health outcomes? Does the interpreter have the requisite medical knowledge to make this call? Also, if interpreters act as advocates in such situations, where does that leave the healthcare professionals?

2.5.1 Research on the role of medical interpreters

There is evidence of medical interpreters acting as advocates even though such an approach is clearly diametrically opposed to the approach laid down in codes of ethics, where the emphasis is on impartiality, on not getting involved. Angelelli sees a dichotomy between theory and reality for healthcare interpreters. For her, 'the complexity of the role must vary in accordance with each specific setting in which it is performed (courts of law, hospital, business negotiations)' (2006: 176). The examples given by Angelelli prompt agreement on the part of the reader but of course business negotiations are not public service interpreting. While there are obvious differences between interpreting in court and interpreting in a hospital, the role itself is the same. Similarly, Leanza suggests that neutrality 'may be pertinent in legal settings, but not in medical or social settings, where personal involvement may be in the interest of both patient and service provider' (2005: 171). But personal involvement can go either way and it may not be in the interest of the patient at all. For example, Dysart-Gale documented examples of interpreters who were far from impartial:

> The doctor was telling a pregnant girl that she needed a test – an amniocentesis, I remember, and the interpreter said 'Oh, she's telling you get this test, but it's not a good one and you don't need it, so forget it.'
>
> *(2005: 96)*

> I caught an interpreter, on two occasions, telling the wife, as I was walking up, 'Listen to your husband, you need to obey your husband. You need to obey your husband because a good Hispanic, Christian woman obeys her husband!' ... When I approached the person, she said, 'Well, in our countries women need to be subservient and obedient to their husbands. You know that makes for a happy household.'
>
> *(ibid.: 96)*

These interpreters allowed their own values and beliefs to influence what they said to patients. They are exercising agency – but is it really desirable for an interpreter to influence a woman's decision on an amniocentesis test or to tell a woman to obey her husband? The difficulty is that interpreters, like all members of society, have their own beliefs, prejudices and unconscious bias.

Rosenberg et al. in their Montreal, Canada, study, recommend that 'To obtain the maximum benefit from a professional interpreter, the physician must invite the interpreter to act as an advocate for the patient and a culture broker' (2008: 87). Referring to professional interpreters, they maintain that 'If they are to only serve as a conduit, they are not permitted to show empathy for the patient' (ibid.: 92). The conduit argument where the interpreter is seen as a machine or a robot, like the discussion about (in)visibility, is a tired one nowadays and has been long discredited (see Wadensjö 1998; Hale 2004: 8–14; Skaaden, Part 3 in this volume); it is inevitable that when an extra person is required for a medical consultation or other event, that person, the interpreter, will change the dynamics of the interaction. Interpreters can show empathy by their behaviour, their professional approach to the task at hand, the way they listen, their body language; words are not essential. The idea of physicians inviting interpreters to act as advocates signals that the authors do not appreciate that the interpreter is present for two parties, the patient and the physician, both of whom need the assistance of an interpreter in order to speak and be understood. When a physician thinks of advocacy, presumably they envision the dictionary definition of championing, pleading or campaigning for patients rather than the restricted approaches that would only apply in certain circumstances as suggested by the IMIA, NCIHC and CHIA. Acting as advocates places a considerable extra burden on interpreters. Interpreting is a very intensive cognitive activity requiring high levels of concentration, excellent short-term memory for what has just been said and long-term memory to understand the context and to retrieve terms rapidly. The extra task of acting as an advocate seems unreasonable in such circumstances and also opens the prospect of individual interpreters, depending on their own views on matters, acting differently from each other. Such practice would inevitably lead to unpredictability and arbitrariness in interpreted sessions, depending on the individual interpreter's predilections.

Angelelli makes a valid point regarding impartiality and advocacy: 'It is difficult for interpreters to reconcile the ethical principle of impartiality when in many healthcare institutions and interpreting agencies where they work they are asked to play the role of an advocate or a social worker' (2008: 150–151). This point relates to a lack of understanding on the part of health professionals of the interpreter's role boundaries. Such views are echoed by a number of researchers. For example, Graham et al. (2008: 215) note that in the University of Washington hospitals and clinics, the role of the medical interpreter is a broad one: 'In our system, interpreters act as advocates for patients, help clarify management and follow-up plans, notify patients of appointments, and assist patients to obtain financial counseling and social work services.'

Hsieh found that some interpreters (most of whom had attended a 40-hour training course developed by the Cross Cultural Health Care Program) in the Midwestern United States took on an advocacy role which could take one of three forms. The first approach was for the interpreter to act as an overt advocate by seeking information, providing answers and requesting services for a patient without consulting the patient (2008: 1373). The second advocacy approach was as a covert advocate, where the interpreter provided information or made suggestions as to what the patient could ask or request (ibid.: 1374). The third approach, which is really not advocacy at all, was to 'assume that patients are competent individuals who act on their own behalf' (ibid.: 1375).

In their survey of professional and family members involved in interpreted consultations with GPs in the UK where the professional interpreters were provided by NHS Interpreting Services but their exact qualifications are not clarified, Greenhalgh *et al.* found that: 'The interpreter occupies multiple social roles, including translator, interpersonal mediator, system mediator, educator, advocate, and link worker. The essence of professionalism in interpreting is shifting judiciously between these potentially conflicting roles' (2006: 1170). This chaotic juxtaposition of what are, as Greenhalgh suggests, potentially conflicting roles, is not intrinsic to the role of the interpreter but may well be linked to lack of clarity at the level of society, healthcare professionals and interpreters themselves concerning the interpreter's role or function. Two interpreters gave examples of patient advocacy with one insisting that a woman's husband be allowed into the consulting room and another citing her attempts to 'protect patients from hurtful information'. Most of the examples, however, are not of patient advocacy but rather of ensuring that the doctors' wishes are facilitated, with interpreters encouraging patients to keep to the point and to focus on one or two medical problems. Time was an issue because GPs did not want consultations to go on over the scheduled time and preferred to focus on medical issues rather than wider social problems. Professional interpreters in this study acted on behalf of doctors to ensure that the purpose of the consultation could be fulfilled.

Davidson (2000) reports similar findings for Spanish-English staff interpreters whom he describes as 'institutional gatekeepers' who are keen to keep consultations 'on track' and to save time wherever possible. Similarly, Robb and Greenhalgh found that 'A good interpreter was also seen [by clinicians] as one who could safely edit out "irrelevancies" offered by the patient' (2006: 449). While it is unclear how interpreters judge what is relevant to the medical practitioner, it is very clear that interpreters who behave in this fashion are moving away from the ethical principle that they should be impartial, interpret everything that is said and not omit information.

Similarly, Hsieh (2007) explored the role of interpreters in interviews with 26 interpreters and analysis of recordings of two Mandarin interpreters. She found that the interpreters, who all either had training or had passed certification programmes, wanted to help doctors achieve their aims within the consultations and that they took on a co-diagnostician role. Hsieh identified five strategies for the co-diagnostician role. These were 'assuming the provider's communicative goals; editorialising information for medical emphasis; initiating information-seeking behaviours; participating in diagnostic tasks; and volunteering medical information to the patients' (ibid.: 924). None of these strategies correspond to any interpreter code of ethics, not even to any of the three US codes that allow for advocacy in certain circumstances. The healthcare professionals in these cases apparently handed over control of medical consultations to the interpreters, despite the risk of jeopardising the patient's access to healthcare. Key questions arise from this: Where does this leave the medical professional in a worst case scenario where something goes wrong, there are negative consequences and an inquiry is set up or someone decides to take a court case? Who would be held responsible?

These research studies raise the question of training for healthcare personnel who may be unaware of the precise role of the interpreter. Because the interpreter can communicate with patients in their own language, it can be a convenient solution to delegate other work, for which they are unqualified and do not have any training, to the interpreters. Rather than accepting a role imposed by healthcare personnel, there is a need for interpreters to challenge this vision of their role and to provide cogent reasons why it is inappropriate for them to step outside their interpreting role. No matter how experienced they may be, medical interpreters are not qualified to act as advocates for patients or healthcare professionals, to provide medical advice or to be social workers. Healthcare professionals need to be trained in how best to work with interpreters in a professional manner and to understand their role.

The examples of advocacy in the research demonstrate the undesirability of this approach and the importance of impartiality. Advocacy for one party is a betrayal of the trust of the other party.

By contrast, Tebble suggests how medical interpreters in Australia could approach their work:

> the interpreter [who] is expected to take the initiative by contacting the physician usually by telephone for a briefing lasting usually no longer than 5–10 minutes, or by email. The briefing should establish the nature of the patient's physical condition; what the physician hopes to achieve from the consultation; what procedures the physician intends to use including physical examination; if there is to be an interpretation of results, for example, from pathology or medical imaging; if bad news is to be delivered; whether a nurse will be present and or a relative or an accompanying carer; any anticipated difficulties or complications; if any documents are to be sight translated such as consent forms; if the dynamics of the consultation require simultaneous or just consecutive interpreting; if the physician needs help in preparing the pronunciation of names or in understanding any cultural practices or other information; whether the location is subject to interference from external noise; and the patient's capacity to hear well.
>
> *(2012: 29)*

While this is an example of best practice, in many countries it is difficult to imagine doctors and other health professionals taking calls from medical interpreters or responding to their emails. Obviously, training courses for medical personnel should encourage this sharing of information. Such an approach would help ensure that interpreters can prepare for assignments both mentally and practically and that both patients and medical professionals could have access to the best possible standard of interpreting.

2.6 Company codes of ethics for interpreters

In Ireland, Spain, England, Wales, Scotland, and Northern Ireland, where interpreting has been outsourced, company codes of ethics are potentially of greater importance than those of national associations because, from a legal point of view, unless the relevant government body has their own code, interpreters will be expected to abide by the company code. In England and Wales, a company called thebigword provided interpreters to the whole public service interpreting sector at the time of writing. Their code of conduct, an appendix to their Interpreting Services Agreement, consists of 36 points. Ozolins acknowledges that issues can arise with some interpreters:

> Difficult interpreter behavior may include a random approach to punctuality (from tardiness in arrival to hastiness in leaving), a 'yes boss' attitude to agency management, failure to communicate on important matters, or pursuing a completely idiosyncratic personal code of ethics and practice.
>
> *(2007: 123)*

However, the provisions in point 13 of thebigword code hint at more serious issues: 'You shall be of good character and not engage in any anti-social behaviour (including impairment through drugs or alcohol, social misconduct, violence, intimidation or abusive behaviour)' (n.d., unpaginated).

Point 16 focuses on non-discrimination, in line with the Equality Act 2010:

> I must not discriminate between parties (to their advantage or disadvantage) or act in any way that might result in prejudice or preference on grounds of sex, disability, age, gender reassignment, sexual orientation, religion, political belief or affiliation, or race.
>
> *(ibid.)*

According to thebigword code of conduct, interpreters are expected to abide by the Official Secrets Act 1989 and the Modern Slavery Act 2015 and are expected to raise any concerns about the safety of a child or vulnerable adult with the 'responsible person leading the assignment' or with the relevant authority.

LanguageLine Solutions has a short code of ethics (2013) for telephone interpreters who work for their company, who are expected to 'limit him/herself to interpreting' and 'shall not give advice, express personal opinions, or engage in any other activity that may be construed to constitute a service other than interpreting'. An unusual point in the code relates to professional courtesy: 'Interpreter shall provide excellent customer service. He/she shall maintain a professional demeanor, be courteous and use the tone of voice appropriate to the situation. Interpreter shall defer to instructions from clients' (unpaginated). It is not entirely clear from the code who exactly are the clients – possibly both parties or perhaps whoever is paying the bill (see the definition of 'client' in Part 3).

What does the future hold for procurement outsourcing? Ozolins (2007: 125) suggests that there is a need for codes of industry practice to define standard practice in the industry. Since then, three standards have been introduced. ISO Standard 13611:2014 Guidelines for Community Interpreting has been introduced to provide guidance for the provision of community interpreting services. ISO 18841: 2018 is a general standard for all types of interpreting while ISO 20228: 2019 focuses on legal interpreting. Ozolins also suggests that companies could be accredited to ensure that they have 'complaint and feedback mechanisms, and reporting requirements including reporting on professional issues faced by interpreters in their practice' (ibid.: 129). This would be an important step forward; perhaps regional organisations such as the European Union of Associations of Translation Companies (EUATC) could play a role in such accreditation.

2.7 The Norwegian example

Norway provides an example of what can be done when interpreter provision is taken seriously by the authorities. The Norwegian Interpreters' Code was originally drawn up in 1997 by a working group which consisted of representatives from four key areas:

- interpreter trainers from the University of Oslo;
- the Ministry of Regional Affairs (the then licensing body for interpreters);
- the Directorate of Immigration, which was in charge of implementing public service interpreting policy;
- the Norwegian Interpreters' Organisation which adopted the code in 2004.

The Norwegian Interpreters' Code applies to practising public service interpreters on the Norwegian Register of Interpreters (tolkeportalen.no) which is administered by the interpreter accreditation body, the Norwegian Directorate of Integration and Diversity (IMDi). According to the tolkeportalen.no website, there are five categories, ranging from a basic level which is tested by a written vocabulary test and attendance at a basic introductory course on interpreter ethics and interpreting techniques to proficiency. The top three categories are for interpreters 'with accreditation by authorization' and/or who have completed university-level interpreter training. Oslo and Akershus University College of Applied Science (HiOA) provides training and organises examinations. At the time of writing, there were plans to introduce legislation to oblige all public bodies in Norway to use registered interpreters.

The Norwegian Interpreters' Code recommends that interpreters should not respond to questions, fill in forms, defend either party, or act as either party's representative. Nor should they act as a cultural informant or mediator or offer an expert opinion because by doing so they could create a perception that they are not in fact impartial, or, indeed, if they provide incorrect information, they could cause harm. If circumstances are detrimental to the provision of interpreting, for example, poor acoustics, unrealistic expectations regarding the amount of time an interpreter can interpret, inappropriate seating arrangements, insufficient number of interpreters – the interpreter is expected to give warning that he or she cannot provide 'responsible interpreting'.

2.8 Intercultural mediators

It would be remiss not to mention intercultural mediators in this book. Advocacy is one facet of the multifaceted role of intercultural mediators, who work in Belgium, Italy, Spain and Switzerland, and also act as interpreters. Verrept and Coune define intercultural mediation as 'all activities that aim to reduce the negative consequences of language barriers, socio-cultural differences and tensions between ethnic groups in health care settings' (2016: 5). In Belgium, a law from 2002–2005 (Arrêté royal 2002) allocated a budget for intercultural mediators at hospitals and outlines appropriate qualifications for the post. These qualifications ranged from secondary school education to a diploma in social studies or in the paramedical area to a university degree in medicine, psychology, anthropology, languages, sociology, translation and interpreting. All intercultural mediators had to speak one of the three Belgian national languages (French, Dutch, German) and a foreign language that is in demand and must have undergone intercultural mediator training. The duties of intercultural mediators (Verrept 2009: 1–2) include:

1. Liaison interpreting
2. Cultural brokerage
3. Helping patients access care, fill in forms
4. Listening and providing support
5. Conflict mediation
6. Advocacy
7. Visiting patients in hospital to check if there are any issues
8. Raising problems with hospital administration
9. Providing information to patients.

The remit of the intercultural mediator in Belgium consists of an array of tasks that go far beyond the work of a medical interpreter even in the United States. They are expected to act as interpreters, clarify cultural issues, provide practical help filling in forms, act as a kind of counsellor by listening and providing support, mediate in case of conflict, act as an advocate, visit patients in hospital, raise any issues with hospital administration and provide information. Paradoxically, the guidelines for the task of liaison interpreting are based on the Massachusetts Medical Interpreters Association 1995 Standards (Verrept 2008: 196) which, as mentioned above, do not include advocacy.

2.9 Conclusion

Associations have created codes of ethics which vary greatly in length and level of detail. While all mention confidentiality, not all cover other key ethical principles and some, perhaps in reaction to instances of bad practice, include issues such as payment of taxes, illegal activities, bribery and corruption, and criminal records. In jurisdictions where it is not obligatory to be a member of an association, many interpreters operate outside this sphere. Interestingly, in Australia, 'a large number of agencies, institutions, language service providers and purchasers of interpreting and translating services' require interpreters, whether they are AUSIT members or not, to abide by the AUSIT Code (AUSIT Code of Ethics 2012: 3). While some associations have disciplinary committees and can impose sanctions, the majority are in reality toothless because, although they may be able to suspend or expel a member, few can prevent sanctioned interpreters from continuing to work.

The codes in the United States that allow for advocacy in restricted circumstances are outliers; the majority of codes include impartiality and a minority prohibit advocacy in all circumstances. It will be interesting to see if the relevant organisations shift their position in the future. There is no evidence of demand from working interpreters for a right to have agency because they know very well that the nature of their work, where they are very often the only person who speaks both languages, is that they already have agency. Impartiality is the fairest way to proceed for all parties and is the best protection for interpreters as well. However, this does not preclude interpreters from requesting repetition, clarifying matters, explaining that they need more context or acknowledging that they have got something wrong. Indeed, it would be remiss of interpreters not to do so.

Other professionals understand the boundaries of their role, thanks not only to their training but also to the opportunity to observe and learn from colleagues in the workplace. The work of public service interpreters is such that they do not have the opportunity to learn by observation. With or without prior training, they find themselves in new situations, all too often working with people who do not know how to work with them. While some codes of ethics could no doubt be tweaked or improved, despite their limitations, they are, and will continue to be, extremely important.

2.10 Introduction

In this section we consider examples in which the topic of interpreter ethics has entered the public domain, giving examples from real-life cases.

2.11 Ethics in real-life cases

Public service interpreters do not always have access to training or an opportunity to receive feedback on their skills. For example, in the European Union, specialised training 'is the exception rather than the rule' and, where it is available, it is expensive and does not meet the needs of speakers of languages of lesser diffusion (Giambruno 2014: 190). There are obvious questions around the reasons why the unsatisfactory situation of lack of training and accreditation is allowed to persist. Interpreters who have not had the opportunity to access training, who have not been assessed to establish their competency, may be doing their best but their best may not be good enough. Incompetent interpreting has most likely led to many more miscarriages of justice and injustices in asylum and court cases than the lack of agency and the 'impartial interpretation of utterances' (2012: 49) described by Inghilleri.

The ethical issues covered in this section relate to interpreting quality, impartiality, neutrality, bribery, the role of the interpreter and whether or not interpreters should comment publicly on cases where they have previously acted as interpreter. It is not our intention to imply that all interpreting is problematic; rather, the aim is to establish what types of ethical issues move into the public arena. Despite broad consensus on the role of legal interpreters, many examples relate to infringements of codes of ethics by interpreters working in courts and police stations.

2.11.1 Interpreting quality

The right to the free assistance of an interpreter in criminal proceedings is widely accepted. Despite this, a lack of understanding on the part of the police and the courts in a number of jurisdictions about the need for interpreter training and testing has allowed situations to arise where some interpreters were unable to carry out the work for which they were recruited. The examples relate to court cases in the United States, Canada, South Africa, Norway and the United Kingdom. Two are asylum cases and just one is a medical interpreting situation.

Layer upon layer of inadequate interpreting, transcription and translation were factors in a miscarriage of justice in Ohio. In 1997, a party was held at the house Alejandro Ramirez shared with 11 other Mexicans. An intruder came along, refused to leave, and was shot. At the time, it was thought he had been injured and Ramirez agreed to take the blame. In fact, the intruder had been killed. The interpreter at the police station had studied Spanish at college for less than two years, was not fluent in the language and had no interpreter training. The police interview was recorded and later transcribed by a professor from a local college who had no training in this type of work and it seems that the transcription included a 'sanitised' version of the Miranda warning in Spanish. In court, interpreting was provided by a 'secretary for the county probation department' whose interpreting was challenged in open court. Ramirez was found guilty of murder. However, he was very fortunate in that he had the help of experts who proved that there were serious problems with the interpretation at the police station and his conviction was overturned in 1999 (Framer 2000).

Framer (2001) also writes about a 1998 case where a Honduran man called Santos Adonay Pagoada appeared in court in Kentucky on a murder charge, was found guilty and sentenced to 40 years in prison. He appealed the sentence and

Framer was asked to review the video tapes of the arraignment (when a defendant is charged in court), suppression hearing (to exclude evidence that is considered inadmissible at trial) and the trial. She found that during the arraignment the interpreter was not actually interpreting and only did so when instructed to tell the defendant the date of his next hearing. At the hour-long suppression hearing, the same interpreter was present again and 'spoke only sporadically'. The judge challenged the interpreter who claimed that the defendant had told him that he understood the proceedings in English. The judge was concerned about the lack of interpreting and it was agreed that another interpreter would be called to interpret at the trial. However, the new interpreter was also problematic, did not interpret everything that was said and was unfamiliar with medical terminology. Framer's analysis of the interpreting at trial demonstrates that the Spanish rendering was nonsensical. In 2002, the defendant won the right to a new trial where he was provided with two federally certified court interpreters. He was found guilty of reckless homicide and released from prison for time served (Nebula).

In 2004, in Florida, Juan Ramon Alfonzo was under the impression that he had pleaded no contest to stealing a toolbox and was expecting to be given probation. In fact, unbeknownst to him, he had pleaded guilty to stealing a dump truck and was sentenced to 15 years in jail. The case went to appeal where an expert witness testified that the interpreting provided in court to Alfonzo was incomprehensible. A very interesting fact about this case is that the court interpreter had been working in the system for nine years and had interpreted on over 5,000 occasions (de Jongh 2008). In this case, experience was no guarantee of competency.

In 2009, in Ohio, a Spanish language interpreter who had been working at Franklin County Municipal Court for two and a half years was fired after a public defender who was learning Spanish heard him interpret Spanish 'semana' meaning 'week' as 'month'. According to a newspaper report, the interpreter invented words, including his own translation for 'defendant' and guessed legal terms when he did not understand them in English (Czekalinksi 2009).

The previous four cases all involved Spanish, which is very widely spoken in the United States. Interpreter provision can be more difficult for less widely spoken languages. In 2014, in Rensselaer County court, New York, a mistrial was declared in a rape case where the alleged perpetrator and the complainant, both immigrants from Myanmar, spoke the Karen language. The interpreter for the defence suggested to the defence attorney that the prosecution's interpreter 'may not have a firm grasp of the English language' whereupon the attorney asked the interpreter to provide English definitions of words or phrases that he had used during the hearing – 'interpersonal', 'forced entry', 'pre-marital' 'dimension' and 'in physical contact'. The interpreter was unable to provide definitions of the terms or phrases and the defence interpreter also had difficulty with two of the phrases. The judge found that the complainant may not have understood the questions she was asked (Gardiner 2014).

The Supreme Court of Canada judgement in the *R v Tran* case (1994) found a number of problems with the interpretation of a witness's testimony revolving around the issue of identification, a topic that was crucially important to the Vietnamese defendant, who was convicted of sexual assault. Unusually, the court interpreter was also a witness in the case; the defence asked him to testify about the accused's appearance at the time of the assault. The Supreme Court found that the interpreter had summarised both questions and answers and had not provided any interpretation for his exchanges with the judge. The court found that the summarising approach meant that there was a lack of precision in the interpretation and also found that information that had not actually been said was 'interpreted'. The court also found that the interpreting should have been done contemporaneously.

Another Canadian case involved Janusz Rybak, a Polish immigrant in Canada, who spoke English but was not proficient in the language. The interpreter at his trial for murder was not accredited although the court was assured that he was. Rybak did not complain about the interpreter and actually requested that she work with him for the whole trial. The fact that the interpreter was not accredited was one of the grounds for appeal but this was rejected by the court. The appeal was dismissed as the court found that the onus was on the accused to demonstrate that he needed the assistance of an interpreter, and that the assistance of the interpreter was below the standard required under the constitution (*R v Rybak* 2008). The approach taken by the Court of Appeal for Ontario in this instance is similar to that taken in appeal cases in Australia between 1991 and 2008 where there were 119 appeals on the grounds of the standard of interpreting at trial. In the years 2006–2008, of 50 such cases, only eight appeals were allowed because interpreting errors had to be found to be 'directly related to an issue of specific significance in the case and constitute jurisdictional error' (Hayes and Hale 2010: 119). As there were no recordings of the court cases, the appeals courts had to rely on the English language trial transcripts. Most Australian judges did not enquire into interpreters' qualifications and did not seem to understand the task of the legal interpreter. Hayes and Hale recommend that court interpreters should be trained in legal interpreting and that the judiciary undergo training about court interpreting (ibid.: 130).

The Ontario Superior Court of Justice judgement in *R v Sidhu* (2008) provides a fascinating insight into the workings of court interpreter provision in Brampton, a Canadian city with a very high immigrant population. From 1999, there was an awareness that there were some issues with a Punjabi interpreter called Mr Dhir, particularly in sexual assault cases and spousal assaults where staff observed that he was rude to female victims and often interrupted their testimony. In August 2002, Mr Dhir acted as interpreter in the Bhullar case which was declared a mistrial after complaints about the accuracy of his interpreting from both the prosecutor and Mr Bhullar's lawyer in British Columbia and Ontario. The audio tape was reviewed by Ms Jhooty, a certified Punjabi-English court interpreter, who found that Mr Dhir had said 'Henh?' nine times – meaning either he had not understood or had not heard. She also found 'inaccuracies, judgmental translations, vital omissions, and witness clarifications and side conversations not reported to the court' (*R v Sidhu* 2008: 50). There was clearly a problem with Mr Dhir's work but despite this he was allowed to continue working as an interpreter. In 2001, Avtar Sidhu was allegedly involved in an assault. At his first appearance in court, he requested a Punjabi interpreter for his next appearance but no interpreter was provided. There were various delays while other suspects were sought and the case came to trial a year later when Mr Dhir appeared as interpreter but was not sworn in. The interpreter intervened about 20 times to say that he could not hear a witness or to ask witnesses to speak more slowly; this would become a pattern over subsequent days of the trial. The defendant was reluctant to criticise the interpreter and did not want the case to go on for any longer than absolutely necessary. Crown counsel was advised that there was a problem and suggested that the audio tape be transcribed by Ms Jhooty. This was done and it was found that Mr Dhir had said 'Henh?' to a witness 27 times over 36 pages of transcript. In addition, the interpreter had, according to the reviewer, who gave examples in court, led the witness and given incomplete and inaccurate interpretations. A mistrial was declared and a second trial scheduled, this time with Ms Jhooty as interpreter, and in June 2003 the defendant was sentenced to six months' imprisonment. On appeal, the conviction was set aside and it was found that Mr Sidhu's rights under the Canadian Charter of Rights and Freedoms had been breached. According to the judgement, unaccredited interpreters regularly worked in the courts as did interpreters who had actually failed the Standard Aptitude Test for Court Interpretation.

In 2012, Brampton was in the news again when Superior Court Justice Casey Hill declared a mistrial in the case of Vishnu Dutt Sharma due to substandard Hindi interpreting. The problems came to light because the defendant's lawyer spoke Hindi. Audio tapes were sent to Umesh Passi, a member of the New York State Bar and a qualified Hindi interpreter (Brean 2011), who wrote a 182-page transcription, including his translations of what the interpreter said in Hindi. According to the newspaper report, Passi found that the interpreter 'did not interpret verbatim, summarised most of the proceedings and was not able to interpret everything that was said on the record'. The newspaper included specific examples such as 'sexual assault' translated as 'physical assault', 'genital area' as 'between legs' and 'two days' as 'a couple of weeks' (Aulakh 2012).

In 2014, there was another mistrial in Brampton. Two Jamaicans who spoke Jamaican Patois were accused of drug trafficking but the interpreter at the trial was deemed incompetent. According to the newspaper report, one of the defendants had used Patois 'dash wey' meaning 'to kill' but this was interpreted as 'throw away'. Two-minute chunks of testimony were abbreviated to brief 30-second interpretations and all parties in court, from a defence lawyer to one of the defendants to a Jamaican-Canadian juror to the judge himself realised that there was a problem (Hopper 2014).

In 2010, in Sweden, the Legal, Financial and Administrative Services Agency (Kammarkollegiet), the body that authorises interpreters, received notification that a certified interpreter for Swedish and Southern Kurdish had provided inaccurate interpretation at a trial in Norrköping. The agency assessor for the language combination listened to five hours of digital voice recordings where the interpreter was working into Swedish and found errors relating to gaps in idioms, syntax, morphology and semantics in both languages along with lack of terminology. The interpreter, whose Swedish vocabulary was described as 'fairly limited', lost his licence to interpret (*The Local* 2010). What is of interest here is that despite a limited knowledge of Swedish, the interpreter was accredited.

In 2014, on the first day of the trial of Oscar Pistorius in South Africa, the assigned court interpreter reportedly took fright when she saw the media circus, photographers, satellite vans, not to mention cameras inside the courtroom, and decided it was not for her. Another interpreter for Afrikaans-English had to be found at extremely short notice, meaning that she had no opportunity to prepare for this high-profile case (Smith 2014). Witness Michelle Burger corrected the interpreter's English and then switched to English herself. A new interpreter was recruited from day two of the trial but, according to newspaper reports, there were continued difficulties with lawyers interrupting to correct translations (*Sowetan Live* 2014).

In 2016, in Cape Town, South Africa, three months after two Chinese people had been found guilty of human trafficking for sexual purposes and one of keeping a brothel, their lawyers launched an application to stop the case on the grounds that the interpreter had been incompetent. An expert engaged by the defence team who had checked part of the court record had found that the Mandarin interpreter had made 140 serious errors, including omitting essential information and adding incorrect information (van Hees 2016).

In 2012, a burglary trial in Snaresbrook Crown Court, London, collapsed when it was realised that the interpreter for Romanian had mistakenly said 'bitten' instead of 'beaten'. Apparently, the interpreter realised her mistake but did not declare it to the court. However, the mistake came to light on the fourth day of the trial when the defendant was asked for evidence that he had been bitten, and replied that he had been beaten, not bitten (BBC News 2012).

In 2019, the BBC reported problems relating to agency interpreters who were not on the National Register of Public Service Interpreters and who had worked at police interviews. Defence lawyers had recordings of police interviews checked by a qualified interpreter who found that the original interpreter 'was making mistakes, making his own little interviews, he wasn't asking what the police officer was asking and he was advising the suspect'. The interpreter, who was unable to interpret the police caution, reportedly told a suspect to 'not say too much' to police. The same interpreter, along with two others, acted as interpreter in a modern slavery case in 2018. Once again, recordings were checked. The BBC suggested that court delays and the collapse of a case had cost thousands of pounds (Goymer 2019).

Issues around interpreting were raised in an asylum case in 2000 when the United States Court of Appeal found in favour of the applicant in *Mamadou Amadou v Immigration and Naturalization Service*. The Board of Immigration Appeals had turned down Amadou's application for asylum as he had been found not credible due to inconsistent testimony, dispassionate demeanour and his failure to establish his identity and citizenship. Amadou, who was from Mauritania and spoke Fulani, maintained that his interpreter, who was from Sierra Leone, was incompetent and spoke a different dialect. The judge found that Amadou did not seem familiar with the ethnic groups in Mauritania and ordered that he be deported to Senegal. The Court of Appeal examined the record and found a number of instances where the interpreter had commented that he did not understand Amadou. The inconsistencies in Amadou's evidence arose from inconsistencies in the interpreter's renditions. In particular, the interpreter was not familiar with the ethnic groups in Mauritania. Moreover, there were instances on the tapes where the interpreter and Amadou spoke but their exchanges were not translated for the court.

In 2011, in Canada, an asylum seeker from Kenya spoke Swahili at a refugee hearing through an interpreter whose English was described by a lawyer as 'gibberish'. Despite this, the adjudicator did not accept concerns about the poor standard of interpreting and the refugee claim was denied. Two Swahili translators later listened to a recording and found that the interpreter was incompetent (Humphreys 2011). The Federal Court of Canada quashed the Board's decision and gave the asylum seeker and her daughter another opportunity to state their claim (*Mohamed Neheid v Canada*).

Examples of poor interpreting in medical settings are less common, not because there is no poor interpreting in the sector, but because there are no recordings, appointments are often held in private and there may be no third bilingual party. In 2008, in Norway, it was reported that a Kurdish woman asked a doctor about contraception but her message was altered by the interpreter to request sterilisation. On the day of the operation, the doctor, through a different interpreter, checked with the woman that she was sure that she did not wish to have any children whereupon she explained that she wanted to access contraception (*Aftenposten* 2008).

Examples of incompetency come to light accidentally or occasionally because the standard of interpreting is so poor. They are more common in the legal setting, often because recordings are available and defence lawyers request transcriptions and translations. However, it is likely that the examples that do come to light are only a tiny fraction of the cases where incompetent interpreting leads to miscarriages of justice, to asylum seekers being refused refugee status, and to patients being given incorrect treatment. These cases highlight the importance of training and accreditation for interpreters; the interpreters concerned did not have the language and interpreting skills to be able to provide accurate interpreting. Competency to act as an interpreter is a core tenet in many codes of ethics for interpreters; those who cannot provide a competent service are expected to withdraw from the assignment.

2.11.2 *Impartiality*

An interpreter behaved very ethically in a case heard in New York in 2013 but his efforts went unappreciated. In *People v Lee*, an appeal was brought on the grounds that the trial court had refused the defence lawyer's request that the state-employed court interpreter for Cantonese be replaced because he knew the complainants whose house had allegedly been burgled. The interpreter explained to the trial court that his father had had business dealings with the husband and had met the wife a number of times. He was aware that the husband had served time in prison and that he had an 'intimidating, violent nature'. The court refused the request to replace the interpreter because he was a state employee who had taken an oath and established that he did not know the facts of the case and would not be uncomfortable interpreting for the complainant wife. On appeal, the majority of the judges agreed with the trial court decision. However, one judge, Rivera, dissented. He complimented the interpreter on 'a commendable level of professionalism and sensitivity to his ethical obligations' and stated that:

> If the fact that the interpreter has taken an oath to faithfully discharge his or her duties is sufficient to overcome a challenge of bias or conflict, then there would never be grounds to remove even the most obviously conflicted interpreter.
>
> *(People v Lee 2013)*

Rivera referred to Canon 6 of the Unified Court System (UCS) Court Interpreter Manual and Code of Ethics which provides that:

> Court interpreters shall not engage in, nor have any interest, direct or indirect, in any activity, business or transaction, nor incur any obligation, that is in conflict, or that creates an appearance of conflict, with the proper discharge of their interpreting duties or that affects their independence of judgment in the discharge of those duties.

He went on to say that the need for this provision 'illustrates the real possibility that a court interpreter can be biased or burdened by a conflict of interest, regardless of the interpreter's lack of knowledge of the facts of a case'.

Experienced court interpreters may be tempted to advise clients on what they should do. For example, in 2007, in Nashville, Texas, Zacarias Quinteros claimed that a court interpreter had told him to plead guilty to driving without a licence and that he had not had access to legal advice from his lawyer. It was also alleged that this was not an isolated case and that about ten other defendants had received the same advice from the interpreter. While Quinteros lost his case, a deputy public defender was quoted as saying that 'We do have some translators who like to tell people what the law is, they think they're helping' and mentioned that one interpreter who had advised defendants 'what they really ought to do' no longer worked in the court (Tobia 2007).

In 2003, in Ireland, a male Chinese witness to a double murder who was being questioned through a female interpreter asked the police for her telephone number. The police obliged and the witness subsequently went on a date with the interpreter. However, the status of the witness changed to suspect and then to defendant and he was tried in court where he was found guilty. The fact that the interpreter had gone on a date with the defendant was obviously problematic and, most unusually, a Chinese Interpol officer acted as court interpreter (*Irish Times*, 5 March 2003).

In another case in Ireland, a complainant told the court that 'she had called an interpreter involved in the case to ask her to tell gardaí [Irish police] she wanted to drop the case' (*Breaking News*, 30 November 2007). In addition, on the same case, the judge told the jury that the court interpreter had received a phone call from the defendant to the effect that he had been involved in an accident (*Irish Independent*, 6 December 2007). No questions were asked in court about why and how the complainant and defendant had access to the interpreters' telephone numbers.

In Italy, in 2007, Amanda Knox was questioned at a police station about a murder with the help of police station employees who acted as interpreters (their actual job is unclear). One of the grounds for the successful case taken by Knox to the European Court of Human Rights was that one interpreter shifted from the impartial role to a mediator role and told Knox that after a very serious road accident, she could not remember what had happened for a year. She suggested that something similar had happened to Knox, that she had seen something terrible and could not recall it because she was traumatised (*Affaire Knox c. Italie* 2019).

2.11.3 Neutrality

Few codes of ethics for interpreters mention neutrality specifically, opting instead to deal with the related overlapping heading of impartiality. Impartiality implies freedom from prejudice or bias while neutrality also has the meaning of not being on any side (*Oxford English Dictionary*), something that is taken up by the National Register of Public Service Interpreters (NRPSI):

> Practitioners carrying out work as Public Service Interpreters, or in other contexts where the requirement for neutrality between parties is absolute, shall not enter into discussion, give advice or express opinions or reactions to any of the parties that exceed their duties as interpreters.

In 2006, a Polish suspect was interviewed with the help of an interpreter in an English police station and later appeared in court accused of groping nine women in the street. According to the *Evening Standard* newspaper, the Russian-born interpreter was also the director of a charity called British Eastern European Support for Foreign Prisoners, in itself a potential conflict of interest. She told the police that the man's behaviour was a bit of 'cultural naughtiness' and was not against the law. She went on to say:

> As an interpreter I would like to add, and if you need I will file a statement, that Eastern European society is much more flirtatious. It is based on mutual information and is not breaking respect and if a person has no aggressive intention usually they can get away with it, even if a female doesn't like it.
>
> *(Metro, 8 November 2006)*

This is an example of advocacy taken to an uninformed extreme. According to the *Evening Standard*, a spokesman for the Polish Embassy said indecent assault was against the law in Poland and was not 'normal behaviour'.

In 2010, in Florida, Mexican David Luna Sanchez requested a lawyer a number of times while being questioned by police about the alleged stabbing of a man in self-defence in Waynesboro, Virginia. However, the interpreter did not convey this information to the police officers. For example, the suspect stated in Spanish that 'Yes, I would like to have a lawyer present here now to tell him – well, whatever it would be' but the interpreter responded, also in Spanish, 'Listen to what I'm saying. She only wants to listen to the side of your story' (Purdy 2011).

2.11.4 Bribery

We have seen that the Institute of Translation and Interpreting Code of Professional Conduct (2013) includes a provision on bribery: 'No member shall accept remuneration from any party that could be construed as a bribe.' Two particular areas seem to be particularly susceptible to bribery – driver theory tests and migration.

Prior to 2014, the system in the UK was that driving theory test candidates could access a voiceover translation in one of 19 languages or they could bring an interpreter with them when they took the theory and practical driving tests. Interpreters were required to read out the following statement: 'I confirm I will not do anything to affect the integrity of the test and understand that by assisting a candidate I may be committing a criminal offence.' Interpreted theory tests were recorded. According to the gov.uk website, between 2008 and 2014, over 1,300 passes on the driver theory test were revoked after suspicions were raised by the popularity of some interpreters and investigations carried out into fraudulent interpreters. The Driving Standards Authority discovered that at least two interpreters had allegedly accepted bribes in exchange for providing help with the tests. These findings ultimately led to the abolition of the use of interpreters and voiceover translation for driving theory and practical tests in the UK in April 2014 (gov.uk). Three interpreters, two of whom were on the NRPSI register, were convicted and received prison sentences. Each of the three had developed a technique to indicate the correct answer to multiple choice questions. One interpreter said 'yes' in Mandarin when the candidates had located the correct answer (Silverman 2013). Another said 'you' in Urdu to signal the correct answer (Buckley 2014) while the third interpreted the correct answer into Ukrainian and the incorrect answers into Russian (Phillips 2017).

In Hungary, in 2009, unqualified interpreters were instrumental in providing the correct answers to the driver theory test for up to 225 candidates from Romania, Vietnam and China. This was quite an elaborate scam involving fake papers to certify that the candidates were both resident and employed in the country. The investigation led to the recording of all driving theory tests (Zimányi 2010).

In Norway, in 2004, the *Aftenposten* newspaper reported that four interpreters had been caught taking the driver theory test on behalf of candidates (*Aftenposten* 2004). In December 2013, it was alleged that two 'mafia groups' were organising 'interpreting help' during the same test in exchange for cash with some candidates using a spy camera and Bluetooth technology to communicate with people in a car outside the test centre (*Dagsavisen* newspaper 2013).

Spanish newspaper *20 minutos* (2009) reported that three interpreters in Tenerife had been sentenced to four years in prison for advising immigrants from Senegal not to speak French and to say they were from the Ivory Coast, a country that did not have a repatriation agreement with Spain. The interpreters allegedly demanded money in exchange. In addition, they reportedly advised accomplices in Africa on the best time to travel by boat to the Canary Islands (*20 minutos* 2009).

At a District Court in Louisiana in 2015, an interpreter pleaded guilty to soliciting illegal payments from undocumented migrants and their relatives. It seems that the interpreter who worked for lawyers was able to identify people who faced criminal charges and were likely to be deported. She allegedly contacted these people directly and claimed that if they gave her between $2,000 and $4,000, she could bribe immigration officials so they would not initiate a prosecution or commence removal proceedings against them (de Santis 2015).

2.11.5 The role of the interpreter

Mohamed Yousry worked as a US Justice Department-approved Arabic-English translator at the 1995 trial of blind Egyptian cleric, Sheikh Omar Abdel-Rahman, for plotting a series of bombings and assassinations. Abdel-Rahman was sentenced to life in solitary confinement without parole. Yousry had never been trained as an interpreter; nor was he a member of any interpreter association. After the trial, he acted as interpreter for Abdel-Rahman's lawyer, Lynne Stewart, during prison visits. Abdel-Rahman was entitled to only three visits per year and, in effect, his only visits were those of Stewart and Yousry. Unbeknown to prisoner, lawyer and interpreter, their prison and telephone conversations were recorded by the authorities. Stewart had signed an agreement to abide by the terms of Special Administrative Measures, whereby she agreed she would 'only be accompanied by translators for the purpose of communicating with inmate Abdel-Rahman concerning legal matters' and that she would not 'use her meetings, correspondence or phone calls with Abdel-Rahman to pass messages between third parties (including, but not limited to, the media) and Abdel-Rahman' (findlaw.com). Yousry was never asked to sign such an agreement. Stewart was convicted of aiding terrorism by conveying messages from Abdel-Rahman to an Islamic network in Egypt. Her original sentence of 28 months was later increased to ten years. Yousry was convicted of supporting terrorism by translating a letter from Abdel-Rahman to his lawyer in Egypt and sentenced to 20 months in jail.

Angelelli and Osman (2007) analyse 12 extracts from conversations that took place between Abdel-Rahman, Stewart and Yousry on two days in 2000. It is quite clear from the conversations that Yousry is not actually acting as an interpreter; after five years of contact with the other two parties, he has become a co-participant, an interlocutor. In fact, Stewart can hardly get a word in; it is largely a conversation between the two men. Angelelli and Osman use this case as an example of the interpreter as co-participant rather than a conduit who lacks agency. They go on to express the following view:

> How can a person with no agency merit a conviction? Only when it is accepted that interpreters do indeed exercise agency in every communicative event will professional organisations take it upon themselves to develop best practices for the exercise of that agency.
>
> *(ibid.: 77–78)*

However, it could also be argued that if Yousry had undergone interpreter training and learnt about interpreter ethics and strategies to uphold them, he would have been able to act more in line with these principles rather than falling into the role of co-participant. It is precisely because associations are all too aware that interpreters exercise agency that codes of ethics seek to delineate role boundaries.

2.11.6 Public comment

The final case in this section involves a very highly qualified interpreter and how he acted in a particular situation. Interpreters rarely comment publicly about cases in which they have been involved. There was an interesting exception in 2008. The background to the case was that Erik Camayd-Freixas, Professor of Spanish and Director of the Translation and Interpretation Program at Florida International University, was recruited, along with 35 other federally certified Spanish-English interpreters, to work on an assignment in Postville, Iowa. The case involved 306 Guatemalan and Mexican immigrants who were employed at a meatpacking company. The defendants were charged with aggravated identity theft and given two options: if they pleaded guilty to knowingly using a false Social Security number, they would serve five months in jail and be deported without a hearing but if they pleaded not guilty they would be remanded in custody for six to eight months while awaiting trial for aggravated identity theft, with the possibility of receiving a two-year jail sentence, followed by deportation. This was a highly unusual case at the time, given the number of people involved (plus their families) and the decision to fast track the cases to ensure that the whole operation was completed as speedily as possible. The charges were criminal ones, and the possibility that some of the defendants could have rights under immigration law was deliberately avoided.

Anyone reading Camayd-Freixas' personal account (2008a) or his article (2013a) would likely assume that he was a lone voice, but that was not the case at all; many individuals, lawyers and organisations spoke out about the Postville raids and there was extensive media coverage of the case at both state and national level – the

Des Moines Register, *USA Today*, the *New York Times*, the *Telegraph Herald* in Dubuque, Iowa, the *Associated Press* news agency, the *Washington Post*, *Cox News Service*, *Time* magazine. The American Civil Liberties Union (ACLU) issued a statement condemning 'the unnecessary use of criminal prosecutions to coerce hundreds of foreign-born workers detained … into waiving their rights to individually demonstrate why each of them should be allowed to remain in the U.S.' There was a rally of about 500 people outside the National Cattle Congress where the detainees were being held and a film of the event was uploaded on YouTube (Gravelle 2008). The American Immigration Lawyers Association (AILA) wrote to the District Court Chief Judge for the Northern District of Iowa and to the Attorney General and to the Homeland Security Secretary (AILA 2008a; 2008b). Defence lawyer David Nadler was 'dismayed that prosecutors had denied them probation and insisted the immigrants serve prison time and agree to a rarely used judicial order for immediate deportation upon their release, signing away their rights to go to immigration court' (Preston 2008a). In addition, there was most likely also a great deal of coverage on radio, television and on social media which is more difficult to capture. All in all, there was extensive coverage of Postville over a sustained period of time.

Camayd-Freixas, who was employed as a court interpreter over a two-week period, became concerned that the defendants were being obliged to plead guilty to *knowingly* using a false Social Security number, when he believed that they did not even understand what a Social Security number was. Unusually, at the end of the proceedings, he availed himself of an opportunity to express his concerns about the jail interviews to one of the presiding judges. After the hearings and when the time allowable for appeal had passed, he completed a 15-page personal account of events which he circulated first to a judge and then to the other interpreters who had worked on the case, some of whom forwarded it to a wider audience. He also sent it to the American Translators Association for possible publication in the *ATA Chronicle*. He then sent the article to the *New York Times* which published a front-page article about Camayd-Freixas and the issue of interpreter confidentiality (Preston 2008b), followed by an editorial two days later (*New York Times* 2008). The personal account is passionate and polemical, and, as Hennessy (2008) has indicated, uses language in a manner aimed at manipulating the reader in an article that is 'weakened by exaggeration, use of emotional manipulation, sentimentality, and visible bias'. The article reads quite differently from the dispassionate, factual newspaper reports. Because it so unusual for an interpreter to speak out, the article and the associated media coverage of Camayd-Freixas no doubt helped keep Postville in the limelight.

On 24 July 2008, Camayd-Freixas testified at the Subcommittee on Immigration, Citizenship, Refugees, Border Security and International Law, as did a number of lawyers (2008c). He would go on to devote a lot of time to 'helping journalists with interviews and reports, lobbying labour unions, faith groups, NGOs, and government officials for a moratorium on raids, and advocating for immigration reform' (2013a: 18), something that could raise concerns for his future impartiality, and he wrote a book (2013b) about the affair. When Camayd-Freixas did all of these things, he was getting involved, he was becoming an actor, a player. Did he do the right thing when he went public? His own view on interpreter interventions is:

> I do not recommend any intervention by other interpreters in a case, except as a last resort in extremely extenuating circumstances – and then, only if no one else can assume that burden. Moreover, before intervening, the interpreter must know exactly in what manner and how far to intervene, and must previously discharge the obligation of consulting with colleagues.
> *(Camayd-Freixas 2009, unpaginated)*

In the Postville case, as we have seen, many other people did assume the burden of intervening. Camayd-Freixas justifies his willingness to go public by saying that as an interpreter he was in a unique position of being able to follow the entire process from beginning to end (2008a: 9). However, he also had other advantages that gave him added status and protection compared to many interpreters; in addition to being an experienced certified Federal court interpreter, he was a university professor, highly qualified academically and presumably not totally dependent on his earnings as a court interpreter. Even if he never worked in Iowa again, he could continue to work in Florida and other states. In short, he was in a privileged position and could afford to speak out without fear of possible consequences.

A question arises about which code of ethics applies in such a situation. In his article (2008a), Camayd-Freixas mentions his contract for the assignment, which was accompanied by a copy of the Standards for Performance and Professional Responsibility for Contract Court Interpreters in the Federal Courts. Therefore, from a legal or contractual point of view, it can be assumed that he was expected to conform to the Standards, which specifically restrict public comment:

> [Canon] 6: Restriction of Public Comment Interpreters shall not publicly discuss, report, or offer an opinion concerning a matter in which they are or have been engaged, even when that information is not privileged or required by law to be confidential.

Canon 6 appears quite restrictive and all-encompassing, because it covers both current and past cases; it is essentially a gagging clause. It even states that restriction of public comment applies 'when the information is not privileged or required by law to be confidential'. However, in Camayd-Freixas' opinion, there was no longer a conflict of interest after the case had been heard:

> Again, canon 6 refers to public comment that may conceivably affect the outcome of an ongoing case. For example, the interpreter has participated in a previous, related case and gives statements to the press, which may find

their way back into court and affect the outcome of the ongoing case. That was not the case here: the cases were closed, and I was not involved in any new, related case. Furthermore, canon 6 conflicts with other responsibilities of the interpreter as expert officer of the court, as outlined above, and also conflicts with canon 9: Duty to Report Ethical Violations. Finally, canon 6 does not survive the final disposition of a case. It is a limited restriction, not an absolute prohibition, and therefore cannot be construed as requiring perpetual or indefinite secrecy on the part of the interpreter about every case in which she or he has been engaged. After the case is closed and the interpreter contract ends, canon 6 becomes subordinate to every citizen's first amendment right to free speech.

(2009, unpaginated)

If we consider the wording of canon 9, Camayd-Freixas' argumentation does not stand up to scrutiny because reporting is to 'the proper judicial authority' – something that he himself had done according to his own account – and not to the media. Moreover, the duty to report is restricted to violations of the interpreter standards and policies to do with court interpreting. The full text of canon 9 Duty to report ethical violations is: 'Interpreters shall report to the proper judicial authority any effort to impede their compliance with any law, any provision of these Standards, or any other official policy governing court interpreting and legal translating.'

Also, it is somewhat worrying that Camayd-Freixas has to resort to his right to free speech under the First Amendment. Where does that leave interpreters in other jurisdictions who may not enjoy such protection? Are they covered under whistleblower protection? Camayd-Freixas is a proponent of the Massachusetts Code of Professional Conduct for Court Interpreters of the Trial Court, which formerly allowed interpreters to speak out once a case had been heard and the time permissible for an appeal had elapsed: 'A court interpreter shall not discuss publicly, report or offer an opinion concerning a matter in which he/she has been engaged and while such matter is pending.' However, in 2009, the wording of the Massachusetts Code was altered to mirror that of the Federal Courts, thus restricting all public comment by interpreters: 'Court interpreters shall not publicly discuss, report, or offer an opinion concerning a matter in which they are or have been engaged, even when that information is not privileged or required by law to be confidential.'

This discussion raises a question: is it really appropriate for interpreters to pick and choose the elements of codes that best suit their circumstances? Camayd-Freixas argues that codes of ethics should be amended to cater for exceptional cases like Postville. He describes court interpreter codes in the US as 'supervisory codes' (2013a: 21) and argues for an acceptance of professional discretion of court interpreters. Camayd-Freixas was a member of both the National Association of Judiciary Interpreters and Translators (NAJIT) and the American Translators Association (ATA) in 2008 but the two associations were reluctant to come out in his favour, or indeed in favour of interpreters speaking out. While canon 2 of the NAJIT code of ethics provides that 'Court interpreters and translators shall abstain from comment on matters in which they serve', in contrast, the ATA code makes no mention of public comment. It should be noted that there is no legal or professional obligation on court interpreters in the United States to join professional associations.

While Camayd-Freixas received support from many individual interpreters and has been praised by Morris for his 'courage, moral fiber, and professionalism' (2010: 36) and by Inghilleri, who has stated that 'There is no question that Camayd-Freixas played a significant role in bringing many of the questionable practices … to public attention' (2012: 68), he was disappointed at the lack of official support from the boards of ATA and NAJIT. He sees this as a sign that 'a revision of ethical codes and the role of professional organizations is overdue' (2013a: 20). However, professional associations are not in agreement for good reason as they believe that the core principles of impartiality and confidentiality are essential and if issues are to be raised, that should be done by the lawyers, as happened in the Postville case.

The experiences of Camayd-Freixas provide an insight into the difficulty of impartiality; his work placed him in a situation where he was an unwilling participant in bad practice and his sympathies lay with the defendants. In other words, a conflict arose between his personal and professional ethics. This is not unusual; for example, Palma has outlined the vicarious trauma experienced by interpreters for immigrant parents who have been separated from their children under the Trump administration 'zero tolerance' policy (Palma 2018). Camayd-Freixas' article (2008a) and book (2013b) are of interest because interpreters' personal accounts, particularly contemporaneous accounts such as the former, are such a rarity apart from the occasional conference or diplomatic interpreter memoir, usually written many years after the events concerned.

2.12 Conclusion

The examples in this second section demonstrate that interpreters have agency. They also show the importance of codes of ethics with their emphasis on accuracy, impartiality and neutrality. Most breaches of ethical codes covered in the second section relate to unqualified interpreters who may not have had any training or been tested to establish if they were competent. Technology and the increased use of recordings are not yet the norm everywhere but when available in police stations, courts and asylum settings, they can enable checking of interpreters' work. However, it is likely that only the most blatant cases, where an interpreter is doing a very poor job, attract attention and are checked.

Rather than focusing on various versions of advocacy, on a supposed need for agency and a right for interpreters to involve themselves in public debate, there is a need to get back to basics and focus on key issues of training, testing and indeed codes of ethics.

References

Angelelli C.V. (2006). Validating professional standards and codes: challenges and opportunities. *Interpreting* 8(2), 175–193.

Angelelli, C.V. (2008). The role of the interpreter in the healthcare setting: a plea for a dialogue between research and practice. In C. Valero-Garces and A. Martin (eds), *Crossing Borders in Community Interpreting: Definitions and Dilemmas* (pp. 147–163). Amsterdam: John Benjamins.

Angelelli, C.V. and Osman, G. (2007). 'A crime in another language?' An analysis of the interpreter's role in the Yousry case. *Translation and Interpreting Studies*, 2(1), 47–82.

Associated Press (2008). 85 sentenced in connection with Postville raid. 20 May.*Associated Press State & Local Wire* (2008a). Postville raid detainees ushered through hearings, 15 May.

Associated Press State & Local Wire (2008b). Miles away, Postville raid's impact is still acute, 25 May.

Aulakh, R. (2012). Mistakes by Hindi interpreter lead to mistrial in Brampton sex assault case. *The Star,* 5 January. Available at: www.thestar.com/news/crime/2012/01/05/mistakes_by_hindi_interpreter_leads_to_mistrial_in_brampton_sex_assault_case.html (accessed 17 January 2017).

BBC News (2012). Trial collapses at Snaresbrook court after interpreter error, 13 April. Available at: www.bbc.com/news/uk-england-london-17709440 (accessed 17 January 2017).

Boéri, J. (2015). Key internal players in the development of the interpreting profession. In H. Mikkelson and R. Jourdenais (eds), *The Routledge Handbook of Interpreting* (pp. 29–44). London: Routledge.

Brean, J. (2011). Translation derails sex assault trial. *National Post,* 18 September. Available at: http://news.nationalpost.com/news/canada/translation-derails-sex-assault-trial (accessed 17 January 2017).

Buckley, J. (2014). Urdu translator jailed after helping prospective lorry drivers cheat their way through theory test. *Mirror,* 15 November. Available at: www.mirror.co.uk/news/uk-news/urdu-translator-jailed-after-helping-4634832 (accessed 10 June 2016).

Camayd-Freixas, E. (2008a). Interpreting after the largest ICE raid in US history: a personal account. *New York Times,* 13 June. Available at: http://graphics8.nytimes.com/images/2008/07/14/opinion/14ed-camayd.pdf (accessed 6 January 2016).

Camayd-Freixas, E. (2008b). Response letters to Camayd-Freixas article on Postville raid 24 July. Available at: http://cdm15897.contentdm.oclc.org/cdm/ref/collection/post/id/865 (accessed 6 January 2016).

Camayd-Freixas, E. (2008c). Subcommittee on Immigration, Citizenship, Refugees, Border Security and International Law. 24 July judiciary.house.gov/_files/hearings/pdf/Camayd-Freixas080724.pdf. (accessed 6 January 2016).

Camayd-Freixas, E. (2009). Statement to the Profession (statement dated 16 July 2008), followed by Appendix: Some questions and answers. *Translation Journal,* 13(1).

Camayd-Freixas, E. (2009). Brief to the Senate Judiciary Committee regarding the nomination of AUSA Stephanie Rose for US Attorney for the Northern District of Iowa and the Inquiry into the Postville prosecutions of May 12–23, 2008. 4 November. Available at: http://justiceforsholom.org/wp-content/uploads/2011/03/DR.-ERIK-CAMAYD-FREIXAS-on-Rose-Nomination.pdf (accessed 6 January 2016).

Camayd-Freixas, E. (2013a). Court interpreter ethics and the role of professional organisations. In C. Schäffner, K. Kredens and Y. Fowler (eds). *Interpreting in a Changing Landscape* (pp. 15–30). Amsterdam: John Benjamins.

Camayd-Freixas, E. (2013b). *US Immigration Reform and Its Global Impact: Lessons from the Postville Raid*. Basingstoke: Palgrave Macmillan.

Cox News Service (2008). Hispanic lawmakers denounce 'inhumane' immigration raids, 20 May.

Czekalinksi, S. (2000). Court interpreter fired. *The Columbus Dispatch*, 8 January. Available at: www.dispatch.com/content/stories/local/2009/08/01/MISINTERPRETED.ART_ART_08-01-09_B1_C3EL5FK.html/. (accessed 18 January 2017).

Davidson, B. (2000). The interpreter as institutional gatekeeper: the social-linguistic role of interpreters in Spanish-English medical discourse. *Journal of Sociolinguistics*, 4(3), 379–405.

de Jongh E.M. (2008). Court interpreting: linguistic presence v. linguistic absence *The Florida Bar Journal*, 82(7), unpaginated.

de Santis, J. (2015). Interpreter faces up to 80 years after plea. *The Times* (Louisiana), 12 August. Available at: www.houmatimes.com/news/interpretor-faces-up-to-years-after-plea/article_55262606-4045-11e5-98f1-b34639eed11b.html (accessed 6 January 2017).

Duara, N. and Petroski, W. (2008). Hundreds arrested in Iowa immigration raid. *USA Today*, 12 May. Available at: http://usatoday30.usatoday.com/news/nation/2008-05-12-iowa-immigration_N.htm (accessed 6 January 2017).

Duara, N., Petroski, W. and Schulte G. (2008). Claims of ID fraud lead to largest raid in state history. *Des Moines Register*, 12 May. (unavailable online 10 February 2017).

Dysart-Gale, D. (2005). Communication models, professionalization, and the work of medical interpreters. *Health Communication* 17(1), 91–103.

Framer, I. (2000). Interpreters and their impact on the criminal justice system: The Alejandro Ramirez case. *Proteus*, IX(1–2).

Framer, I. (2001). Through the eyes of an interpreter. *The Advocate*, 23(3).

Gardiner, B. (2014). When language can make or break a case. *Times Union*, 20 July. Available at: www.timesunion.com/default/article/When-language-can-make-or-break-a-case-5634577.php (accessed 17 January 2017).

Giambruno, C. (2008). The role of the interpreter in the governance of sixteenth and seventeenth century Spanish colonies in the 'New World': lessons from the past for the present. In C. Valero-Garcés and A. Martin (eds), *Crossing Borders in Community Interpreting* (pp. 27–50). Amsterdam: John Benjamins.

Giambruno, C. (2014). *Assessing Legal Interpreter Quality Through Testing and Certification: The Qualitas Project*. Alicante: Publicaciones de la Universidad de Alicante.

Gov.uk (20170. Foreign language driving tests end. Available at: www.gov.uk/government/news/foreign-language-driving-tests-end (accessed 17 January 2017).

Goymer, P. (2019). Translators were 'not qualified' for police interview work. BBC News. Available at: www.bbc.com/news/uk-england-46838858?ref=BNTMedia&utm_medium=facebook (accessed 17 March 2019).

Graham, E.A., Jacobs, T.A., Kwan-Gett, T.S. and Cover, J. (2008). Health services utilization by low-income limited English proficient adults. *Journal of Immigrant Minority* Health, 10, 207–217.

Gravelle, S. (2008). Postville rally supports immigrant detainees. *Gazetteonline*, 19 May. Available at: www.youtube.com/watch?v=H7iZHN7eh2M (accessed 16 January 2016).

Greenhalgh, T., Robb, N. and Scambler, G. (2006). Communicative and strategic action in interpreted consultations in primary health care: a Habermasian perspective. *Social Science & Medicine*, 63, 1170–1187.

Hale, S. (2007). *Community Interpreting*. Basingstoke: Palgrave Macmillan.

Hayes, A. and Hale, S. (2010). Appeals on incompetent interpreting. *Journal of Judicial Administration*, 20, 119–130.

Hennessy, E.B. (2008). Whistle-blowing and language professionals: the case of Postville and Professor Erik Camayd-Freixas. *Translation Journal*, 12(4).

Hernandez-Iverson, E. (2010). *IMIA Guide on Medical Interpreter Ethical Conduct*. Available at: www.imiaweb.org/uploads/pages/376_2.pdf (accessed 3 January 2017).

Hopper, T. (2014). Jamaican patois interpreter shortage causes mistrial, leaving alleged drug smugglers in legal limbo. *National Post*, 30 April. Available at: http://news.nationalpost.com/toronto/na0501-mistrial (accessed 17 January 2017).

Hsieh, E. (2007). Interpreters as co-diagnosticians: overlapping roles and services between providers and interpreters. *Social Science & Medicine*, 64, 924–937.

Hsieh, E. (2008). 'I am not a robot!' Interpreters' views of their roles in health care settings. *Qualitative Health Research*, 18(10), 1367–1383.

Hsu, S.S. (2008). Immigration raid jars a small town. *Washington Post*, 18 May. Available at: www.washingtonpost.com/wp-dyn/content/article/2008/05/17/AR2008051702474.html (accessed 6 January 2017).

Humphreys, A. (2011). Translator error sinks woman's refugee hearing. *National Post*, 18 July. Available at: http://news.nationalpost.com/news/canada/translator-error-sinks-womans-refugee-hearing (accessed 20 January 2017).

Inghilleri, M. (2012). *Interpreting Justice: Ethics, Politics, and Language*. London: Routledge.

Irish Independent (2007). Hunt for Lithuanian guilty of rape and threatening to kill, 6 December.

Irish Times (2003). Murder accused dated interpreter, 5 March.

Leanza, Y. (2005). Roles of community interpreters in paediatrics as seen by interpreters, physicians and researchers. *Interpreting*, 7(2), 167–192.

Mairs, R. (2011). 'Translator, traditor': the interpreter as traitor in classical tradition. *Greece & Rome*, 58(1), 64–81. Available at: www.jstor.org.dcu.idm.oclc.org/stable/41306148

Mayoral Asensio, R. (2011). Discusión crítica de los códigos deontológicos. *Boletín de la Asociación de Traductores e Intérpretes Jurados*. Available at: www.ugr.es/~rasensio/docs/etica.pdf (accessed 24 October 2015).

Metro (2006). 'Polish Borat' groped women, 8 November. Available at: http://metro.co.uk/2006/11/08/polish-borat-groped-women-344767/ (accessed 27 February 2017).

Morris, R. (2010). Images of the Court Interpreter: professional identity, role definition and self-image. *Translation and Interpreting Studies*, 5(1), 20–40.

Ozolins, U. (2007). The interpreter's 'third client'; interpreters, professionalism and interpreting agencies. In C. Wadensjö, B. Englund Dimitrova and A.-L. Nilsson (eds), *The Critical Link 4* (pp. 121–131). Amsterdam: John Benjamins.

Ozolins, U. (2014). Rewriting the AUSIT Code of Ethics: principles, practice, dispute. *Babel* 60(3), 347–370.

Phillips, T. (2017). Interpreter helped driving theory test candidates cheat by giving answers in secret Ukranian code instead of Russian. *Sussex News*, 23 February. Available at: www.getsurrey.co.uk/news/surrey-news/interpreter-helped-driving-theory-test-12642869

Pöllabauer, S. (2004). Interpreting in asylum hearings: issues of role, responsibility and power. *Interpreting*, 6(2), 143–180.

Preston, J. (2008a). 270 illegal immigrants sent to prison in federal push. *New York Times* 24 May. Available at: www.nytimes.com/2008/05/24/us/24immig.html (accessed 6 January 2017).

Preston, J. (2008b). An interpreter speaking up for migrants. *New York Times*, 11 July. Available at: www.nytimes.com/2008/07/11/us/11immig.html (accessed 6 January 2017).

Purdy, C. (2011). Interpreter's actions jeopardise evidence. *Daily Progress*, 14 January. Available at: www.dailyprogress.com/news/interpreter-s-actions-jeopardize-evidence/article_bf3222d1-c1c1-5780-9ff1-c94d307ba0c2.html

Robb, N. and Greenhalgh, T. (2006). 'You have to cover up the words of the doctor': the mediation of trust in interpreted consultations in primary care. *Journal of Health Organization and Management*, 20 434–455.

Rosenberg, E., Seller, R. and Leanza, Y. (2008). Through interpreters' eyes: comparing roles of professional and family interpreters. *Patient Education and Counselling*, 70, 87–93.

Rubiner, B. (2008). After immigrant raid, Iowans ask why postcard: Postville. *Time* magazine, 27 May.

Rudvin, M. (2006). The cultural turn in Community Interpreting: a brief analysis of epistemological developments in Community Interpreting literature in the light of paradigm changes in the humanities. *Linguistica Antverpiensia Taking Stock: Research and Methodology in Community Interpreting*, 5, 21–41.

Saulny, S. (2008). Hundreds are arrested in U.S. sweep of meat plant. *New York Times*, 13 May. Available at: www.nytimes.com/2008/05/13/us/13immig.html. (accessed 6 January 2017).

Schweda-Nicholson, N. (1994). Professional ethics for court and community interpreters. In D. L. Hammond (ed.), *Professional Issues for Translators and Interpreters*. Amsterdam: John Benjamins Publishing Company.

Silverman, R. (2013). Chinese interpreter helped drivers cheat at UK theory. *The Telegraph*, 6 August. Available at: www.telegraph.co.uk/news/uknews/crime/10224856/Chinese-interpreter-helped-drivers-cheat-at-UK-theory.html. (accessed 6 January 2017).

Skaaden, H. (2013). *Den topartiske tolken. Lærebok i tolking*. Oslo: Universitetsforlaget.

Smith, D. (2014). Oscar Pistorius: a runaway interpreter, then the trial of the century begins. *The Guardian*, 3 March. Available at: www.theguardian.com/world/2014/mar/03/oscar-pistorius-reeva-steenkamp-murder-trial-opens (accessed 17 January 2017).

Sowetan Live (2014). Anger over Pistorius trial interpreters, 14 March. Available at: www.sowetanlive.co.za/news/2014/03/14/anger-over-pistorius-trial-interpreters (accessed 17 January 2017).

Tebble, H. (2012). Interpreting or interfering?' In C. Baraldi and L. Gavioli (eds), *Coordinating Participation in Community Interpreting* (pp. 23–44). Amsterdam: John Benjamins.

The Local (2010). Interpreter loses licence for poor Swedish skills, 22 July. Available at: www.thelocal.se/20100722/27934 (accessed 17 January 2017).

Tobia, P.J. (2007). Language barrier. *Nashville Scene*, 22 November. Available at: www.nashvillescene.com/news/article/13015482/language-barrier (accessed 18 January 2017).

Van Hees, B. (2016). Interpreter's incompetence delays human trafficking trial. *IOL*, 5 August. Available at: www.iol.co.za/news/crime-courts/interpreters-incompetence-delays-human-trafficking-trial-2054084 (accessed 22 January 2017).
Verrept, H. (2008). Intercultural mediation: an answer to health care disparities? In C. Valero-Garcés and A. Martin (eds), *Crossing Borders in Community Interpreting: Definitions and Dilemmas* (pp. 187–201). Amsterdam: John Benjamins.
Verrept, H. (2009). Intercultural mediation at Belgian hospitals. Available at: www.mfh-eu.net/public/files/conference/mfh_paper3_Hans_Verrept.pdf
Verrept, H. and Coune, I. (2016). *Guide for Intercultural Mediation in Health Care*. Available at: www.health.belgium.be/sites/default/files/uploads/fields/fpshealth_theme_file/en_2016_04_20_leidraad.pdf (accessed 6 January 2017).
Wadensjö, C. (1998). *Interpreting as Interaction*. London: Routledge.
Zimányi, K. (2010). Hundreds of Hungarian driving licences issued to illiterate Romanians. *ITIA Bulletin*, March.

Websites

ACLU (American Civil Liberties Union) (2008). Statement concerning due process after ICE Raid in Postville, Iowa by R. Ben Stone, Executive Director 13 May. Available at: www.aclu-ia.org/iowa/wp-content/uploads/2012/01/PR_20080513_Postville_Raids.pdf (accessed 15 February 2016).
Affaire Knox c. Italie (2019). European Court of Human Rights. Available at: http://hudoc.echr.coe.int/eng?i=001-189422 (accessed 1 September 2019).
Aftenposten (2004). Available at: www.aftenposten.no/osloby/Bestikker-tolken---jukser-seg-til-forerkortet-508126b.html (accessed 3 January 2017).
Aftenposten (2008). Available at: www.aftenposten.no/norge/Prevensjon-ble-sterilisering-595410b.html (accessed 1 September 2019).
AIIC (2012). Recommendations on social media issued by Heads of Interpreting Services, 4 April. Available at: http://aiic.net/p/3870 (accessed 12 January 2017).
AILA (American Immigration Lawyers Association) (2008a). Letter to Attorney General www.aila.org/advo-media/aila-correspondence/2008/letter-proceedings-surrounding-agriprocessors-raid (accessed 15 February 2016).
AILA (American Immigration Lawyers Association) (2008b). Letter to Chief Judge of United States District Court. Available at: www.aila.org/advo-media/aila-correspondence/2008/proceedings-surrounding-agriprocessors-raid (accessed 15 February 2016).
AITI (Asociazione Italiana Traduttori e Interpreti) (2013). Code of Professional Ethics and Conduct. Available at: www.aiti.org/english/code-of-professional-ethics-and-conduct (accessed 3 January 2017).
APTIJ (Asociación Profesional de Traductores e Intérpretes Judiciales y Jurados) (2010). Code of Ethics for Court and Sworn Interpreters and Translators. Available at: www.aptij.es/img/doc/CD%20APTIJ.pdf (accessed 3 January 2017).
Arrêté royal relatif à la fixation et à la liquidation du budget des moyens financiers des hôpitaux (2002). 25 April. Available at: www.ejustice.just.fgov.be/cgi_loi/change_lg.pl?language=fr&la=F&cn=2002042549&table_name=loi (accessed 1 September 2019).
ASETRAD (Asociación Española de Traductores, Correctores e Intérpretes) Code of Professional Conduct. Available at: https://asetrad.org/en/the-association/codigo-deontologico (accessed 3 January 2017).

Codes of ethics 143

Associated Press (2008). Immigration raid spurs calls for action vs. owners. *Washington Post*, 1 June. Available at: www.washingtonpost.com/wp-dyn/content/article/2008/06/01/AR2008060101059_pf.html (accessed 6 January 2017).

Association of Translators and Interpreters of Alberta (2015). Code of Ethics and Supplemental Code for community, conference, court and medical interpreters. Available at: www.atia.ab.ca/about/code-of-ethics

ATA (American Translators Association) (2010). Code of Ethics and Professional Practice Available at: www.atanet.org/governance/code_of_ethics.php (accessed 3 January 2017).

ATA (American Translators Association) Code of Ethics and Professional Practice – Commentary. Available at: www.atanet.org/governance/code_of_ethics_commentary.pdf (accessed 3 January 2017).

ATA (American Translators Association) (2013). Policy on Ethics Procedures. Available at: www.atanet.org/docs/p_dm_ethics.pdf (accessed 10 January 2017).

AUSIT (Australian Institute of Interpreters and Translators) (2012). Code of Ethics and Code of Conduct. Available at: http://ausit.org/AUSIT/Documents/Code_Of_Ethics_Full.pdf (accessed 3 January 2017).

Bancroft, M. (2005). *The Interpreter's World Tour: An Environmental Scan of Standards of Practice for Interpreters*. Available at: www.ncihc.org/assets/documents/publications/NCIHC%20Environmental%20Scan.pdf (accessed 10 January 2017).

BDÜ (Bundesverband der Dolmetscher und Übersetzer e.V.). (2014). Code of Professional Conduct. Available at: www.bdue.de/en/bdue/codes/code-of-professional-conduct/ (accessed 3 January 2017).

Beal, A. C. (n.d.). National Council on Interpreting in Health Care develops National Standards for Interpreters. Available at: www.ncihc.org/ethics-and-standards-of-practice (accessed 25 February 2017).

CHIA (California Healthcare Interpreting Association) (2002). California Standards for Healthcare Interpreters. Available at: www.chiaonline.org/Resources/Documents/CHIA%20Standards/standards_chia.pdf (accessed 3 January 2017).

CIoL (Chartered Institute of Linguists) (2013). Disciplinary Procedures. Available at: http://ciolweb.nfpservices.co.uk/sites/default/files/DiscProc.pdf (accessed 3 January 2017).

CIoL (Chartered Institute of Linguists) (2015). Code of Professional Conduct. Available at: http://ciolweb.nfpservices.co.uk/sites/default/files/CPC15.pdf (accessed 3 January 2017).

Collins English Dictionary. Available at: www.collinsdictionary.com/dictionary/english (accessed 3 January 2017).

Dagsavisen (2013). Available at: www.dagsavisen.no/betaler-15-000-for-jukselappen-1.278442 (accessed 6 January 2017).

EUATC (European Union Association of Translation Companies). Available at: www.euatc.org/ (accessed 5 January 2017).

EULITA (European Association of Legal Interpreters and Translators) (2013). Code of Ethics. Available at: www.eulita.eu/sites/default/files/EULITA-code-London-e.pdf (accessed 3 January 2017).

EXPERTIJ. Available at: www.net1901.org/association/EXPERTS-ET-TRADUCTEURS-INTERPRETES-JUDICIAIRES-EXPERTIJ,1783728.html (accessed 27 February 2017).

Findlaw. Available at: http://news.findlaw.com/cnn/docs/terrorism/uslstwrt111903sind.html (accessed 10 October 2015).

Finnish Association of Translators and Interpreters (2016). Code of Ethics. Available at: www.sktl.fi/@Bin/1015311/Tulkin_etiikka_englanti.pdf

FIT Translator's Charter (1963, 1994). www.fit-ift.org/translators-charter/ (accessed 27 February 2017).

IAPTI (International Association of Professional Translators and Interpreters). Code of Ethics. Available at: www.iapti.org/code_of_ethics/ (accessed 20 June 2016).

IMIA (International Medical Interpreters Association) (1995). Medical Interpreting Standards of Practice. Available at: www.imiaweb.org/uploads/pages/102.pdf (accessed 3 January 2017).

IMIA (International Medical Interpreters Association) (2006). Code of Ethics. Available at: www.imiaweb.org/code/ (accessed 3 January 2017).

ISO Standard 13611: 2014. Guidelines for Community Interpreters. Available at: www.iso.org/iso/catalogue_detail.htm?csnumber=54082 (accessed 6 January 2017).

ISO Standard 18841: 2018 Interpreting Services – General Requirements and Recommendations https://www.iso.org/standard/63544.html (accessed 1 September 2019).

ISO Standard 20228: 2019 Interpreting Services – Legal Interpreting – Requirements https://www.iso.org/standard/67327.html (accessed 1 September 2019).

ITI (Institute of Translation and Interpreting) (2013). Code of Professional Conduct. Available at: www.iti.org.uk/attachments/article/154/Code%20of%20professional%20conduct%2008%2009%202013_Final.pdf (accessed 3 January 2017).

Judicial Council of California (2013). Professional Standards and Ethics for California Court Interpreters. Available at: www.courts.ca.gov/documents/CIP-Ethics-Manual.pdf (accessed 1 September 2019).

LanguageLine Solutions Interpreter Code of Ethics (2013). Available at: http://lcsokcps.weebly.com/uploads/1/7/8/5/17851241/interpreter_code_of_ethics.pdf (accessed 3 January 2017).

Massachusetts Court System. Code of Professional Conduct for Court Interpreters of the Trial Court. Available at: www.mass.gov/courts/docs/admin/interpreters/code-of-conduct.pdf (accessed 3 January 2017).

Merriam-Webster Dictionary. Available at: www.merriam-webster.com

NAJIT (National Association of Judiciary Interpreters & Translators). Code of Ethics and Professional Responsibilities. Available at: https://najit.org/wp-content/uploads/2016/09/NAJITCodeofEthicsFINAL.pdf (accessed 3 January 2017).

NCIHC (National Council on Interpreting in Health Care) (2004). A National Code of Ethics for Interpreters in Health Care. Available at: www.ncihc.org/assets/documents/publications/NCIHC%20National%20Code%20of%20Ethics.pdf (accessed 3 January 2017).

NCIHC (2005). National Standards of Practice for Interpreters in Health Care. Available at: www.ncihc.org/assets/documents/publications/NCIHC%20National%20Standards%20of%20Practice.pdf (accessed 27 February 2017).

Nebula. Available at: http://nebula.wsimg.com/c72d2839eaa09ccdde7ea73ba0d1a854?(accessKeyId=5AF78834A5D9003DD559&disposition=0&alloworigin=1 (accessed 27 January 2017).

New York Times (2008). Editorial: The shame of Postville, Ohio, 13 July. Available at: www.nytimes.com/2008/07/13/opinion/13sun2.html (accessed 6 January 2017).

NRPSI (National Register of Public Service Interpreters) (2016a). Code of Professional Conduct. Available at: www.nrpsi.org.uk/for-clients-of-interpreters/code-of-professional-conduct.html (accessed 3 January 2017).

NRPSI (National Register of Public Service Interpreters) (2016b). Disciplinary Framework and Procedures. Available at: www.nrpsi.org.uk/downloads/NRPSI_Disciplinary_Framework_and_Procedures_22.01.16.pdf (accessed 3 January 2017).

Palma, J. (2018). The cat is out of the bag. NAJIT. Available at: https://najit.org/cat-out-of-bag/

SFT (Société française des traducteurs) (2016). Code of Professional Conduct. Available at: www.sft.fr/code-de-deontologie-des-traducteurs-et-interpretes.html#.VZVlhRtVhHx (accessed 3 January 2017).

SITA (Scottish Interpreters and Translators Association). Code of Conduct for Individual Members. Available at: www.si-ta.yolasite.com/resources/NEW%20SITA%20CODE%20OF%20CONDUCT%20SEPTEMBER%202010<1].pdf (accessed 3 January 2017).

Subcommittee on Immigration, Citizenship, Refugees, Border Security, and International Law of the Committee on the Judiciary House of Representatives (2008). Serial No. 110–198. Immigration raids: Postville and beyond. 24 July. Available at: http://judiciary.house.gov/_files/hearings/printers/110th/43682.PDF (accessed 6 January 2017).

Telegraph Herald (14 July 2008). article no longer available online.

Thebigword. Interpreting Services Agreement. Available at: www.thebigword.com/static_file/OP3_App%2061a_INTERPRETING%20Services%20Agreement%20v5.2.pdf (accessed 15 January 2017).

UCS (Unified Court System New York) (2008). Court Interpreter Manual and Code of Ethics. Available at: www.nycourts.gov/COURTINTERPRETER/pdfs/CourtInterpreterManual.pdf (accessed 27 January 2017).

UNETICA (Union Nationale des Experts Traduteurs Interprètes près les Cours d'Appel). Available at: www.unetica.fr/

US Federal Courts Standards for Performance and Professional Responsibility for Contract Court Interpreters (n.d.). Available at: www.scd.uscourts.gov/interpreter/StandardforPerformanceandProfessionalResponsibility.pdf (accessed 3 January 2017).

Washington State Department of Social and Health Services. Code of Ethics Interpreter, Translator, and Licensed Agency Personnel Code of Professional Conduct. Available at: www.dshs.wa.gov/fsa/language-testing-and-certification-program/code-ethics (accessed 3 January 2017).

20 minutos (2009). Condenan a tres traductores de la Policía por amañar la nacionalidad de los inmigrantes, 9 March. Available at: www.20minutos.es/noticia/455470/0/tenerife/traductores/inmigrantes/ (accessed 10 January 2016).

Cases cited

Mamadou Amadou v Immigration and Naturalization Service 2000. https://caselaw.findlaw.com/us-6th-circuit/1193816.html (accessed 1 September 2019).

Mohamed Neheid v. Canada (Citizenship and Immigration), 2011 FC 846. https://www.canlii.org/en/ca/fct/doc/2011/2011fc846/2011fc846.html (accessed 1 September 2019).

People v Lee 2013 New York Court of Appeal. http://law.justia.com/cases/new-york/court-of-appeals/2013/111.html (accessed 1 September 2019).

R v Rybak. www.canlii.org/en/on/onca/doc/2008/2008onca354/2008onca354.html (accessed 18 January 2017).

R v Sidhu. www.canlii.org/en/on/onsc/doc/2005/2005canlii42491/2005canlii42491.pdf (accessed 17 January 2017).

R v Tran. http://scc-csc.lexum.com/scc-csc/scc-csc/en/item/1166/index.do (accessed 19 November 2016).

3
ETHICS AND PROFESSION

Hanne Skaaden

In this part of the book, the aim is to explore *ethics* and the activity of *public service interpreting* (PSI) in light of the process of *professionalisation*. How well does the interpreter's societal function fulfil the criteria of being a profession? What is the link between ethics and profession? In exploring these topics, we observe the activity of interpreting through the lenses of concepts such as *profession*, the *exercise of discretion*, *trust*, *virtue* and *quality* in performance. Hence, we examine interpreting in terms of a general model of professionalisation that divides the process into a *performative* aspect and an *organisational* aspect, as outlined in the sociology of professions (Molander and Terum 2008; Grimen 2008a; 2008b; Grimen and Molander 2008; Molander and Grimen 2010; Molander 2016, Skaaden 2013; 2016; 2018a; 2018b). The analysis shows that the interpreter function fulfils the criteria of a profession's performative aspect, while the organisational aspect – pertaining to society's licence and mandate for professional practice – is less developed, mainly due to the lack of educational options for interpreters.

The field of PSI appears torn over the values of its core ethics, the principles of accuracy and impartiality, two principles that clearly differentiate the interpreter's societal function from those of other professions. An analysis of metaphors used to depict the interpreter's 'role', as well as the concept of 'role' itself, shows that the different positions on 'role' represent different delineations of the domain within which the interpreter exercises discretion. It is further established that trust is a vital link between ethics and professional integrity, that is, 'what counts as legitimate grounds for professional action' and 'loyalty to profession-specific ends' (Eriksen 2015: 3, 14). An issue that receives particular attention here is the basis upon which clients should place their trust in an interpreter. Because this issue relates to the organisational aspect of profession, its 'licence and mandate', the final subsections draw attention to the interrelationship between the performative and organisational aspects of interpreting as a professional activity and the development of the profession's knowledge base. In other words, how does the interplay between practice, research and education affect interpreters' ethics and their professional status?

As outlined here, the specific nature of the activity of interpreting and the interpreters' double allegiance to clients on both sides of the table unequivocally raise questions that point beyond the professional integrity of interpreters. This part of the book therefore concludes by raising an issue that requires attention in future education, practice and research: how do interpreters' professional ethics affect the work and integrity of their clients who are themselves professionals – often practising in the established professions of medicine and law?

3.1 Why do we need professional ethics?

In their handbook, *Liaison Interpreting*, Gentile, Ozolins and Vasilakakos make the following note on the relationship between ethics and profession:

> In the vernacular, the adjectives 'professional' and 'ethical' are often synonymous, as are their opposites 'unprofessional' and 'unethical'. Among professionals and their clients, there is the perception that professionalism and ethics are inextricably linked, that you cannot claim to possess the former without also possessing the latter.
>
> *(Gentile et al. 1996: 56)*

The authors go on to quote the *Webster's Dictionary* definition of ethics, stating that ethics are 'the principles of conduct governing an individual or a profession' or simply 'standards of behaviour'. Gentile *et al.* compare the function of interpreting with the functions of medicine, teaching and the law, that is, professions where 'the client's welfare is usually affected directly' and which share 'the basic philosophical premise that providing a service which affects the welfare of the client demands ethical practices' (ibid.: 57). The authors conclude that the same applies to the profession of interpreting, not only because interpreters work in the context of the other professions 'but also because interpreting has its own particular kinds of knowledge, skills and practices which require particular ethical considerations' (ibid.: 57).

Professional ethics may often run counter to personal ethics or common sense regarding what is 'good' or 'right'. For illustration, we may look to the classic professions of medicine and law. Generally, it is not ethical to cut open a person's skull, but brain surgeons do so for a living and are highly respected for it. Similarly, it is not evident that it is ethical to defend perpetrators of serious crimes, but defence lawyers do it and enjoy one of the highest ranks in terms of professional status.

The reason professional ethics exist has to do with the nature of professions. To close in on the nature of professional ethics and their impact on the professionalisation of interpreting, the following questions are crucial: What is a profession? How well does the interpreter's societal function fulfil the criteria of being a profession? After a brief look at the aim of professional ethics in general and in relation to the

> **TEXTBOX 3.1** The difference between professional ethics and personal ethics comes to the fore in the defence of serious crimes. The trial after the terror attacks in Norway in July 2011 may serve to illustrate this point. The defence was (upon the terrorist's own request) led by defence attorney Geir Lippestad, a member of the Norwegian Labour Party – the body that the terrorist himself proclaimed his main enemy by attacking its youth organisation's summer camp and killing 77 people. Despite the defence attorney's background, people soon identified him with his client, and Lippestad, his family and co-workers received threats. Lippestad (2013: 67) quotes some of the hostile comments directed at him, such as 'How dare you walk the streets of Oslo?' In his memoir on the case, the experienced lawyer describes the relief he felt when the newspaper *Aftenposten* explained *the societal function of a defence lawyer* in a commentary, stating that, in a law-abiding society '[e]ven a mass murderer's interests must be taken care of. In this manner, the defence lawyer becomes something more than "just" the criminal's defence attorney. He becomes defender of the law-abiding society itself" (ibid.: 70–71).

practice of interpreting in particular, we shall examine aspects of the activity of interpreting from the vantage point of the sociology of professions.

With reference to the Aristotelian concept of *good*, the Norwegian sign language interpreter and philosopher Patrick Kermit (2002, see also Kermit, Introduction, in this volume) describes professional ethics in terms of *virtues*. He states that the ethical norms of professions refer to what is 'good' behaviour in the sense of 'good at', 'virtuous' or 'capable' rather than 'good to' in the sense of 'kind'. In a comparison of the professional functions of physicians, engineers and translators, the scholar of translation Andrew Chesterman (2001) similarly emphasises that professional ethics pertain to 'virtues' and 'duties' in that professional practices depend on phenomena such as *loyalty* and *trust*. In this sense, codes of ethics express professional practitioners' *responsibility* to behave in a certain way towards their clients and colleagues. Accordingly, professionals must strive for virtue – in terms of 'excellence' – in their practice to deserve the trust of their clients. It follows that because practising professionals rely on their clients' trust, they must deliver to the best of their ability according to a norm. Otherwise, the reputation of their profession will suffer, and their livelihood may be threatened. Comparably, Kinsella and Pitman (2012a: 2), who discuss 'virtue' in the context of medical training and practice, relate virtue to applied knowledge and 'the knowing how', as in the Aristotelian concept of *phronēsis*. The phenomenon of *virtue*, as in quality performance, connects professional ethics with the *exercise of discretion*, and thereby with gaining the clients' trust. From the perspective of sociology, professional ethics are norms or values that direct the behaviour of professionals so that the professions do not exploit the power that their specialised task accords them. As norms, professional ethics are general directions of action that describe 'how to behave or what to do in a certain type of situation' (Grimen and Molander 2008: 183; cf. Molander and Grimen 2010). The sociologist Eliot Freidson (2001: 12) links the ethical constraints of the individual practitioner to 'the institutional ethics of professionalism' and holds that '[i]f the institutions surrounding them fail in support, only the most heroic individual can actively concern themselves with the ethical issues raised by their work'. We therefore return to the relationship between professional ethics, virtue and trust and the organisational aspect below.

In summary, professional ethics serve both to secure the welfare of the client and the livelihood of the practitioner. We keep this in mind as we examine the interpreter's task from the vantage point of the sociology of professions, addressing the questions: What are the criteria of being a profession? And how well does the interpreter's societal function or task fulfil these criteria?

3.2 What is a profession?

The American sociologist Talcott Parsons, who in many respects 'fathered' the sociology of the professions, states that professions are 'occupational groups that perform certain rather specialized functions for others ("laymen") in the society on the basis of high-level and specialized competence, with the attendant fiduciary responsibility' (1978: 40).

In line with his 1978 definition, Parsons (1968) also identifies a number of criteria that are necessary for a societal task or function to develop into a profession. For instance, a set of norms or professional ethics that are widely shared are vital for a task to be professionalised (ibid.: 536). The observation relates to the fact that for professionalisation to take place, the task in question must be clearly delineated. Also of importance is the practitioners' ability to keep personal needs and professional function separate. Accordingly, *emotional neutrality* towards both clients and tasks is a core requirement in any profession's ethical norms. The criterion follows from the fact that the livelihood of professionals rests on the trust their clients have in their 'specialised competence'. Therefore, it is important for professionals to approach both tasks and clients with an altruistic rather than an egotistic attitude. Finally, Parsons stresses that organised *training* and *authorisation* are necessary for professionalisation to develop. The emphasis on training relates to society's need to secure high-quality services as represented by the professions' 'specialised competence' and 'attendant fiduciary responsibilities'. Because clients lack the specialised competence and cannot control the quality of the services themselves, society must rely upon licence and mandate to assure quality service (Molander and Terum 2008: 18–20). For the established professions, society secures its need for quality service through organised education in that the completion of education leads to authorisation, which can be revoked in the case of ethical misconduct. As a basis of licence and mandate, education is thereby intrinsically linked to the practitioner's professional integrity and ethical behaviour.

Parsons' interest was in the development of professions in general and of the medical profession in particular (Fauske 2008: 42). When we approach the professional status of interpreters, who typically serve practitioners of medicine and law alike, it is interesting to note Parsons' emphasis that 'the institutionalization of medicine as a profession, like that of law, was a process beset with serious difficulties' (1968: 540). Accordingly, he recognises that professionalisation is a *process*. Parsons' predictions for the future power status of professionals where they rule over state and capital have not been fulfilled, however, Freidson (2001: 195) notes. Nevertheless, since Parsons' time, the sociology of the professions has grown into a branch of science in its own right, and numerous professions have evolved since the birth of the professions labelled the classic professions – those of medicine, law and theology (Slagstad 2008: 57).

The sociologists Molander and Terum (2008: 18–20) elaborate on Parsons' definition of 'profession' and divide 'profession' into a performative aspect and an organisational aspect. In examining the interpreter function in light of this model, we shall let the organisational aspect in terms of education and authorisation rest for now and explore the performative aspect, asking 'How well does the interpreter's task coincide with sociology's requirements for professional performance?' The performative aspect of a profession pertains to 'what "practice" in the sense of professional activity means', according to Molander and Terum (2008: 19–20).[1] They go on to list several performative criteria that an activity or enterprise must fulfil to be labelled a 'profession'. In essence, what characterises professional activity is the offering of a service to clients who depend upon the professionals' specialised skills to solve a 'how-to' problem. In doing so, the professionals apply their specialised skills in unique situations that are difficult to standardise. Hence, professionals *exercise discretion*.

Table 3.1 displays how these criteria apply to the interpreter's societal function or task (Skaaden 2013; 2016; 2018ab).[2]

TABLE 3.1 The performative aspect of the process of professionalisation

	The professional	*The interpreter*
1	offers a service	offers a service by rendering someone else's talk in another language
2	for clients who depend upon the professional's specialised skills	for clients, i.e., the speaker and listener, who both depend on the interpreter's specialised skills
3	to solve a 'how to' problem	to solve their problem of how to communicate (verbally)
4	by applying specialised skills in unique situations that are difficult to standardise	by applying specialised interpreting skills in unique situations that are difficult to standardise
5	hence, the professional exercises discretion	hence, the interpreter exercises discretion

The interpreter (1) *offers a service* by rendering someone else's talk in another language (2) *for clients*, that is, speakers *and* listeners, (3) who both *depend on the interpreter's specialised skills* to solve their *problem of how to* communicate (verbally).

Consequently, (4) by *applying interpreting skills in unique situations* that are difficult to standardise, (5) the interpreter *exercises discretion*.

Evidently, the criteria in Table 3.1 elaborate on Parsons' (1978) definition of a profession. Supplementary to these basic criteria, Molander and Terum (2008: 19–20) list three interrelated criteria. First, professional activity is 'change-oriented' in that the activity should promote change, for instance, from sick to healthy or from non-functioning to functioning. Second, professional activity is carried out according to a *norm* and is consequently a 'fallible' activity. The criterion follows from the nature of the exercise of discretion. Third, as the authors observe, the professional '*applies* a systemized *amount of knowledge* to unique cases' (ibid.: 19, emphasis in original).[3] How do these additional criteria apply to the activity of interpreting? Interpreting is clearly a fallible activity. Furthermore, the move from 'non-communicating' to 'communicating (verbally)' represents *change* in interpreting. The activity of interpreting thus readily fulfils two of the additional criteria. As the systematisation of knowledge is in itself a process, the final criterion pertaining to a codified knowledge base cannot be absolute, however (Skaaden 2013: 218; cf. Skaaden 2016; 2018a). Moreover, the systematisation of knowledge pertains to the interrelation between *practice*, *research* and *training*, as elaborated on in Section 3.5 in exploring the organisational aspect of the interpreters' professionalisation. At this point, we simply note that both the setting of norms and the systematisation of knowledge form an important bridge between the performative and organisational aspects of professionalisation.

As pointed out in the sociology of the professions, the idea is that when practitioners behave in accordance with the professional standards for good practice, the profession's norms or standards serve to make the profession independent of the individual practitioner's personal morals (Molander and Terum 2008: 18; Eriksen 2015: 14). It follows that the practitioners' education has an impact on their ability to apply universal criteria in specific situations of action, that is to say, their ability to exercise discretion (Molander 2016: 24). An additional role of education is that it 'provides a foundation for the claim to be more than narrow technical specialists', Freidson (2001: 96) observes.

When we examine the activity of interpreting in light of the performative aspects of professional activity as listed above, it becomes evident that the interpreter function fulfils the core criteria of '"practice" in the sense of professional activity' with good margin. However, specific to the activity of interpreting is the fact that the interpreter always has *two* clients – speaker *and* listener – who equally depend upon the interpreter's skills to solve their mutual problem of how to communicate verbally. Importantly, because interpreters constantly serve two clients, their allegiance is always double (Skaaden 2013: 25–28; 2018a: 8–9). Moreover, the interpreters' double allegiance influences the drawing of boundaries around the domain within which they exercise discretion. Before returning to the interpreter's clients in Section 3.2.3, the following questions are addressed: What does the exercise of discretion in professional activity mean? What does the exercise of discretion entail in the case of interpreting?

3.2.1 Professions and the exercise of discretion

Professionals who apply their skills in practice constantly make judgements and on-the-spot decisions in real-life situations that are each unique. Even though some situations may resemble each other in type, no two situations are identical. All professionals therefore exercise discretion in one form or another Grimen and Molander (2008: 179) find. They explain that as a type of activity, the exercise of discretion pertains to the ability to apply knowledge and skills in real situations, so as to discern between good and bad solutions within an area of expertise (ibid.: 182). In their decision-making, professional practitioners rely on the norms and values manifested in their codes of ethics, the standards of their profession's accumulated knowledge base and the individual practitioners' previous experiences.

Grimen (2008c: 144) states that while norms and values represent the profession's morals, professional ethics are the reflections of such norms and values. Codes of ethics are in turn understood as 'norms of action'. By definition, however, all norms and standards are *general* because if too detailed, they would become dysfunctional, according to Grimen. Correspondingly, Grimen and Molander (2008: 181), who rely on the works of Galligan (1986) and Dworkin (1978) in describing the structure and nature of the exercise of discretion, hold that discretionary powers come into play because the norms of action cannot cover every detail or coincide fully with all aspects of the situation at hand. The general norms therefore leave 'a sphere of autonomy within which one's decisions are in some degree a matter of personal judgment and assessment' (Galligan 1986: 8). This vagueness then leaves the practitioner with 'an area left open by a surrounding belt of restrictions', as described by Dworkin (1978: 31). It is in order to cover 'the area left open' that the practitioner exercises discretion, Grimen and Molander (2008: 181) explain (cf. Molander and Grimen 2010: 171). In terms of *applied knowledge*, it follows that the exercise of discretion is 'an evaluating enterprise under the conditions of vagueness' (Grimen and Molander 2008: 182). Consequently, all professional activity is fallible and characterised by a certain degree of indeterminacy. In fact, the indeterminacy is essential to the mere existence of professions, and Grimen and Molander state:

> Without decision-making, in situations with a certain degree of indeterminacy – and the exercise of discretion, in the execution of tasks – there would hardly be any basis for a profession to lay claim to the legitimate control over certain work tasks. In the absence of indeterminacy, the tasks could be carried out more or less mechanically. It would then make no difference really who carried them out.
>
> *(2008: 179; author's translation from Norwegian)*

What causes the indeterminacy is that the norms of action, due to their general nature, give only vague clues as to what is an acceptable solution to the problem at hand. Still, a licence to exercise professional discretion 'is not a license to do what one wants' (Molander 2016: 24). The 'surrounding belt of restrictions' indicate that the individual practitioner's judgements must obey certain standards: What does the interpreter's 'surrounding belt of restrictions' embody? What does the domain for the interpreter's exercise of discretion comprise?

3.2.2 *The interpreter's exercise of discretion*

The code of ethics represents a 'surrounding belt of restrictions' for the activity of interpreting. In line with those of other professions, the interpreter's code of ethics are general norms. This also goes for the core *principle of accuracy in rendition* and the accompanying *principle of impartiality*. The two principles in concert outline the specific profile of the interpreters' societal function and form the base of the code's remaining principles, such as the important principle of confidentiality. At the same time, the core principles differentiate the interpreters' responsibilities from those of the professionals that the interpreters serve in institutional encounters. As an additional set of 'rules of action', interpreters must rely on the units and structures established by the *linguistic conventions* of their two working languages (Skaaden 2013: 190). Here, linguistic convention is used in the Langackerian sense, referring to the inventory of a linguistic system as units that are being 'widely shared (and known to be shared) by members of the relevant speech community' (Langacker 1991: 156, 546). With its usage-based perspective, the term *convention* captures the phenomenon of language as a social occurrence without the limiting factor of the community's (or register's) status. Thus, convention embraces any linguistic register shared by a community of speakers according to a number of uniting factors, such as social or regional affiliations, age, class, gender, religion or profession. Because linguistic units depend on cues provided by the context to attain their precise meaning, in interpreting, further indeterminacy occurs due to the very substance that makes up the interpreter's work material, that is, situated spoken utterances.

The following Example 3.1 from a Norwegian courtroom sheds light on the indeterminacy of the work material and the nature of the interpreter's exercise of discretion. The example demonstrates that the domain that the interpreter must cover by exercise of discretion is indeed narrow yet is one designated by complexity.

The linguistic unit that illuminates the interpreter's exercise of discretion here is the witness' nickname, *Dada*, in line 3. This linguistic unit happens to coincide phonetically with a more frequent unit in the source language, Bosnian, Croatian or Serbian. In the source language, [da:da] also means 'yes, yes'. Such a coincidence is difficult for the interpreter to anticipate. At the same time, the highly frequent unit is a logical answer to the prosecutor's question 'Did you have a nickname?' The interpreter's first reaction to the witness' response in line 4, the translation 'ja, ja', meaning *yeah, yeah/naturally* in the target language Norwegian, is therefore a plausible choice. The interpreter's quick response and repair here give the observer a glimpse into the narrow, yet complex, domain within which interpreters must balance their judgements when they are to determine the most fitting rendition of a specific utterance. In essence, the example illustrates how the interpreter exercises discretion at the multifaceted interface between *cognition*, *convention* and *context*

Ethics and profession 155

> **EXAMPLE 3.1**
>
> 1. *Prosecutor*: Hadde du et kallenavn? – *Hadde du et kallenavn?* (did you have a nickname? — *did you have a nickname?*)
> 2. *Interpreter*: Jeste li Vi imali kakav nadimak? (did[-Polite] you[-Polite] have[-Polite] some kind of nickname?)
> 3. *Witness*: Dada.
> 4. *Interpreter* (to the court): Ja, ja (Yeah, yeah).
> 5. *Interpreter* (to the witness): Dada?
> 6. *Witness* (confirming): mhm.
> 7. *Interpreter* (to the court): Dada. Tolkens feil, *Dada* (Dada. Interpreter's mistake. *Dada*).
>
> *(Skaaden 2013: 152; cf. 2018a: 7)*

(Skaaden 2013: 214). Moreover, the instantiation illustrates that in their exercise of discretion interpreters must collaborate with the interlocutors on both sides to reach the most fitting solution. The interpreter's coordination is here made necessary by the indeterminate nature of the material handled by the interpreter, the spoken, situated utterance, and is part of the interpreter's domain for the exercise of discretion.

The fact that the 'matter' handled by the interpreter, the spoken utterance, is in itself characterised by indeterminacy is not specific to the activity of interpreting, however. For comparison, the symptoms managed by the medical profession and the evidence that the legal professionals must process are far from unambiguous. Hence, the indefinite nature of the units processed by the interpreter does not *per se* disqualify the activity of interpreting from the ranks of professions. Nor does the fact that interpreters must make their judgements spontaneously disqualify the activity from the category. In fact, Grimen (2009: 96) stresses the speed with which reasoning is carried out as a prominent characteristic of the exercise of discretion as such. The swift decisions made by surgeons exemplify this.

The exercise of discretion brings us to the question of who is in need of the interpreter's services in the institutional encounters of the public sector. In other words, who are the interpreter's clients? Examples from the Norwegian public sector are examined next, bringing to the fore the interpreters' specific position between two clients who are equally in need of the interpreter's services.

3.2.3 Who are the interpreter's clients?

In the interpreted encounter, the possibility for the parties to solve their mutual how-to problem – that is, to communicate verbally – rests on the interpreter's exercise of discretion for each utterance. The interpreters' exercise of discretion thereby affects both speaker and listener. In other words, the interpreter has *two* clients according to the criteria of professional activity listed in Table 3.1. The core meaning of the word *client* is 'dependent'. By definition, therefore, 'clients are dependent in the sense that they seek assistance from the professional in order to handle issues that are to them important' (Molander and Terum 2008: 19).[4] From the perspective of interpreting, the 'clients' on both sides of the table represent Parsons' aforementioned laymen. An objection to this observation may be that in institutional encounters, one of the interpreter's 'clients' is by definition a highly ranked professional herself/himself – often a practitioner of medicine or law. As far as the services offered by the interpreter go, however, even judges and doctors are laymen in that they do not possess the specialised skills of the interpreter (Skaaden 2013: 219; 2018a: 8).

In the public sector setting, the interpreter works within institutional discourse, that is, encounters where 'one person who represents an institution encounters another person seeking its services' (Agar 1985: 147). The information exchange in such encounters seeks to prevent the professionals from misusing the power instilled in them by their profession and thus infringing upon the individual's life in an unwarranted manner. Each professional's need to stay true to the institution's standards is mirrored in the classic structure of institutional encounters, that is, the phases of *diagnosis*, *directive* and *report* (ibid.: 156). The professional standards of both medicine and law, accordingly, stress the importance of *verbal communication* between professionals and their clients.

Talking to the clients, defendants, victims and witnesses is accordingly a necessity for legal professionals, as dialogue is one of their main tools due to the legal principle of immediacy – a principle that requires the court to hear the parties 'first hand' (Vogler 2014: 239). For the legal professions in general, a fundamental principle is equality of arms. As expressed in the European Convention of Human Rights, the principle states that 'everyone who is a party to [legal] proceedings shall have a reasonable opportunity of presenting his case to the court under conditions which do not place him at substantial disadvantage vis-à-vis his opponent' (Gooch and Williams 2007; Giambruno 2014; Toma 2018).[5] The Convention takes on the perspective of the adversaries and therefore focuses on their *right* to information and voice. Legally, rights and duties are two sides of the same coin, however.

The right and duty to receive and impart information are not restricted to the confines of the courtroom. They influence all communication between individuals and institutions through the professionals that represent them, as Agar's definition shows. For the police, the investigative interview is an important tool in obtaining 'a detailed and reliable account from the interviewee while remaining objective and impartial' (Kepinska Jakobsen *et al.* 2017: 427). With reference to the profession of medicine, Woloshin *et al.* (1995: 724) state that 'the conversation between doctor and patient is the heart of the practice of medicine'. Evidently, to be able to diagnose and treat their patients, the doctors need to talk to them (Gulbrandsen and Finset 2014: 14). Wadensjö (1998a: 51) states accordingly that 'Practitioners can hardly provide adequate health-care if they are unable to communicate (if they do

Ethics and profession 157

> **TEXTBOX 3.2** The duties pertaining to institutional communication are part of the legislation that regulates professional activities within both medicine and law in some countries, such as Norway and Sweden (Felberg and Skaaden 2012: 99–100).[6] To exemplify, the Courts Act regulating court procedures in Norway affirms the court's need to communicate, stating that 'if anyone who does not know Norwegian is to take part in the proceedings, an interpreter, whom the court has approved of or appointed, is to serve' (Courts Act 1915, §135; author's translation from Norwegian). Thus, the Courts Act has a wider perspective than the European Convention on Human Rights and EU directives, with the latter documents' focus on the defendant's rights.
>
> The medical professionals' obligation to inform, guide and hear their patients is stated in Norway's Patients' Rights Act (2001; §§3-1, 3-2). The Norwegian Public Administration Act from 1967 does not mention interpreting explicitly but states the professionals' duty to inform, guide and hear their clients. By annex to the Public Administration Act (§11e) in 2016, the use of children as interpreters is explicitly banned in Norway. In March 2019, Norwegian authorities sent out for hearing a general act on institutions and professionals' explicit duty to call upon an interpreter in cases of language barriers.

not understand their patients' problems correctly, and if they cannot make themselves adequately understood).'

The need for information exchange in institutional encounters relates to the professions' standards and ethics, as well as their clients' and patients' basic human right to information and voice (Skaaden 2018a: 8). When confronted with a language barrier, professionals of medicine and law are themselves in the role of speaker/listener dependent on the interpreter's specialised skills in their communication with their clients and patients. Consequently, interpreting in institutional encounters 'enables professionals and officials to inform, guide and hear the parties in the case of language barrier' (NOU 2014: 18; cf. Jahr et al. 2005: 28; author's translation from Norwegian). The definition mirrors the client's and the professional's equal need to communicate in institutional encounters.

After a brief look at the interpreters' double allegiance and professional status in the public sector, the remainder of this part of the book explores factors that contribute to the interpreters' professional status in the PSI setting.

3.2.4 The interpreter's double allegiance and status in the public service setting

Legal and medical professionals do not seem to associate interpreting with the quality of their own work or professional integrity, despite their need to communicate with clients and patients. Rather, in cases of language barriers, they ascribe the ownership of the problem of communication to the party speaking the

158 Hanne Skaaden

minority language. Typically, medical professionals explain their own reluctance to call upon a trained interpreter by stating that '"their" [i.e. the patients'] culture does not allow them to use interpreters', as documented by Felberg and Skaaden (2012: 100) in a focus group approach. The courts' unawareness of the interpreters' working conditions and failure to link interpreting quality to their own work mirror a similar attitude among legal professionals. A survey directed at courtroom interpreters in Norway (Jahr et al. 2005) shows legal professionals' reluctant attitude towards interpreting quality:

EXAMPLE 3.2

It is my impression that it is 'boring' when a court case has to be interpreted ... Therefore they often ask us to only interpret 'the most important parts', which is totally impossible, since the interpreter then has to decide what is important.

...

Often I wish I did not have to ask for a copy of a text that is handed out to everybody else in the courtroom, but not to the interpreter, even though it is expected that all test results in the distributed examination report, or all paragraphs, dates etc. ... are to be interpreted.

(State-authorized interpreter in Jahr et al. 2005: 37; author's translation)

Descriptions such as those in 3.2 indicate that legal professionals commonly associate the interpreter with the speaker of the minority language and not with their own need for communication. The court's reported habit to seat the interpreter next to the defendant mirrors the same tendency (Jahr et al. 2005: 37).

There is no reason to assume that the Norwegian courts represent an exception. In fact, reports from courtrooms around the world indicate that the courts pay little attention to interpreting quality and the interpreters' work conditions. Case descriptions from the courts of Canada, Israel (Morris 2008), Italy (Garwood 2012), the US (Wallace 2015), and Belgium (Balogh and Salaets 2016; 2018) display the courts' reluctant attitude (see also Section 3.5.1). Moreover, observations that medical professionals accept working with untrained interpreters or even people who lack the most basic interpreting skills indicate that professionals fail to see the impact of interpreting on the quality of their own work. Early studies from Vienna hospitals document how medical professionals allow family members and even children to serve as interpreters (Pöchhacker 1997; Pöchhacker and Kadrić 1999). Studies from around the world have since documented that medical professionals allow laypeople to act as interpreters (Meyer 2001; Meyer et al. 2003; Angelelli 2004; Kale 2006; Merlini 2009; and studies referred to in Hale 2007 and Tipton and Furmanek 2016). Some studies even emphasise that

> **TEXTBOX 3.3** Despite the court's own need for interpreting, a biased image of the courtroom interpreter has come to the fore in the Norwegian media. A court case reported on in the newspaper *VG* (2002) serves to illustrate. In a high-profile triple murder case, the 'Orderud case', everyone involved spoke Norwegian except for an expert witness, the British forensic psychologist Gisli Guðjónsson. When, due to a misunderstanding, an English interpreter did not arrive, the lawyers first tried to take care of the interpreting themselves. The prosecution and defence could not agree on proper translations, however. The court then installed Natalia, a woman working in the court's cafeteria, in the interpreter function. The *ad hoc* interpreter reveals to the journalist that she is not a native speaker of either Norwegian or English and has never worked as an interpreter before. Her immigrant background appears to be the qualification for her assignment to the interpreter function.
>
> *(VG 2002)*

the doctors are 'happy to make do' with this kind of communication (Meyer *et al.* 2003: 75).

The tendency to associate the interpreter with the speaker of the minority language appears widespread in the medical domain and beyond. A discussion between four interpreter students in Example 3.3 sheds light on the possible consequences of the reluctance regarding interpreting quality displayed in the studies just mentioned. The students who already practise as interpreters draw on their own experiences from the public sector when they, as part of a university-level course, engage in synchronous chat discussions on professional integrity. The topic under discussion in Example 3.3 is the interpreters' work conditions in institutional encounters and the danger of burnout. Interestingly, when asked to name factors that may drain the interpreters' energy and even lead to burnout, the students first mention their professional clients' tendency to regard the interpreter as 'the minority speaker's representative'. The attitude comes to the fore when the professionals in charge of institutional encounters address their own client and the interpreter jointly, 'even using the pronoun '"dere"', that is, the plural form of 'you' in Norwegian, as noted by the student in posting 2.

The strong association between the interpreter and the speaker of the minority language observed in posting 2 is a recurrent problem mentioned by the interpreter students and practitioners. The 'scepticism' sensed towards the interpreter described in posting 5 similarly indicates the identification of the interpreter with the 'other', the speaker of the minority language. Posting 6, however, comments on incidents that have been reported in the Norwegian media of 'interpreters' under investigation for sitting the theoretical driving test on behalf of candidates (Riaz 2004). Such incidents bear witness to the fact that the professional in charge of an institutional encounter, here the examiner for the theoretical driver's test, is as much in need of

> **EXAMPLE 3.3**[7]
>
> 1. *Facilitator*: 18:24. If one of the speakers signals his or her distrust towards the interpreter, e.g., because of ethnicity. How may this drain the interpreter's energy? Any examples?
> 2. *mSora1*: 18:25. One thing [that] I have noticed [that] is that some people regard the interpreter as the client's representative. They even use the word 'dere' [i.e. 'you – plural'; the two of you about the interpreter and client].
> 3. *fSora1*: 18:26. Right, I have experienced that too, several times. In particular, at the ODE [Official Driving Examination].
> 4. *mPers1*: 18:27. What happened at the ODE?
> 5. *fSora1*: 18:28. That the examiner was very sceptical, and seemed suspicious. It's something that is really annoying, and you can't help but think about it.
> 6. *fPers2*: 18:30. I have heard that some interpreters have misused their position at the ODE [referring to cases where the interpreter has been accused of doing the theoretical drivers' test on behalf of the candidate].
>
> *(Skaaden and Wattne 2009: 83–84)*

the interpreter's services as the speaker of the minority language. Evidently, assigning the 'helper' image to the interpreter may ultimately threaten the professional party's integrity, as the driver's test cases elucidate.

The opinion that the interpreter is the 'helper' of the party who speaks the minority language, is not limited to the professionals in charge of legal and medical encounters. The perspective appears even in the research literature on interpreting. For instance, Tipton and Furmanek (2016) describe interpreters as serving 'when *patients* need an interpreter' (ibid.: 113; emphasis added, cf. ibid.: 35; 115). Similarly, definitions of community interpreting often delineate the interpreters' work from this vantage point. As exemplified here by Venuti (2000: 500, emphasis added): 'the oral, two-way, translating *done for refugees and immigrants* who must deal with the social agencies and institutions of the host country'. When contrasted with the above delineation, which emphasises that interpreting in institutional encounters *enables professionals and officials to inform, guide and hear the parties in the case of language barriers* (Jahr et al. 2005: 28), it becomes clear that placing the focus solely on the non-professional party represents a bias. In fact, it can be claimed that the quality of the interpreters' performance is of particular importance to the professional party. The claim is based on the professionals' duty to communicate with their clients or patients that follows from both legal–institutional and professional standards (Felberg and Skaaden 2012: 108; cf. Skaaden 2013: 192; 2018a: 9). Yet, the association of the interpreter with the speaker of the minority language appears to be quite common among professionals who rely on interpreting to fulfil their own tasks and duties in institutional encounters.

Deliberations over the 'role' of the interpreter reveal that the field is torn over the value of its core ethics – the principles of accuracy and impartiality. A closer look at the controversy, next, shows that the positions taken on the core ethics represent different views on the extension of the domain over which the interpreter should exercise discretion or the interpreter's area of expertise.

3.3 How extensive is the domain for the interpreter's exercise of discretion?

The previous sections established the interpreter's double allegiance, that is, the interpreter is equally important to the clients on both sides – both speaker and listener, both doctor and patient or both judge and witness. How do we delineate the extension of the domain within which the interpreter exercises discretion? How extensive should this domain be? In other words, for which areas of expertise should the clients trust the interpreter to take on responsibility? In approaching these essentially ethical questions, this section first examines some of the metaphors used and the positions taken in determining the extension of the interpreter's area of expertise and subsequently looks into the dual meaning of the concept 'role'.

The discourse on interpreter ethics often appears to discuss 'role', but in fact it comprises several issues and layers. On one level, the value of the code of ethics and its core principles of accuracy and impartiality is under debate, resulting in at least five alternative role identities, as discussed by Hale (2008: 102). On another level, the controversy reveals a rift between the interpreters' three main arenas of performance, the community, the courtroom and the conference setting. This mirrors an internal conflict within the ranks of an emerging profession, as pointed out by Mikkelson (1996: 126). (See also Textbox 3.4.) Sometimes portrayed as a difference between the medical and legal settings (e.g. Tipton and Furmanek 2016), the division harbours under its surface an attitudinal cleft that pertains to the image of the interpreter as the 'helper' of the party who speaks the minority language. Finally, ambiguities associated with the concept of 'role' itself add to the controversy (Skaaden 2018a: 7).

3.3.1 A 'mediated approach' vs a 'directly interpreted approach'

Metaphors frequently used in descriptions of the interpreter's 'role' are *conduit* and *machine*, on one hand and *helper* and *advocate*, on the other. The metaphors often play the role of red herring in the debate on ethics where the first pair serves to signify critique of the principle of *accuracy* in rendition. The second pair serves to oppose the principle of the interpreter's *impartiality* towards the communicating parties. Roy (1993 [2002]: 349), with reference to sign-language interpreting, observes that metaphors depicting the interpreter as 'invisible' or 'machine' were originally used to create distance from an image of the interpreter as a deaf person's 'helper'. Referring to Roy, Llewellyn-Jones and Lee (2014: 26) describe the machine metaphor as 'one of the first steps in the moves to professionalise the field of signed–spoken language interpreting' with the intent 'to counter the notion that deaf people, by definition, needed "help"'. Interestingly, the metaphors portraying the interpreter as 'machine' and 'invisible' later appear as arguments against the code of ethics' core principles. When used to argue *for* expanding the interpreter's role into 'cultural mediator', the metaphors then serve as a rhetoric tool in construing *agency* in terms of *advocacy*. Thus, in effect, a return to the *helper* image of the interpreter.

With the explicit aim of demonstrating that the image of the 'invisible' interpreter is a myth, Angelelli (2004: 2) argues in favour of extending the interpreter's role to cultural mediation based on her observations in a US hospital. In her proposed *mediated approach*, the interpreter abandons the core principles of accuracy and impartiality and gets involved in deciding on what to render and what to omit or add (ibid.: 75–77). In order to demonstrate the interpreter's 'visibility' and 'agency', Angelelli adopts images of the interpreter as 'detective' (ibid.: 129), 'miner' (ibid.: 132) and 'multi-purpose bridge' (ibid.: 130). An example from Angelelli's (2004: 98) book *Medical Interpreting and Cross-Cultural Communication* illustrates the impact that a 'visible' interpreter engaged in mediation may have on the communication between doctor and patient, as shown in Example 3.4.

When responding 'Okay' in line 17, the doctor does not know that the patient never answered the question in line 1, or that the patient probably never grasped the question in the first place. Medical professionals stress the importance of successful communication between doctor and patient for the practice of medicine, as seen above. Understanding successful communication as 'expanding common knowledge' and 'managing misunderstandings' (Scollon and Scollon 2001: 61, 134), we notice that the 'visible' interpreter in Example 3.4 does not promote communication between doctor and patient. Rather, the interpreter here expands the distance between the interlocutors, as Angelelli (ibid.: 138) herself notes. The fact that the interpreters in Angelelli's study lack training (ibid.: 130) weakens the claims in favour of the mediated approach. The observed practitioners' lack of interpreting skills and bilingual resources may cause these interpreters' need for extra 'mining' or mediation. Discussing the above example from Angelelli and examples from courtroom interpreting, Hale (2008: 111) illustrates how the interpreter's attempt to 'help' often backfires. More often than not, rather than facilitating communication the 'helping' interpreter, as shown here, gets in the way, Hale (2008: 106) observes.

Analysing different delineations of the interpreter's role, Hale (2007: 42–43) identifies two opposing poles in the debate on 'role', that is, the *mediated approach* and the *directly interpreted approach*, respectively. Between the poles Hale (2008: 102) isolates five different demarcations: (1) 'advocate for the powerless'; (2) 'advocate of the powerful'; (3) 'gatekeeper'; (4) 'filter'; and (5) 'faithful renderer of the original utterances'. Only the final position of 'faithful renderer' coincides with the ethical code's core principles in that it limits the interpreter's agency to rendering and coordinating others' talk, that is the directly interpreted approach. The remaining positions to some degree align with the mediated approach in that they involve mediation in a conciliatory form.

EXAMPLE 3.4

1. *Doctor*: On a scale from one to ten, how would she rate her pain?
2. *Interpreter*: A ver, Señora Rita, en una escala de uno a diez ¿qué número le pondría a su dolor? Por ejemplo, si el uno es que está para irse a bailar y no tiene nada y el diez es que se está muriendo, dónde estaría el dolor ... (Let's see, Mrs. Rita, on a scale from one to ten, what number would you assign to your pain? For example, if one is a pain that would allow you to go dancing, you almost don't feel anything and ten is so painful that you are dying from that pain ...)
3. *Patient*: ¿Cómo dice? (What did you say?)
4. *Interpreter*: ¿Qué ... ¿qué número le dariá a su dolor? (What ... what number would you give to your pain?)
5. *Patient*: Pos, ... a mí me duele mucho. (Well, ... it hurts a lot.)
6. *Interpreter*: ¿Cuánto es mucho, señora? ¿Mucho que se está muriendo del dolor? (How much is lot, Ma'am? Does a lot mean you are dying from the pain?)
7. *Patient*: Pos ... no., muriendo no, pero ... (Well, ... no ... not dying ... but ...)
8. *Interpreter*: ¿Qué cosas puede hacer con el dolor? (Which things can you do when you are in pain?)
9. *Patient*: Pos no sé ... cuando me duele mucho, me siento (Well, I don't know ... when it is very hard, I sit down.)
10. *Interpreter*: Pero ¿puede cocinar con el dolor? (But can you cook when you are in pain?)
11. *Patient*: A veces me pega fuerte y no. (Sometimes it is very hard and I can't.)
12. *Interpreter*: Y, esas veces, ¿siente como que se va a morir o no tanto? (And at times, does it feel like you are going to die or it is not so hard?)
13. *Patient*: No, morir no, no más pega fuerte. (No, not like I'm going to die, it's just hitting me hard.)
14. *Interpreter*: ¿Le ponemos un ocho o un nueve? (Do we give it an eight or a nine?)
15. *Patient*: Pos yo no sé, pos sí ... (I don't know, yes ...)
16. *Interpreter*: When it is most painful it would be close to an eight, doctor.
17. *Doctor*: Okay.

(Angelelli 2004: 98)

In opposition to mediation in the conciliatory sense, Hale (2007: 42–43) argues in favour of the directly interpreted approach and describes the difference between the two approaches in the following way:

> Whereas under the mediated approach the interpreter is involved in deciding on the content of the utterances (i.e. what to interpret and what to omit), in the direct approach the interpreter is involved in deciding how to render most accurately what the other two parties themselves have chosen to communicate to each other.
>
> *(Hale 2007: 42–43)*

The direct approach does not imply that the interpreter is in any way 'invisible', Hale (ibid.: 42) explains. Rather, in the direct approach the interpreter needs to be 'fully involved in the complex interpreting process' in order to render the utterance just heard. The direct approach, therefore, does not mean that the interpreters 'must act like mindless machines' Hale (2008:119) emphasises; '[i]t means attempting to be as accurate as possible within human limitations'.

3.3.2 What are 'culture' and 'cultural mediation'?

According to Angelelli (2004: 99), what makes it necessary for the interpreter to act as mediator in the sense illustrated in Example 3.4 are the *cultural* differences between doctor and patient. The line of argumentation hinges on the complexity of 'culture' as such. A closer look at the concepts of 'culture' and 'mediation' sheds light on some effects of interpreters' using their agency in terms of advocacy. The deconstruction of 'cultural mediation' shows that the approach has repercussions not only for the professional integrity of interpreters but also for the high-status professionals they serve (Felberg and Skaaden 2012; Skaaden 2013: 180).

The dual meaning of the concept of *mediation* confuses the image of the interpreter's role, Pöchhacker (2008: 24) observes, and draws attention to the meanings of the concepts *mediator* or *mediation* in the German, English and Italian languages. In one sense, a mediator may act as a *contractor* or *arbitrator* in terms of advocacy, while in another sense a mediator simply serves as an *intermediary* in communication. The extended meaning allows for 'the professional function of cross-cultural mediation (in the contractual, conciliatory sense)' (ibid.: 24), while 'mediation' in the restricted sense produces the 'function of enabling intercultural communication by relaying and coordinating other's talk', Pöchhacker states (ibid.: 23). Identifying this conceptual tripwire in the delineation of the interpreter's domain of expertise, Pöchhacker does not analyse the first part of the metaphor *cultural mediator*.

Culture is a fuzzy concept that also requires deconstruction, however. Authors in the fields of anthropology, intercultural communication, linguistics and interpreting point out that 'culture' is a concept that raises more questions than it answers (e.g. Langacker 1994; Scollon and Scollon 2001; Wikan 2002; Piller 2011; Felberg and Skaaden 2012; Nilsen *et al.* 2017). First, cultural differences do not follow the borders of states or nations but rather the dividing lines of a range of other factors, such as *class, gender, generation, profession* and *religion* (Scollon and Scollon 2001: 3). Second, the phenomenon's nestedness makes culture unsuitable for capturing aspects of importance in the communication between individuals (ibid.: 138). Much in line with Scollon and Scollon's point, the anthropologist Unni Wikan (2002: 83) accentuates that 'cultures do not meet, people do'. She draws attention to the difficulties with defining culture and its boundaries, as follows.

> What would it mean if we said that there must be agreement in a population on knowledge and values for a culture to count as such? The question would logically be: Among how many people? A thousand? A hundred? Ten? The question is unanswerable.
>
> *(ibid.: 80)*

With reference to ongoing debates within anthropology, Wikan holds that instead of fostering interpersonal understanding, '"culture" has become a tool, or weapon, for pursuing particular interests and building barriers between people' (ibid.: 81–82). Correspondingly, the linguist Ingrid Piller describes culture as 'an ideological construct called into play by social actors to produce and reproduce social categories and boundaries' (2011: 16). One reason for this state of affairs, according to Piller (ibid.: 32), is that intercultural studies have remained within the structuralist paradigm of the 1960s and their cultural categorisation at the level of nations or states, while the field of linguistics has moved on from this paradigm. Her critical approach to 'culture' illuminates the concept's tendency to create stereotypes. *Stereotyping*, according to Scollon and Scollon, is 'the process by which all members of a group are asserted to have the characteristics attributed to the whole group' (2001: 168). Stereotypes are often manifested through *othering*, that is, the construction of dualisms through statements that underscore the 'difference and division between *us* and *them*' (Maccallum 2002: 87–88). Used as an explanatory tool for challenges experienced in actual encounters between individuals, 'culture' may readily contribute to 'othering', Felberg and Skaaden argue (2012: 97). The term *othering* originates from the philosopher Emmanuel Lévinas' discussions on the relations between Self and Other and pertains to the reduction of '"your neighbor" into "a categorically abstract otherness"' (Finkielkraut 1997 [1984]: xiv–xv). The association of the interpreter with the speaker of the minority language through the plural 'you' (*dere*) in Example 3.3 illustrates such constructions of 'the other'. Felberg and Skaaden (2012) show that in various ways medical personnel ascribe problems in communication with minority patients to 'their' culture, even when other explanations – such as the lack of linguistic skills – may apply to the situation. Similarly, Nilsen *et al.* (2017) document *othering* in the discourse practices of teacher educators' talk about the 'cultural diversity' of minority students in that they negatively ascribe 'culture' as a feature of 'them'. As a result, minorities are 'excluded from the large "we"' (ibid.: 41) through discourse practices 'in which the "ordinary" represents us and "unordinary" represents them via implicit or explicit discursively constructed contrasts' (ibid.: 44). Nilsen *et al.* argue that teacher educators have special responsibility in their awareness of othering (2017: 48). The same could be held for educators and researchers of interpreting.

Apparently, culture is a dynamic phenomenon. The aspects just mentioned may all negatively influence the clients on both sides of the interpreter. An obvious danger if an interpreter acts as a *cultural mediator* relates to the manifestation of stereotypes. Wadensjö (1998b: 51–52) warns that the individual interpreter's focus on 'how things usually are' may 'block the interpreter's recognition of the situation's uniqueness'. Still, interpreters are in practice often met with expectations from clients on both sides of the table to perform services that not only violate their code of ethics, but also exceed their area of expertise by far. The trend comes to the fore when interpreting students describe their clients' expectations in a chat discussion in Example 3.5. The four students, whose first languages are Arabic, Sorani Kurd and Bosnian, Croatian or Serbian, communicate in Norwegian, their second language (Skaaden 2013: 223). The chat log is rendered here in English, and each posting indicates student, time and order of posting.

EXAMPLE 3.5

1. *Facilitator*: 18:09. In which situations might it be that the interpreter feels pressured to act on behalf of the parties? Examples?
2. *Student 1*: 18:11. Interpreters who interpret for the driving test and help the candidate for money.
3. *Student 2*: 18:11. I have experienced being asked by the police after the interrogation whether I thought that the suspect was telling the truth.
4. *Student 3*: 18:13. I was asked by the social services whether I thought the client was telling the truth.
5. *Student 4*: 18:15. I have also experienced people from my own hometown, and even from my home country, expecting me to speak on their behalf.

As illustrated, the interlocutors on both sides of the table may have expectations that go far beyond the interpreter's area of expertise, such as 'help' the candidate pass the driver's test, differentiate truth from lies or speak on behalf of a whole country. With their *double allegiance*, the interpreters face an impossible task in serving as 'cultural advocate', as the parties' interests often diverge. Moreover, the nested nature of culture makes the interpreter's mediation difficult. On one hand, interpreters by definition lack full insight into the 'culture' that the professionals in charge share through *their* area of expertise. On the other hand, interpreters may lack in-depth knowledge of recent developments in 'their' country, as well as access to all subcultures in the country – sometimes countries – where their working languages are spoken.

Finally, interpreters' cultural knowledge typically varies, simply because they are individuals with different experiences and opinions. The Example 3.6 illustrates this point when a group of interpreting students discuss the concept of *mahram* and whether Muslim women can receive the services of male doctors and interpreters. The students, both women (f) and men (m), who take part in the online discussion represent the working languages Persian, Sorani Kurd, Urdu, French, Vietnamese and Mandarin. Hence, they have background experiences from Iran, Iraq, Pakistan, China (Mandarin), Vietnam and Africa (French). A student had initiated the topic 'the interpreter's gender' earlier in the chat session. The student, who here reappears in posting 6 (mSorani3), had been rejected for an assignment because he was a man and felt the rejection was unjust. When we enter the discussion, it has taken a topical turn toward the gender of doctors before moving on to the Muslim concept *mahram* (Example 3.6).

EXAMPLE 3.6

1. *mSorani1*: 20:28. It's not only Muslims who wish to have a female doctor; there are many NORWEGIAN women who want a female doctor.
2. *fUrdu1*: 20:29. A Muslim woman is reluctant to shake hands because it is forbidden to have body contact with men other than those closest to them, something which is difficult to understand for Norwegians.
3. *mPersian1*: 20:29. How many percent of doctors in all Muslim countries are women?
4. *mSorani1*: 20:31. There are very few women doctors in the Islamic countries.
5. *mSorani2:* 20:31. If you are really sick, you cannot wait to see a woman doctor.
6. *mSorani3*: 20:31. But it's not only doctors they refuse to see, it also concerns the use of male interpreters.
7. *mPersian1*: 20:33. According to Islam, a doctor is *mahram*.
8. *mVietnamese1*: 20:34. What is *mahram*?
9. *fUrdu1*: 20:35. A male doctor cannot be *mahram*, can he?
10. *mPersian2*: 20:36. If what mPers1 says is true, then it is not such a big deal whether the doctor is male or female.
11. *fMandarin1*: 20:37. What does the concept *mahram* mean?
12. *mSorani1*: 20:40. *Mahram*? Many different people can be *mahram* to a woman, but they feel ashamed to talk about certain things. Hence, it has to do with shame.
13. *mFrench1*: 20:41. Hey, you really have to explain *mahram*!!!!
14. *fUrdu1*: 20:41. A woman's brother, father, husband and son are *mahram*.
15. *mPersian1*: 20:41. Plus doctor.
16. *mSorani1*: 20:42. Agree with mPers1.

(Felberg and Skaaden 2012: 106)

With backgrounds from Iran, Iraq and Pakistan, the main participants in this chat exchange originate from societies identified by Norwegians as part of the 'Muslim cultural sphere'. Yet, they do not ascribe the same meaning to the 'cultural' concept *mahram*. The exchange in Example 3.6 mirrors the linguist Ronald Langacker's (1994) description of the interplay between language, cognition and culture. While language and culture are partly overlapping social or conventionalised phenomena, Langacker (in defence of 'cognitive linguistics') emphasises that we have no guarantee that the representations of a convention are identical for individual members of that community:

> [L]anguage and meaning are not exclusively (or even primarily) psychological phenomena – they do not reside in individual minds, but have a distributed representation, emerging in context and being continually renegotiated in the social interaction of actual speech. The same can be argued for culture. Now I would certainly not claim that all aspects of language and culture are fully represented in individual minds, nor that any single individual has complete knowledge of a language or a culture in all its vast, detailed complexity. At the same time, I think it is simply wrong (if not incoherent) to deny that individual minds are the primary locus of linguistic and cultural knowledge. To put it bluntly, empty heads would not have any basis for talking or engaging in sociocultural interaction …
>
> *(Langacker 1994: 26)*

Langacker goes on to emphasise that due to the dynamic nature of both language and culture 'the strongest kind of dependency of language on culture is the fact that language is itself a cultural entity, at least to the extent that linguistic structures are conventional and acquired through social interaction' (ibid.: 31). An example from the psychiatric evaluation of the defendant after the aforementioned 2011 terrorist attacks in Norway sheds further light on the dynamic interrelationship between the individual's cognition, community or culture and its conventionalised language (Felberg and Skaaden 2012: 105). In their first assessment of the terrorist, two of Norway's leading forensic psychiatrists deemed the defendant psychotic based on his use of certain concepts that to them appeared to be *neologisms*, that is, words coined by an individual but not shared by society. However, had the renowned psychiatrists Googled the novel terms, they would have found them to be conventionalised linguistic units in certain communities on the internet (Giæver 2011: 12–15).

In summary, the examples considered shed light on some unfortunate aspects of interpreters acting out their agency in the extended function of cultural mediators or advocates. First, the interpreter, an individual, will necessarily lack an overview of all 'cultures' embraced by the numerous communities of his working languages – and particularly the cultures of the different professions that the interpreter must serve while lacking full insight into their expertise. Second, instances of 'mediation' where the interpreter is 'sitting the driver's test on behalf of the candidate' highlight an unfortunate effect of interpreters enacting their agency. Due to the double allegiance inherent in their professional function, interpreters serving as 'advocate' for one party may soon harm the interests of the other, as the Examples 3.3–3.5 show. Such examples bring to the fore the importance of keeping the interpreter's 'agency' separate from that of 'advocacy', an aspect addressed next.

3.3.3 Role: participant status and occupational function

Interpreters' professional ethics are recurrently discussed under the heading of 'role' (Gentile 1997; Wadensjö 1998a; Hale 2007; 2008; Pöchhacker 2008; Rudvin 2009; Llewellyn-Jones and Lee 2014; Tipton and Furmanek 2016). In terms of the model of professionalisation presented above, the dispute over 'role', as argued elsewhere (Skaaden 2016; 2018ab), concerns the question of *how extensive the domain within which the interpreter exercises discretion should be*. A closer look at the concept of role brings further clarification to the controversy over the interpreter's professional profile. 'Role' is commonly associated with the works of the sociologist Erving Goffman (1974; 1981) and his analyses of how we organise our experiences and present our *self* in talk. In his discussions on role Goffman (1974: 128–129) explicitly distinguishes between role as 'an equivalent to specialized capacity or function' – an 'occupational role' – and role in the sense of a 'part', as in a play (ibid.: 129). The latter meaning is an abstraction of the 'parts' that may represent a speaker's/hearer's footing *within* the micro-ecology of the conversation in terms of *participation status*. Interestingly, in defining participation status (in talk), Goffman states that 'a special participation status [is] that of the interpreter who can (and only can) relay messages between participants who would otherwise be cut off from each other' (ibid.: 224).

The meaning of role as in participant status and its importance to our understanding of the onsite interpreting of dialogues was brought to the fore by the seminal studies of Cecilia Wadensjö (1992; 1998a; 1998b). Her model of dialogue interpreting employs Goffman's concept in his sense of 'part' or 'participation status' to illustrate the interpreter's possible 'positions' within the dynamics of an interpreted dialogue. In line with Goffman's distinction, Wadensjö (1998a: 86) keeps participation status apart from the interpreter's societal function or occupational role.

Despite the fact that Goffman and Wadensjö both stress the difference between the two meanings of 'role', the important distinction tends to be lost in discussions on the interpreters' code of ethics. Gentile (1997: 111) accordingly observes that the *persona* of the interpreter rather than the *function* of interpreting more often receives attention in studies from the community compared to those from the conference setting. He emphasises the importance of keeping Goffman's two aspects of 'role' apart to avoid a fragmented understanding of *the interpreter's task* and to avoid losing sight of *the purpose of interpreting*. Some aspects in the practice of interpreting will necessarily differ with setting. To some extent, the tendency observed by Gentile depends on the physical placement in the community setting, where interpreters are often present at the table with the parties. Relationally, interpreters are therefore more exposed here than in the conference setting, where they are typically protected from direct contact because they sit in a separate booth. Another difference pertains to the possibility of controlling the quality of performance. Options for quality control are more limited in police interviews and doctor-patient consultations, which are ruled by confidentiality, than in the open settings of courtrooms and conference venues. Gentile (1997: 118) makes the valid point that, despite these variations, the core *activity* of interpreting is the same independent of arena.

Since the turn of the twenty-first century, interpreting as performed outside the conference and courtroom settings has developed as a branch of empirical study in its own right, and the hierarchy between the settings is becoming less prominent. Yet, in discussions on ethics or 'role', a split between settings remains, although the dichotomy now seems to be between legal and medical interpreting (e.g. Tipton and Furmanek 2016). The fact that a fragmentation remains raises the question of whether the division is based on ideological differences. Certainly, fragmentation does not serve the process of professionalisation, and Hale (2008: 99) makes the

---

TEXTBOX 3.4 A hierarchical division between the three main arenas where interpreters normally practise, the *community*, the *courtroom* and the *conference setting*, has historical roots. Mikkelson (1996: 125–126) notes that the term *community interpreting* was coined with the purpose of promoting the professionalisation of *courtroom interpreting*. She illustrates with a quote from an early textbook on *courtroom* interpreting:

> Community interpreting refers to any interpretation provided by *non-professional interpreters*. *Amateur interpreters* provide services in hospitals, public meetings, medical offices, stores, social service agencies, schools, churches, parent organizations, police departments, real estate offices, and a legion of other agencies both public and private. Their dedication and interest are to be commended, but often the standard for interpretation is set by *their linguistic limitations* rather than by the language needs of the client.
> (González, Vásquez and Mikkelson 1991: 29; emphasis added)

Interestingly, the only setting not mentioned in the above description is the courtroom, Mikkelson observes (1996: 126). She adds that the court interpreters' efforts to distance themselves from colleagues practising in other parts of institutional discourse replicates strategies that conference interpreters had used earlier in their struggle for professional recognition. Mikkelson concludes that in this sense, the battle within the interpreter profession compares to minority groups' fighting each other to gain a seat at the table (ibid.: 126).

important point that 'a multiplicity of conflicting roles leads to confusion among users of interpreting services and to insecurity among practicing interpreters'.

Obviously, interpreters are not 'invisible'. In onsite interpreting in particular, the practitioners must be aware of the 'space' they occupy within the micro-cosmos of the dialogue and be ready to apply strategies in order 'not to get in the way' of the interlocutors. Interpreters who are unaware of their specific position in the dialogue or take it upon themselves to act as advocate risk occupying unrestricted space in exercising their discretion. They thereby appear to be 'invincible' rather than 'invisible' (Skaaden 2018a: 11–12). Metzger (1999: 204) draws attention to the interpreter's interactional strategies when she determines that her critical exploration of the principle of *neutrality* 'has revealed that interpreters have the power to influence discourse'. What remains, she adds, is to examine 'the interpreter's ability to *not* influence interactive discourse'. The realisation necessitates 'more research regarding an interpreter's ability to limit or constrain their influences in interpreted encounters', Metzger concludes (ibid.: 204).

3.4 Interpreting as interaction

Wadensjö's model of *interpreting as interaction* promotes the exploration of the strategies interpreters may apply in order to 'avoid getting in the way' in the onsite interpreting of dialogues. In her seminal study of institutional dialogues interpreted between Russian and Swedish, Wadensjö (1992; 1998a; 1998b) demonstrates how the interpreter who works onsite and in both language directions is at the same time *rendering and coordinating* the interlocutors' talk (Wadensjö 1998a: 105). Wadensjö implements Goffman's concept of 'role' in the sense of 'part' to explore the interpreter's possible positioning in the interaction, and draws on the Russian scholar Mikhail Bakhtin's model of language as inherently *dialogic*. This allows Wadensjö to demonstrate how the interpreter does not 'mechanically' render text but also coordinates the interlocutors' talk in complex interaction that she labels 'a communicative *pas de trois*' (ibid.: 10).

Certain aspects of human interaction come to the fore, as if seen through a magnifying glass, when a dialogue is interpreted, Wadensjö observes (1998b: 154). In a model that depicts language as being in essence dialogic, any conversation involves an interplay between *talk as text* and *talk as activity* (Wadensjö 1998a: 21–23). Moreover, a dialogic view on human language sees the interlocutors' interactions with each other and with the context as 'resources in the meaning-making process' (Linell 2009: 17). The approach is opposed to a *monologic* understanding of language, which draws the individual's cognition to the foreground and pays less attention to the interaction between speaker and listener (ibid.: 40–41). The realisation that linguistic meaning is achieved through continuous negotiation between interlocutors in situated encounters has implications for our understanding of the interpreter's activity, as Wadensjö's model demonstrates. Wadensjö's model pertains to the micro-ecology of the interpreted dialogue, described by her as 'a monologising practice in a dialogically organized world' (2004: 105).

3.4.1 The concept of 'role' in Wadensjö's model

Wadensjö's model reveals the interplay between the interpreter's coordination and rendition of someone else's talk. The employment of Goffman's (1974; 1981) concept of role in talk enables Wadensjö (1998a: 245) to demonstrate how interpreters' constantly (re)position themselves in the roles of speaker/listener between the interlocutors. According to Wadensjö's model, in this positioning on the dialogue's 'stage', an interpreter may take on the roles of *animator/reporter, author/recapitulator* or *principal/responder*, respectively (ibid.: 87–92). In the default mode, the interpreter takes the position of *reporter* or *recapitulator*, thus repeating or 'mimicking' the speaker's utterance in the other language. However, from time to time, the interpreter will need to take on the position of *principal/responder*, that is, someone who takes on full responsibility for an utterance and its content. This is the role we carry as regular interlocutors when we act on our own behalf. For the interpreter, the principal position may serve to explicitly coordinate the participants' talk.

In dialogue interpreting, the interpreter's coordination can be both implicit and explicit and may, for instance, serve to coordinate the participants' turntaking (see Example 3.7), to clarify an ambiguity (see Example 3.8) or to correct a misunderstanding (see Example 3.9). Turntaking, which contributes to significant difference between interpreted and monolingual dialogues, is often smoothly coordinated without the interpreter's explicit instructions, but Wadensjö (1998a: 155) emphasises that interpreted dialogues involve multimodal interaction. An extract of one of her examples (the original includes several exchanges), here rendered as Example 3.7, illustrates multimodality with both talk and movement involved in the coordination.

Here, the police officer (Peter) addresses the interpreter (Ilona) directly as he hands her the passport and in a lowered voice (indicated by the °...°) directs his request at her instead of his interlocutor, an asylum seeker. The interpreter avoids taking over the 'lead role', however, as indicated by her implicit coordinating action, an immediate rendition of the police officer's utterance, while passing on the passport to the primary interlocutor, the asylum seeker (ibid.: 118).

In the onsite interpreting of dialogues, coordination is necessary to enable the interpreter to render the original utterance and manage the turntaking. At the same

---

EXAMPLE 3.7

Peter: °Kan du visa mig var?° [simultaneously handing the passport to the interpreter] (Can you show me where?)
Ilona: а вы можете показать где? [passing the passport to the applicant/interviewee] ([and] can you show where?)

(Wadensjö 1998a: 155)

time, the interpreter must avoid stepping into 'the main part' and risk getting in the way of the interlocutors' communication. In fact, an interpreter who fails to utter necessary coordinating comments may as a result end up 'getting in the way' of the communication (Skaaden 2013: 138). Example 3.8 illustrates this problem when the false friends, *profesor* and *professor*, in the source and target languages, Serbian and Norwegian, present the interpreter with a dilemma.

EXAMPLE 3.8

1. *Nurse*: Hva slags yrke har du? (What kind of profession do you have?)
2. *Interpreter*: Šta ste po zanimanju? (What are you [polite form] by profession?)
3. *Patient*: Radio sam kao profesor matematike. (I [have] worked as a professor of mathematics.)
4. *Interpreter*: Jeg har arbeidet som – sånn – professor i matematikk. (I have worked as – such – professor-[university level] of mathematics.)

(Skaaden 1999: 84)

The discourse marker *sånn* ('such') and pausing in line 4 reveal that the interpreter has detected a problem. In Serbian, 'profesor' is the term used for teachers both at university and high-school levels, while in Norwegian 'professor' is reserved for university-level teachers. Without asking the patient for clarification before delivering the rendition in the target language in line 4, the interpreter ends up with a misleading solution. By adding the discourse marker *sånn*, a signal of insecurity, the listener, a nurse, may be misled into thinking that the patient, an elderly man, is unclear about his own past.

As seen in Example 3.8, the *lack* of coordination may result in the interpreter 'getting in the way' of the interlocutors. A quick clarifying question, for instance, '*profesor fakulteta?*' ('teacher at university level?') directed at the speaker/patient would have solved the problem. At the same time, Example 3.8 displays a case of implicit coordination when the interpreter in line 2 renders the personal pronoun *du* (the unmarked informal-'you' in Norwegian) into the polite verbal form *ste* ('are you') in the target language Serbian. While unmarked in the source language Norwegian, an informal pronoun would have been marked, thus signalling impoliteness in an institutional encounter in the target language Serbian. Failure to coordinate the pronominal form would have added an indication of negative markedness not present in the original utterance.

The interpreter's choice of referents, for instance, in terms of pronoun choice, is one of the implicit coordinating strategies that helps keep track of 'who is who' in the interpreting of dialogues. In certain situations, explicit coordination is also necessary to clarify who is talking as 'principal', as in Example 3.9.

> **EXAMPLE 3.9**
>
> *Interpreter* (to the court): Dada. Tolkens feil, *Dada* (Dada. Interpreter's mistake. *Dada.*)
>
> (Skaaden 2013: 152)

The interpreter, referring to herself as 'the interpreter' here, illustrates the presentation of *professional self* instead of *personal self*. The effect is that the court is not getting confused as to the source of the necessary repair. In a handbook based on their experience with sign language interpreting, Llewellyn-Jones and Lee (2014: 32) fail to see the value of the interpreter's presentation of professional self as opposed to personal self and argue in favour of the 'interpreter' referring to herself/himself as the 'normal I'. Their point of reference is sign language interpreting, where interpreters work simultaneously and between the modalities of sign language and spoken languages. The difference in modalities may perhaps lead to different strategies. For the consecutive interpreting of dialogues between two spoken languages, I will maintain that using the personal self ('normal I') is not an efficient strategy. In this mode, a solution such as the one shown in Example 3.9, with the practitioner's reference to professional self as 'the interpreter', is essential to avoid confusing the listener.

The aim of coordination is 'to promote primary interlocutors' continued focused interaction', as Wadensjö (1998a: 274) puts it, so that the interlocutors can achieve an 'illusion of mutual and shared involvement in an activity in common and their (at some level) shared and mutual understanding'. At the discourse level, the interpreter must coordinate to be able to render the interlocutors' talk. In dialogue interpreting, it is important to keep the dynamics *within the dialogue* itself apart from the encounter's legal or societal function. The micro-level of interactive discourse falls within the realm of the interpreters' responsibility – their domain for the exercise of discretion. The macro-level relates to the primary participants' responsibilities and in particular those of the professional legally in charge of the institutional encounter. Because Wadensjö's model is often referred to and sometimes wrongfully taken into account regarding mediation in an extended sense, it is worth quoting her at some length at this point.

> In dialogue interpreting, the translating and coordinating aspects are simultaneously present, and the one does not exclude the other. As a matter of fact, these aspects condition each other. Seen like this, it is not an empirical question *whether* interpreters are translators or mediators – they cannot avoid being both. However, the coordinating and the translating functions are foregrounded at particular moments, sometimes supporting, and sometimes disturbing one another. The two aspects of interpreting – translation

Ethics and profession **175**

and coordination – are in practice inseparable, but it is possible and indeed fruitful theoretically to distinguish between them and use them as analytical concepts.

(Wadensjö 1998a: 106)

Due to the need for the interpreter's coordination, the structure of interpreted dialogues differs from the interactional patterns of dialogues between interlocutors who share the same language. The differences pertain, for instance, to turntaking, feedback and pronominal references, as the examples presented here briefly illustrate. Wadensjö's model provides tools for interpreters' *presentation of professional self* and their *positioning* within the interpreted encounter. The strategies of coordination and positioning within the ecology of the dialogue must be learnt, as interpreters do not interact in the dialogue in the capacity of their personal self or 'normal I'. The strategies for drawing the line between personal and professional self are part of the interpreter's domain for the exercise of discretion and belong in the curricula of interpreter education and on the agenda of future research – along with knowledge on functional coordinating and interpreting strategies in general.

3.4.2 The interactive interpreter: neither 'invisible' nor 'invincible'

The notion of the 'invisible' interpreter was originally linked to strategies used in the professionalisation process of sign language interpreters and their need to distance themselves from the image as the deaf person's 'helper'. The controversy comes full circle when the metaphor of the 'invisible' interpreter is used in attempts to rebut the code of ethics. Arguing for cultural mediation in terms of advocacy, Llewellyn-Jones and Lee (2014: 21), for instance, claim that the principle of impartiality, which they hold is particular to the interpreter profession, is 'inhibiting and de-skilling'. Impartiality is a characteristic that professional practices in general strive for, however. It even pertains to the function of defence attorneys, as illustrated in Textbox 3.1 above. Impartiality manifests the difference between professional and personal self. Typically, the professional self is difficult to represent when the interpreter has strong personal ties to one party, as follows from Example 3.10 where the daughter acts as 'interpreter'.

EXAMPLE 3.10

1. *Father:* Digli che è un imbecille! (Tell him he is an idiot!)
2. *Daughter* (to third party): My father won't accept your offer.

(Mason and Stewart 2001: 52)

What necessitates impartiality for all professionals is the fact that 'the nature of their work requires trust', Freidson (2001: 214) accentuates. He goes on to explain that the ethics of everyday life are not a sufficient guide for professionals because of 'the special circumstances surrounding their special practices' (ibid.: 215). The stance that the principle of impartiality is 'inhibiting' interpreters' professional practice appears to be a misconception that rests on the dual meanings of 'role' as participation status on the discourse level on one hand and occupational role or function on the societal or legal level on the other. As argued elsewhere (Skaaden 2018a: 11–12), an extended role where the interpreters' agency is enacted through advocacy leads to an 'invincible' interpreter since it ascribes unrestricted discretionary powers to the interpreter.

In a dialogic understanding of language, '[m]eanings are continuously established and re-established *between* people in actual social interaction' (Wadensjö 1998a: 24). Thus, meaning is co-constructed through the interlocutors' interactions. How does the directly interpreted approach as opposed to the mediating approach align with a dialogic understanding of language?

Logically, the interpreter's *exercise of discretionary power* must entail factors over which the interpreter has control. How the parties choose to express themselves through clothing, posture and appearance are aspects of the situation over which the interpreter has no control. Nor can the interpreter control the speaker's choice of linguistic registers or the choice to verbalise vulgarisms or express aggression and disrespect. Such expressions carry important information for the listener in a given situation, whether a therapeutic encounter, police interview or medical consultation. In institutional dialogues, therefore, it is important that the interpreter does not edit out such units or replace them with euphemisms, as seen in Example 3.10. In a study of practising interpreters in Norway, Felberg and Šarić (2017: 10–13) find that practising interpreters report difficulties in handling expressions of impoliteness and may develop various strategies to cope. In my own experience with topicalising these issues during training sessions, awareness of the importance of such expressions in institutional discourse may help students cope with aversions against rendering insults and vulgarisms, as may the awareness of the difference between acting according to *professional self* as opposed to the *personal self*.

Ultimately, due to the indefinite nature of their working material, the spoken utterances, interpreters can never control what the listener actually understands. A dialogue between a prosecutor and a witness in a Norwegian courtroom illustrates the interpreter's lack of control over what the listener may or may not understand, as follows in Example 3.11.

The witness here explicitly states that he does not understand the prosecutor's question (line 3). Because the interpreter's rendition (line 2) is adequate and in line with the working languages' conventions, one may only speculate over the reasons for the witness' response in line 3. His response to the prosecutor's reformulation (lines 5–7) indicates that the term 'ethnicity' causes the initial problem. The witness' response in line 7, *pravoslavac* ('Orthodox Christian'), refers to the faith of most Serbs. The concept's dual religious and ethnic connotations makes it a meaningful answer to a question about *national affiliation*. For the Norwegian courtroom, however, it may seem confusing that a witness answers questions about nationality

> **EXAMPLE 3.11**
>
> 1. *Prosecutor:* Hvilken etnisitet hadde du selv? (Which ethnicity did you belong to (lit. have) yourself?)
> 2. *Interpreter:* A kojeg ste vi etniciteta osobno? (And of which ethnicity are you, personally?)
> 3. *Witness:* — æ::: Nisam razumio pitanje. (— eh::: I did not understand the question.)
> 4. *Interpreter:* Jeg har ikke forstått spørsmålet (I have not understood the question.)
> 5. *Prosecutor:* Hvilken etnisitet har du; hvilken *nasjonalitet* regner du med å ha? (Which ethnicity do you belong to (lit. have); which *nationality* do you reckon you belong to (have)?)
> 6. *Interpreter:* Kojega ste vi etniciteta odnosno kojoj *nacionalnoj grupi* pripadate po svom nahođenju? (Of which ethnicity are you, respectively, to which *national group* do you belong according to yourself?)
> 7. *Witness:* Pravoslavac. (Christian Orthodox.)
> 8. *Interpreter:* Ortodoks. (Orthodox.)
> 9. *Witness:* Pravoslavac. (Christian Orthodox.)
> 10. *Interpreter:* Ortodoks. (Orthodox.)
>
> (Skaaden 2018a: 10)

with a religious category. Had the interpreter taken on the role of cultural advocate here and simply told the court 'Serb' instead of repeating the utterances that each of the parties chose to verbalise, the court might have 'saved time' in the short run. The strategy would have deprived the courtroom insight into the complexity of linguistic, ethnic and cultural categorisation, however. Here, the interpreter's directly interpreted approach allows the court to gain cultural insight.

The need for co-construction testifies to the fact that the interpreter exercises discretion, as seen in Example 3.11. The co-construction of meaning through negotiation does not free the interpreter of restrictions, however. According to Hale (2007: 42–43), the directly interpreted approach implies that the interpreter is involved in deciding how to render as accurately as humanly possible *what the other two parties themselves choose* to communicate to each other. Therefore, the interpreter's loyalty is bound to each utterance rather than to one of the speakers, Hale stresses (ibid.: 42). Obviously, engaging in this interactivity the interpreter is not invisible.

Proposals for an extended mediating approach often accuse a restrictive code of ethics in line with the direct interpreting approach of being 'prescriptive' (e.g. Angelelli 2004: 13; Llewellyn-Jones and Lee 2014: 21; Tipton and Furmanek 2016: 11). However, such claims are seldom followed by reflections on the ethical consequences of the mediating approach, Hale (2008: 101) observes. In a statement that harmonises with the exercise of discretion, as described above (Section 3.2), Hale goes on to make the valid point that:

> There is no escaping prescription as far as professional role or code of ethics is concerned. ... Whether the mandate is to be an advocate or to be a faithful renderer of the utterances, it is equally prescriptive. What is necessary, however, is to move away from prescriptions based merely on personal opinion and towards prescriptions based on consequences. It is also essential that interpreters will always need to resort to their discretion and better judgement to make the appropriate decisions for each situation, led by the general guidelines of the code of ethics
>
> *(ibid.: 101)*

Professional practitioners rely on their clients' trust. Because trust depends on the fulfilment of expectations, it follows that an extensively delineated domain for the interpreters' exercise of discretion will bewilder the clients. At this point, the mediating approach runs into problems. A 'flexible role' that varies with the context or setting and that is characterised by 'fluidity and dynamism of the (re-)positioning processes in intercultural and interlingual mediation' (Tipton and Furmanek 2016: 10) will make it difficult to obtain the clients' trust simply because they will not know what to expect. Consequently, 'an ill-defined, confusing role or an absence of a clear, prescribed role, leads to negative consequences', as Hale (2008: 101) puts it. Obviously, clients who do not know what to expect from an interpreter, will soon lose trust in the interpreter. Furthermore, with the assignment of extensive discretionary powers to the interpreters, their professional clients cannot uphold *their* duties and integrity. Subsequently, the rights and welfare of these professionals' clients and patients are threatened.

In drawing the boundaries of the interpreters' domain for the exercise of discretion, two aspects must be kept in mind, a legal-societal aspect and a linguistic-interactional aspect. On the one hand, the legal-societal aspect concerns the fact that the interpreter's occupational function always serves two clients, speaker and listener, who are equally entitled to the interpreter's specialised interpreting skills. From this vantage point, the need for *impartiality* is intrinsically linked to professional trust and could be claimed to be particularly strong for interpreters due to their double allegiance. On the other hand, the linguistic-interactional aspect, and how the interpreter handles it, determine whether the two parties are to succeed in their communication, that is, expand their common ground of knowledge and sort out misunderstandings. The interactional part of the latter aspect has to do with the nature of the interpreter's *working material*, that is, spoken utterances as they occur in actual encounters. Because linguistic units only obtain their precise meaning in each utterance or *instantiation of use* in the interplay between cognition, linguistic convention and context (Langacker 1987: 68), the interpreter's implicit and explicit *coordination* is necessary to promote the primary interlocutors' continued focus of interaction.

At the discourse level, interpreters must continuously position themselves in such a manner that they *do not get in the way* of the interlocutors' communication. In doing so, interpreters exercise discretion within a narrow but complex domain of spoken utterances as exchanged in a specific context (Skaaden 2013: 188–192; 2016: 59). In discussions on the meaning of interpreters' professional ethics, Chesterman (2001: 140) and Dean and Pollard (2013: 186) both make references to the medical profession's creed of 'doing no harm' that expresses the 'centrality of the consequences of one's work', as the latter authors put it. What does it mean to 'do no harm' for the interpreting profession? It would seem interpreters do least harm when they do not get in the way of the interlocutors so that the latter individuals can observe their duties and rights. To achieve this goal, the interpreter must remain impartial at the legal level by applying strategies of coordination at the discourse level, for instance, by paying attention to the difference between expressions of the personal and professional self.

3.4.3 The exercise of discretion and trust

We seek the services of professionals because we trust they will make better judgements in solving our problems than would laypeople, who by definition lack the virtues that professionals possess due to their specialised skills. The exercise of discretion is accordingly closely associated with the phenomenon of *trust*, as was pointed out in the introduction to this section of the book. Grimen (2008b; 2009) notes that like the exercise of discretion, trust is an abstract phenomenon that is rather difficult to capture. In his approach to the phenomenon, he uses a definition from political science as the point of departure, referring to Warren's statement that: 'trust involves a judgement, however tacit or habitual, to accept vulnerability to the potential ill will of others by granting them discretionary power over some good' (Warren 1999: 311). Grimen (2008b; 2009), who takes on a transactional perspective to the phenomenon of trust, adds that 'trust implies that the giver of trust [i.e. the person who trusts another person] leaves something in someone else's keeping in good faith' (Grimen 2008b: 198). Accordingly, the giver of trust 'always transfers *de facto* discretionary powers over this something to the other' [i.e. the trustee]' (ibid.: 198). Finally, leaving something with somebody 'in good faith' implies an expectation that the trustee will *take appropriate care of* it. The 'something' that the interlocutors as 'givers of trust' leave in good faith to the interpreters' discretionary power are their verbal utterances. What it means to 'take appropriate care of' in the case of interpreting is an issue we return to below, under the heading of *quality in interpreting* and *the organisational aspect* of professionalisation.

Differentiating between personal trust and professional trust, Grimen (2008b: 199, 207), moreover, states that the former type is emotionally founded and is based on individual beliefs, experiences and preferences. The latter type is impersonal and based on knowledge that is attested through licence and mandate, thus, granted only to certain practitioners on the matter in question (ibid.: 197ff.). Society's need to secure high-quality services through licence and mandate pertains to the issue of *virtue* and practitioners' *quality performance*. Licence and mandate are thus society's measures for authorising individuals to carry out a specific task according to certain standards. *Professional trust* in this manner bridges the performative and organisational aspects of professionalisation in that professions 'ask for the public's trust and in doing so, generate a set of legitimate expectations' (Eriksen 2015: 3). Consequently, *professional integrity* is 'a virtue concerned with both fidelity to practice and assurance to the public, connecting these features by emphasizing the role of evaluative judgment' (ibid.: 14–15).

The division between personal and professional trust makes it understandable why patients or clients allow family and friends to perform the interpreter's function. Family and friends are recipients of their personal trust. It is more of a conundrum that the established professions in charge of institutional encounters are willing to rely on the services of non-professional 'interpreters' who often lack the most basic skills necessary to perform the activity of interpreting. Relying on the non-qualified interpreting of minority patients' family or friends, doctors (and other professionals) puts the quality of their own professional performance and integrity at risk. This state of affairs (cf. Phelan, Part II in this volume) represents a paradox, given the fact that for the established professions, such as those of medicine and law, verbal communication with patients and clients is of primary importance in fulfilling their own professional responsibilities.

Trust and *professionalisation* are phenomena that shed light on the consequences of interpreters performing cultural mediation in the conciliatory sense. Proponents of the mediating approach emphasise that the interpreter has 'agency' and identify agency with the interpreter enacting 'co-power' or becoming a 'co-diagnostician' or 'advocate' (e.g., Tipton and Furmanek 2016: 129, 136). With regard to the interpreter's occupational function, Wadensjö (1998a: 281), in contrast, states that '[a]ny mediating person may be taken as inhibiting communicative contact between two individuals rather than promoting it, when they appoint themselves as the *primary participant* and *spokesperson for others*' (italics added). Correspondingly, Pöchhacker (2008: 9) emphasises that 'characterizing interpreting as mediation carries a considerable risk of ambiguity and misunderstanding and may play a role in the very practical difficulties that appear to hamper the professionalisation of interpreting in many countries'. Respectively, Hale (2008: 110) draws attention to the consequences that mediation may have not only for interpreters' professional development but also for institutional discourse as such, in that the interpreter may be 'interfering with the cross-examiner's professional communication strategies'.

Evidently, when the interpreter's discretionary powers expand, the discretionary powers of the professional in charge of the institutional discourse will diminish. How the doctor's professional integrity and ability to *exercise discretion* diminish with the augmentation of the interpreter's 'advocacy' came to the fore in Example 3.4, when the doctor was left out of the patient's description of her pain due to the interpreter's construal of own agency. Accordingly, mediation in the conciliatory sense does not only have implications for the *interpreter's* discretionary powers. Practitioners of medicine or law who accept this type of 'mediation' simultaneously accept that their own professional integrity is reduced (Skaaden 2013: 226–227). Therefore, the mediated approach raises the more far-reaching questions of diminishing the discretionary powers of the professional in charge of the institutional encounter and consequences thereof.

On one hand, a dialogic understanding of language discloses that the 'invisible' interpreter is a dysfunctional metaphor. On the other hand, expanding the interpreter's area of responsibility into 'advocacy' leaves us with an 'invincible' interpreter. An unfortunate consequence of assigning such power to the interpreter would be that the patients and clients are deprived of access to the expertise of the professional they seek, whether in medicine or law. Obviously, such a development will have repercussions not only in terms of the interpreters' professional function but will also infringe on the professional integrity of those served by the interpreter in institutional discourse. The realisation that interpreting quality affects the professional party as well as the client or patient has implications for drawing the boundaries of the interpreters' domain for the exercise of discretion. The direct interpreting approach, which defines the domain narrowly, leaves it to the professionals in charge of the institutional encounter to exercise discretion within their own domain of expertise, be it medicine or law.

Professional trust rests on the integrity of the professionals in performing the specific activity for which they have achieved licence and mandate. That is to say, their clients' trust depends on the quality of the services delivered. In this sense, professional ethics represent the guarantee that clients 'get what they expect'. If the interpreter's task is not clearly defined or is delineated too evasively, the clients' expectations will be unclear and their trust equally hard to gain. This speaks in favour of a narrowly defined domain for the interpreter's exercise of discretion.

3.5 Ethics, trust and the organisational aspect of professions

Professionals exercise discretion in problem-solving within their assigned area of expertise. As all professionals engage in fallible activity, codes of ethics are standards that serve as guidelines for problem-solving in actual situations. Moreover, because the clients are unable to control the quality of the specialised services that professionals provide, society needs ways of granting professional trust through licence and mandate. The *organisational aspect* of professionalisation pertains to the existence of licence and mandate that guarantees the practitioners' ability to produce quality services within their specific area of expertise. For the established professions, licence and mandate appear in the form of several years of education that lead to accreditation (Smeby 2008). Traditionally, in this, organised education has three major goals, as follows:

- the students' development of knowledge and skills;
- the students' development of professional identity and societal status;
- the monopolisation of a certain function, in that it can no longer be handled by laypeople.

Education is an essential component in the professionalisation of any societal function, and its length has a documented impact on the profession's status (ibid.: 89). The ultimate goal of professionalisation is *monopolisation* that serves to protect the practitioners' livelihood in that only those with education are licensed to take on the specific function. Monopolisation appears a graded phenomenon, however. For the classic profession of medicine, monopoly is strong in most countries. In case of shortages, a country like Norway will recruit qualified medical professionals from abroad. In comparison, the important societal function of teachers, for example, is not yet fully monopolised in Norway. Until the educational system produces enough teachers, the function is to some degree handled by substitute teachers, that is to say, pedagogical laypeople.[8]

Through education, interpreters, like practitioners of other professions, need to acquire skills and understanding of the effects of their professional actions. How does society cater for the interpreter profession's organisational aspect? Moreover, what characterises the knowledge base of the interpreter profession? And how does the interplay between *practice, research* and *education* affect the interpreter's process of professionalisation?

3.5.1 Organised education for interpreters: an international spectrum of response

In an overview of how the quality of interpreting services is catered for around the world, Ozolins (2000; 2010) describes an *international spectrum of response* that stretches from 'neglect' through 'ad hoc solutions' and 'generic services' to 'a state of comprehensiveness' (Figure 3.1). Ozolins' (2000: 22) international spectrum of response depicts how different countries provide for the interpreter function's licence and mandate and hence the organisational aspect of professionalisation.

Entering the twenty-first century, few countries had reached 'a state of comprehensiveness', that is, measures that include policy planning, organised education, accreditation tests and professionally organised interpreting services. The situation had not improved a decade later (Ozolins 2010), although Ozolins' overview indicates that some countries provide for interpreting in the courts. However, EU members'

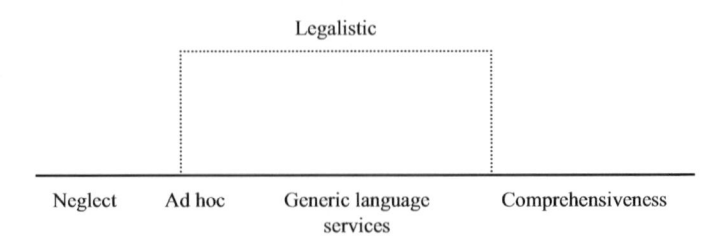

FIGURE 3.1 An international spectrum of response regarding the organisational aspect of the profession of interpreting in the public sector
Source: Ozolins (2000: 22).

attitude to the aforementioned directives (Giambruno 2014) adds to the impression of reluctance as far as the organisational aspect and quality measures, even in courts. In their case study involving courtrooms of Austria and Belgium, Balogh and Salaets (2018: 293) observe that: 'Nobody seems to know how to work with an interpreter.' The courts' negligence of the interpreters' work conditions, as documented in the aforementioned case studies, mirrors the legal professions' unawareness of the impact that the quality of interpreting has on their own professional integrity.

The impact of (poor) communication on human rights is obvious in the legal sphere. A legal aspect is present even within the medical domain, however, and pertains to the individual's legal safeguard in *institutional encounters* in general, as emphasised above. Medical malpractice due to language barriers is difficult to document because of the confidential nature of the encounters, although cases where patients have sued health institutions for failure to provide adequate interpreting have been reported (Ozolins 2010: 7). Ozolins provides an elaboration of factors leading to 'neglect' rather than 'comprehensiveness', and emphasises that policy planning and socio-political organisation, including funding and budgets, have an impact on the situation in any given country. Prior to the phase of policy planning, a change in attitude as to who are the interpreter's clients seems to be necessary, Skaaden and Felberg (2012) note, based on observations from the Nordic countries.

Educational options for interpreters who practise in institutional encounters are poorly developed in most countries. The lack of stable educational options for the language combinations required is due to various factors. First, the need for interpreting in a large number of languages in itself represents a challenge to educational measures. For instance, in a market like the Norwegian, with its five million citizens, there is a registered need for interpreting in more than one hundred languages

TEXTBOX 3.5 An overview of the provision of interpreters' *licence and mandate* within the European Union (Giambruno 2014) shows that accreditation tests and/or organised education are the exception rather than the rule, even for legal interpreters (LI), and Giambruno (ibid.: 185) states that 'specific training for LIs is limited at best, and in some cases is non-existent'. The report shows that few EU member states have organised training for the plethora of languages needed, even though some countries have training options for a smaller number of languages. Other states reportedly have 'registers of interpreters'. However, Giambruno (ibid.: 185) observes that 'a register is only as valid as those included on it', and often 'the lists are tailored to the needs of the agency or entity in question and are sometimes built, at least partially, upon informal connections and relationships, friendships or professional interests' (ibid.: 185). The situation in the European Union is in line with the state of affairs in the rest of the western world. For instance, research reports from the United States show that interpreting is less than satisfactorily catered for within the legal system of most US states (Wallace 2015).

(NOU 2014). In a city like Manchester alone, there is a registered need for interpreting in more than 150 languages (Giambruno 2014: 181). Second, a constant flux as to which languages the market requires encumbers the establishment of education, thus, affects the stability of the profession indirectly. Unless the market establishes organisational measures in addition to education, such as a national register to increase the availability of educated interpreters, educational institutions risk training practitioners who will soon leave the field for other, more secure jobs. Third, the complex nature of the most basic prerequisite for interpreting, the performer's well-developed bilingual skills, in itself represents challenges in establishing accreditation measures for the multitude of language pairs needed (Skaaden and Wadensjö 2014). At the same time, the low passing rates that are common for interpreting tests (Mortensen 2012; Wallace 2013) reveal the need for education. Despite the challenges associated with establishing the organisational measures, education is necessary to professionalise the interpreter function.

An excerpt from the online learning activities of interpreter students in Example 3.12 gives a glimpse into the effects of education on the development of a professional identity. Here, an evolving professional identity manifests itself in the students' differentiation between 'we' and 'they' when they discuss their profession's status, as emphasized in postings 2, 5, 8, and 10. The students who refer to their own professional behaviour and the need to inform the clients about their 'role' add to the impression of an emergent professional identity but also draw attention to the dependence of interpreting quality on the attitude of the interpreters' professional clients.

The students, who interact online in a synchronous chat towards the end of a one-year training course, display their evolving professional identity. Importantly, the students also point to the fact that the virtues of the trained interpreter alone cannot ensure quality in interpreting. The professional in charge of the situation also needs to understand the interpreters' professional function and their particular position at the discourse level. To assure interpreting quality, the future education of practitioners of medicine and law who rely on interpreting to fulfil their professional integrity should give insight into the nature of interpreted discourse.

As yet, few countries have acknowledged the need for interpreter education. In addition to the structural challenges associated with establishing education for the multiplicity of language combinations required, the attitudinal factor that dysconsciously ascribes the ownership of the problem of communication to the speaker of the minority language continues to hamper development in the field. A change in the attitude illustrated above, that the interpreter 'represents the minority speaker' is probably the most important factor in improving the organisational aspect of the interpreters' process of professionalisation. Not only professionals in charge of institutional encounters, but also researchers studying the practice of interpreting in legal and medical settings carry responsibility in changing this attitude.

In summary, the structural challenges associated with organising interpreter education for the volume of language combinations needed can only partially explain the state of affairs. A first step towards comprehensiveness hinges on society's

> **EXAMPLE 3.12**
>
> 1. *Facilitator*: 20:54. What is necessary in order to enhance the interpreter profession's status in the public sector?
> 2. *fStudent1*: 20:54. That *we* all behave like professionals.
> 3. *fStudent2*: 20:54. Inform about the interpreter's role on every assignment.
> 4. *mStudent3*: 20:54. Official Stamp in the b...
> 5. *fStudent4*: 20:54. That *we* act like a group, not only as individuals. And that *everyone represents the same*, behave like professionals, and are *proud of their work*.
> 6. *mStudent5*: 20:55. Agree with fStud2, explain every time the interpreter's role.
> 7. *fStudent6*: 20:55. An interpreter education that is obligatory for everyone who wants to work as an interpreter in the public service sector.
> 8. *fStudent7*: 20:56. *The clients* harm the interpreter profession when *they* hire incompetent interpreters.
> 9. *fStudent1*: 20:56. Mandatory use of the best in the interpreter portal [i.e. the Norwegian National Register of Practicing Interpreters accessible at www.tolkeportalen.no].
> 10. *mStudent3*: 20:57. *We* were once incompetent ... don't forget that *we* were once cubs ...
>
> *(Skaaden 2016: 63; emphasis added)*

political will and its readiness to see that 'poor communication not only threatens minority speakers' legal safeguard, but also poses a threat to the professional integrity of the healthcare workers, police officers, or judges in charge of the institutional dialogue' (Skaaden and Felberg 2012: 8). Consequently, ethical principles of a wider range than those governing the interpreter function are at stake. Education that enhances interpreters' ability to deliver quality services is of the essence, but so is raised awareness and improved knowledge among the professionals that interpreters serve.

3.5.2 *The interplay between practice, research and education in professionalisation*

The sociology of professions considers the development of a *knowledge base* a requirement for the process of professionalisation to take place. What is the nature of such a knowledge base in the professionalisation of interpreting? A brief look into the type of knowledge involved in professional practice and in the exercise of discretion is necessary in addressing this question. Gentile (1995: 55) notes that the integration of theory and practice is a recurrent topic in the training of interpreters. The issue is one that interpreters share with other professions. In their presentation of types of knowledge involved in professional practice, Kinsella and Pitman (2012a: 2) state that, in general, 'professions are plagued with a theory–practice gap'. With their interest in the profession of medicine, they discuss the importance of *phronēsis* in professional practice, that is, applied knowledge that is 'pragmatic, variable, context-dependent, and oriented toward action' (ibid.: 2). The concept originates from Aristotle's classification of different types of knowledge (also see Rudvin, Part I in this volume). *Phronēsis* is of particular interest in the education of professionals because it pertains to the professional's skills in making 'wise' decisions in actual situations (Grimen 2008a: 78; Hibbert 2012: 65; Skaaden 2017). This *knowing how* requires 'reflection in action', according to the sociologist Donald Schön (1987: 14, 22), thus, it relates to the exercise of discretion. It is, therefore, essential for professional practice and education. The above examples that reveal how the interpreter weighs different options 'in action' (e.g. Example 3.1), illustrate how the type of knowledge is involved in interpreting.

The knowing how involved in the mastery of professional skills also has to do with the building of confidence and the experience of making judgements in actual situations (Grimen 2008a: 72). Kinsella and Pitman (2012b: 169) who describe *phronēsis* as 'wise action in context', state that the knowing how involved in the successful practice of the individual practitioner, moreover, relates to a *collective phronēsis*. That is, 'the collective good that a professional community commits itself to through its practice as a profession' (ibid.: 9). Organised education evidently influences the interrelation between the individual and the collective. As the students' discourse in Example 3.12 briefly shows, education motivates the participants' professional identity. Subsequently, the professional identity may improve their confidence when engaging in 'reflection in action'.

Flyvbjerg (1993: 65) observes that the type of knowledge that produces quality in professional performance is difficult to grasp with traditional scientific methods. Moreover, professional activity requires that professionals apply knowledge that is not homogeneous and where different theoretical perspectives are only loosely integrated (Grimen 2008a: 72). As a result, a profession's knowledge base is 'an amalgam of theoretical insights from different fields of knowledge along with practical skills and confidence in concrete situations', Grimen (ibid.: 84) explains. He uses the sciences of medicine and health care as examples (ibid.: 72), but such a description also fits the professional knowledge base for interpreting very well, as I have argued elsewhere (Skaaden 2013: 231; 2017: 325–327).

An understanding of the activity of interpreting rests on knowledge about different – and not very well integrated – branches of linguistics, such as *bilingualism research, cognitive linguistics, comparative linguistics, discourse analysis, psycholinguistics, sociolinguistics*, and *translation studies*. Furthermore, a full grasp of the activity of interpreting and its societal function must include knowledge from branches of science such as psychology, anthropology, law and sociology (Skaaden 2013: 231). Finally, as discussed with regard to the profession of medicine (Grimen 2008a), what brings professional development forward in general is an interplay between *practice, education* and *research*. Ideally, the researchers' observations, analyses and reflections over practice will feed back into education, which in turn improves practice. The continuous interplay may somewhat simplified be imagined as a 'wheel' moving forward, as indicated in Figure 3.2 (cf. Skaaden 2013: 229).

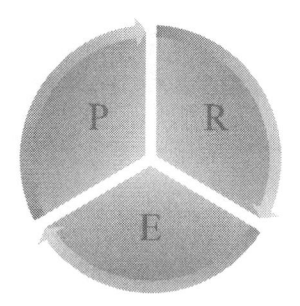

FIGURE 3.2 The interplay between education (E), practice (P), and research (R)
Source: Skaaden (2013: 219).

In PSI, the lack of education for interpreters practising in the setting results in research where 'worst practice' rather than 'best practice' sets the standard of what interpreting in institutional encounters is all about. An excerpt from Meyer (2001) in Example 3.13 illustrates research where a layperson (here, the patient's daughter) serves as 'interpreter' in the consultation between a patient and a doctor preparing the patient for surgery.

EXAMPLE 3.13

1. *Doctor*: Das ist die Leber. (1.2) Das ist die – (That is the liver. – That is –.)
2. *Patient*: hm, hm.
3. *Doctor*: Gallenblase. (1.3) Da sitzen die Steine drin, (.) nech? (.) Und (.) das is (.) ein Speicher für die Galle und de/ (…) die Galle wird (.) über den Gallengang (…) in den Darm abgegeben (xxx) (The gall bladder. (.) The stones are in there, (.) right? (.) And (.) it is (.) a reservoir for the bile and th/ (…) the bile (.) is via the bile duct (…) passed into the intestine (xxx).)
4. *Interpreter*: Also vai pra … Äh (.) aqui é o coisu, ja? Tu dizes que é o veneno dos coelhos. Vai, e depois vai para os (So it moves… er (.) here is the thingy, right? What you call the rabbit's poison. It moves, and then it moves to –)
5. *Patient*: Bom. (OK.)

(from Meyer 2001: 93)

The fact that this type of medical practice takes place is important to document, and the fact that German medical professionals are 'happy to make do' (Meyer *et al.* 2003: 75) with this type of communication is particularly interesting in light of the professional interpreters' double allegiance to their clients on both sides of the table. A problem for the profession's knowledge base arises when research reports label the type of exchange witnessed in Example 3.13 'an archetype of community interpreting' (Meyer 2001: 113). In the research on PSI, discourse analyses of institutional dialogues mediated by untrained practitioners who sometimes lack the most basic bilingual skills are quite common, and Meyer's example is not exceptional (e.g., works referenced in Hale (2007) contain similar examples). The study of laypeople in the interpreter function is partially due to the lack of educational options for interpreters. At the same time, the trend sheds light on the researchers' responsibility in the process of professionalisation. In moving the process of professionalisation forward, the goal must be a knowledge base that does not build its standards on the actions of laypeople who lack the necessary skills to perform the activity of interpreting.

Instances like Example 3.13 show that poor interpreting quality may affect the professional integrity of medical professionals. In light of this, the interpreters' weak professional status in PSI represents a paradox. For interpreters, as for the practitioners in the established professions, the path towards professionalisation is education. In contrast to the layperson 'interpreter' in Example 3.13, Example 3.14 shows the reflections of an interpreter who is developing her skills in an online university-level course on remote interpreting.

EXAMPLE 3.14

fStudent23: 18:36:44. The sequences become longer in onscreen interpreting [i.e. remote interpreting]. I experienced it today, in fact, when I had an assignment via Skype. It was more difficult to seize your turn; every time the interpreter tries to seize the turn, it ends with repetitions and misunderstandings. Therefore, I chose to allow more room for longer sequences, but I was very careful to take notes and had to pose control questions. I noticed another very interesting thing today as well, that the minority language speaker inserted an 'ok' or 'right' after each tiny little sentence. I understand it as a sort of reassurance of 'you heard me, didn't you?', and this alone leads to longer sequences.

(Skaaden 2018c: 843)

The student's reflections on her own practice show the emergence of a *reflective practitioner*, while the reference to a remote assignment earlier in the day reveals that students of interpreting are already practising as interpreters. In this manner, the excerpt indicates that education for interpreters must seek unconventional routes.

At the same time, the excerpt mirrors a setting of PSI where technological distance is rapidly becoming more common. Apparently, the distance of the technology brings new challenges into the interaction of interpreted encounters. As the student observes, some of the strategies efficiently applied in onsite encounters for turntaking and notetaking have an altered effect on the screen (Skaaden 2018c: 844–846). Finally, the student's observations indicate that the novelty of the technological setting bring challenges even for 'normal' speakers/listeners, who reveal their insecurity by seeking frequent feedback. In this sense, the interpreted encounter serves to disclose aspects of communication via technology in general. Moreover, the conditions of communication brought on by technological solutions serve as a magnifying glass for the need to accommodate any setting for interpreting. Interpreters often report that they experience challenges in achieving quality interpreting due to the actions and attitudes displayed by the professionals in charge of the institutional encounters. The challenges experienced onsite do not go away when the interpreter is performing from a remote site, whether via telephone (Wadensjö 2009) or Skype (Skaaden 2018c). Rather, the remote mode appears to alter and sometimes augment challenges experienced in onsite interpreting, in ways that we have just started to explore (Napier *et al.* 2018).

3.5.3 *Professional trust and virtue or quality in performance*

Multiple factors are involved in reaching optimal quality in each instantiation of interpreting, and this makes it difficult to determine what *quality* entails. Nevertheless, Grbić (2008: 231), who investigates the use of the concept in interpreting, finds that 'quality' plays an important role in practice, research and training. At the same time, her investigation shows that the many criteria applied in determining – or constructing – quality are rather subjective. Often concepts such as 'exception', 'perfection', 'excellence', 'exceeds/complies with high standards', describe quality, but without identifying the various components that contribute to quality (ibid.: 242). Whether the quality judgements are carried out by an elite of peers or by the interpreter's clients or customers, a recurrent problem is the fact that real benchmarks are lacking, Grbić observes (ibid.: 245). She describes quality as 'multiperspectivist, multireferential and dynamic' and concludes that:

> thorough understanding of the system(s) is essential if our aim is to establish, revise or expand the canon of criteria that ought to be fulfilled in order to satisfy the various needs and requirements within the systems of research, teaching and practice.
>
> *(ibid.: 252)*

Equivalence, a notion closely tied to that of *accuracy in rendition*, is difficult to escape in descriptions of quality, Grbić (ibid.: 245) furthermore notes. Although some researchers try to avoid the concept altogether, she finds that equivalence often reappears in new forms, such as *optimum quality*, that is 'the quality that an interpreter can provide if external conditions are appropriate' (Moser-Mercer 1996: 44). Throughout the history of translation theory, the debate on equivalence oscillates between keeping the perspective of the speaker or the listener in the foreground (Munday 2001). Rather than seeing equivalence as a norm, the translation scholar Gideon Toury (1995) proposes a model that views the relationship between source and target utterance as an empirical phenomenon. The proposal circumvents the complexity of real instantiations and provides a platform for hypotheses about translation – or interpreting (ibid.: 37). Evidently, the difficulty in reaching consensus on equivalence and quality has to do with the nature of the activity of interpreting and the indeterminacy associated both with the nature of linguistic units and the exercise of discretion (Skaaden 2013: 196). Moreover, due to their double allegiance, interpreters should ideally consider both the *speaker's intentions* and *the rendition's effect on the listener* in every rendition. The problem remains that the interpreter never fully controls either the speaker's *intention* or the rendition's *effect* on the listener. Indeed, as pointed out by Grbić (2008: 238), '"quality" is a fuzzy concept, comprising a multitude of interdependent variables, thus largely defying exact definition'.

Apparently, in reaching quality in interpreting, the practitioner's virtues are just one factor at play – as Moser-Mercer's 'optimum quality' indicates. The quality of any given instantiation of interpreting is the result of the complex interplay between the practitioner's *cognition*, the working languages' *conventions* and the *context* – including the *interaction* between participants (Skaaden 2013: 195–215). A model of interpreting quality must include both the basic tenets of Gile's (2009 [1995]) *effort model* and Kalina's (2002) *factor analysis model*. Respectively, Gile's and Kalina's models portray interpreting quality as a balance between resources required and resources available (to the practitioner) and as a product of the interpreter's basic skills in concert with features of the original utterance and the practitioner's work conditions. The models of Gile and Kalina pay less attention to interaction as their primary focus is the classic conference setting. A model of quality in PSI must also take into consideration the tenets of Wadensjö's model of *interpreting as interaction*. When applying the basic tenets of these three models to the institutional encounter, we identify a number of factors of importance to the quality of interpreting. These factors pertain to aspects of cognition, convention and context, as well as interaction between participants. Table 3.2 suggests a list of factors that play a role in each utterance or instantiation of interpreting.

In summary, quality equals the possibility to produce optimal renditions. This is a process where the interpreter's skills and virtues cover but one of the facets that contribute to the quality of each instantiation. The list of factors is by no means exhaustive. It is merely an illustration of factors pertinent in determining interpreting quality and hence suggest aspects that should receive attention in research, education and the planning of actual interpreted encounters in practice.

The linguistic conventions of the two working languages in question receive special mention because they are the interpreter's main tool but also the practitioner's work material. The complex universe of bilingualism therefore has special bearing on the core activity of interpreting. Obviously, the potential to produce

TABLE 3.2 Factors which impact on the quality of a given interpreting event

Cognition	Convention	Context
The interpreter's skills and virtues along parameters such as	*The degree of coincidence or divergence in and between the two working languages' conventions, along parameters such as*	*The complexity and grammar of the situational context in terms of*
• Bilingual skills • Interpreting skills, including mastery of interpreting mode • Interactional skills • Understanding of own function or role in the communication • Understanding of context and situation • Processing capacity • Memory capacity • Stamina and stress tolerance • Fatigue • Self-confidence	• Grammatical and pragmatic device, e.g. deictic device, etc. • Markedness • Homonymy, including false friends (see Example 3.8) • Loan words • Register variants • Stylistic variants including politeness expressions • Metaphors, proverbs, etc.	• Degree of formality, number of participants • The participants' interactional skills – including awareness of the specific nature of interpreted interaction • Expected mode(s) of interpreting; and accommodation thereof • Participants' mode of speech; dialogue or lecture style; planned or spontaneous speech • Speech quality, e.g. diction, speed, clarity • Accommodation of the situation for interpreting • External interference or noise

quality interpreting depends on the practitioner's bilingual skills. To some extent, it also depends on the interrelationship between the working languages, however. In this sense, the aspects of linguistic convention embrace even the level of typology and grammar. 'No lack of grammatical device in the language translated into makes impossible a literal translation of the entire conceptual information contained in the original', according to Jakobson (2000 [1959]: 140). Although this holds in general, 'in practice the lack of grammatical device can make the translation of "the entire conceptual information" very difficult indeed', as Baker (1992: 86–87) points out in a comment on Jakobson's observation. Certain 'mismatches' between the working languages' inventories either on the structural or lexical level can be difficult to anticipate for the interpreter (in time) and thereby challenge interpreting quality. To exemplify, differences in terms of *markedness*, as illustrated above by different inventories of polite pronoun forms, may cause challenges. Correspondingly, *false friends* on the lexical level as in the case of *profesor/professor* (see Example 3.8) may challenge the interpreter's exercise of discretion. Even similarities *within* a working language, represent potential tripwires for the interpreter in an otherwise stressful situation, as exemplified by homonymy (*da, da/Dada*) in Example 3.1 above.

Moreover, non-linguistic aspects of the situational context, such as the seating and procedures of a courtroom, may have impact on the interpreter's opportunity to produce quality work (e.g., as seen in Example. 3.2). Although the types of factors in Table 3.2 are independent of setting in principle, the co-occurrence of factors may cause interpreting quality to deteriorate when the cognitive resources required exceed the resources available (Skaaden 2013: 214–215). The complexity of the courtroom vividly illustrates a setting where a number of factors that may complicate the interpreter's striving for quality typically co-occur in terms of interactional, contextual and conventional aspects.

The factors summed up in Table 3.2, as first outlined in Skaaden (ibid.: 195–215), in certain respects harmonise with the approach of Dean and Pollard (2013), in that both approaches emphasise that interpreting quality does not depend on the virtues of the interpreter alone. Dean and Pollard describe the interpreter's performance according to a 'Demand-Control Schema'. Whereas their 'control schema' may in certain respects pertain to factors here listed under the practitioner's 'cognition', their 'demand' schema, includes environmental, interpersonal, paralinguistic and intrapersonal categories. These categories correspond with the factors described in Table 3.2 as contextual prerequisites for accomplishing the relative quality of interpreting. In their description of the 'control' schema, Dean and Pollard (ibid.: 16) include interpreters who 'never had formal education as an interpreter'. Certainly, the factors contributing to quality pertain to untrained practitioners as well. However, since an aim of professionalisation is for all practitioners to undergo organised education, the inclusion of laypeople in the model may seem counterproductive.

Moreover, Dean and Pollard's control schema, which pertains to the skills and preparations of the practising interpreter, includes consideration of the participants' 'thought worlds' (ibid.: 6–7). Undeniably, all the individual participants' 'thought worlds' play a part in human interactions, and 'empty heads would not have any basis for talking or engaging in sociocultural interaction', as Langacker (1994: 26) points out. However, the interpreter does not have direct access to the interlocutors' actual understanding and can only rely on the inventory of the working languages' conventions as uttered in instances of a particular context. Therefore, the interpreter assisting the principal interlocutors in their mutual negotiation of meaning can only rely on their verbalisations, as seen, for instance, in Example 3.11 above.

Because the interpreter does not have full insight into the participants' individual histories, their cognition or 'thought worlds', the interpreter's vantage point on the situation can never cover fully those held by the parties on both sides. Figure 3.3 indicates the different vantage points, depicting quite schematically the interpreter's and interlocutors' viewpoints from a bird's-eye perspective.

In the attempt to produce optimal renditions of the interlocutors' utterances, interpreters must rely on the units (of lexicon and grammar) conventionalised in their working languages together with cues provided by the context. Unequivocally, the interpreter, an individual, never has insight into the complete case history and context in the way the parties on both sides do. This is obvious as far as the professional party's 'thought world' goes, as the interpreter does not share their area of expertise. The interpreter's incomplete access to the context and case history is one of the reasons why interpreting, like any other professional activity, is in essence *a fallible activity*. Given that interpreting is a fallible activity, misunderstandings are to

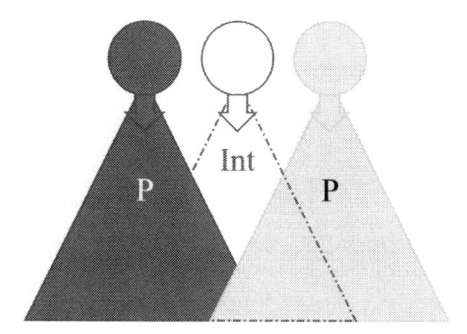

FIGURE 3.3 The interpreter's vantage point indicates that the interpreter does not 'see' all the information that either party has access to about the context. That is, the interlocutors' individual and mutual histories prior to the interpreted encounter, the professional party's criteria and evaluations, etc.
Source: Skaaden (2013: 191).

be expected. It follows that both practitioners of interpreting and their clients must always keep the relative quality of interpreting in mind. The factors contributing to quality in interpreting described here merely indicate the complexity of the activity. Evidently, education is necessary for interpreters to optimise their skills and virtues in performance and Hale states that:

> The better trained, the better prepared, and the better equipped the interpreter is, the better chance s/he has of producing a faithful rendition. Working conditions, including the way they are treated by the other participants and the way those participants express themselves, will also affect performance. The higher the level of bilingualism, biculturalism and of interpreting skills, the higher the level of accuracy will be.
>
> *(2008: 119)*

Due to the interpreter's unique position within the discourse, the education of interpreters will guarantee quality interpreting only to a certain extent. The virtues of the individual interpreter are but one factor that quality depends on. The professional in charge of the interpreted institutional encounter also needs knowledge about this particular type of communicative setting and the activity's inherent challenges and options. Before the true nature of interpreting quality can be determined, the topic of 'how to communicate via an interpreter' must be included in the educational programmes of the lawyers, police officers, doctors and nurses who in their future practice are going to rely on interpreting in their own exercise of discretion.

3.6 Conclusion: ethics, education and professional integrity

Acting according to professional ethics involves a number of aspects that this part of the book has approached in terms of professionalisation, exercise of discretion, clients, trust and virtue or quality in performance. The professionalisation of any societal function includes a performative aspect and an organisational aspect. As established here, the activity of interpreting fulfils the performative criteria to qualify as a profession by good margin. The interpreter, like other professionals, exercises discretion. In the exercise of discretion, interpreters apply their specialised interpreting skills to solve their clients' mutual 'how-to problem', that is, the interlocutors' possibility to communicate verbally. From this perspective, professional ethics have two functions. On one hand, professional ethics serve as general norms of action for the professionals in their exercise of discretion. On the other hand, they serve as a guarantee for their clients that they can trust the quality of the services provided by the professionals. In the latter sense, the code of ethics is a guarantee for clients that professionals own up to their professional integrity by acting according to profession-specific ends.

Specific to the interpreter profession is the double allegiance resulting from the fact that the interpreter constantly serves two clients, that is, both speaker and listener. In rendering and coordinating the interlocutors' talk, the interpreter simultaneously serves both doctor and patient or both judge and defendant. The core principles of accuracy and impartiality in the interpreters' code of ethics accordingly reflect that their professional loyalty is with each utterance rather than with one of the interlocutors, as Hale (2007; 2008) puts it.

From the perspective taken here, the controversy in the field over the values of its core ethics appears as a controversy over the extension of the domain within which the interpreter is to exercise discretion. Should interpreters limit their services to rendering and coordinating others' talk, in line with the directly interpreted approach? Or should interpreters engage in cultural mediation in terms of 'advocate' and 'co-diagnostician', as proposed by the mediated approach? The controversy has more than one source. In order to understand the interpreters' professional ethics in terms of role, one must keep two levels of analysis in mind. On one level, the interpreter fulfils a legal-societal function in institutional encounters that pertains to the duties and rights of the interpreter's two clients. On the other linguistic-interactional level, the interpreter must strive for a participation status within the dialogue so as to 'not get in the way' of the interlocutors' communication. Unless the interpreter succeeds with the latter, the former is not accomplished.

Like other professionals, interpreters engage in a fallible activity. A fundamental question for any profession relates to the trust the clients invest in its practitioners' exercise of discretion. It follows that a multiplicity of conflicting roles fail to provide a base for professional trust. In order to gain their clients' trust, the profession must determine what virtue, thus, quality in interpreting should imply. Regardless of how one chooses to restrict the domain of the interpreters' exercise of discretion, if clients do not know what to expect, their trust will dissolve. Moreover, an extensive domain for the interpreter's exercise of discretion will concurrently narrow the domain of the professional in charge of the institutional encounter. Consequently, the rights of *their* patients and clients will suffer. Incidents and examples discussed in this book where layperson interpreters apply their agency to take over the doctor's task in identifying a patient's symptoms, or sit the theory part of the driver's test on behalf of the candidate, clearly speak in favour of an approach where interpreters adhere to a restricted domain for the exercise of discretion. Even in managing their task according to the directly interpreted approach, the interpreters exercise discretion within a narrow but extremely complex domain.

An obvious paradox relates to the fact that interpreters in the public sector setting typically serve high-status professionals with strongly monopolised functions. For the established professions, professional trust rests on several years of education and the resultant virtues, licence and mandate. Yet, the organisational aspect of professionalisation is underdeveloped for interpreters in most countries. Education will serve to develop the practitioners' interpreting skills, stimulate their reflections on professional ethics and prepare them for the exercise of discretion in real situations. Due to the interpreter's specific position in the communication, the quality of interpreted encounters does not solely depend on the virtues of the interpreter, however. Even the professionals who must rely on interpreting to fulfil their own professional function need knowledge of the possibilities and limitations of interpreted institutional encounters. How to communicate in interpreted encounters – onsite and online – should therefore be included in the education of future professionals within medicine and law, and other relevant professions.

Moreover, fundamental problems remain in developing the field's knowledge base through the interplay between practice, research and education. 'The clients harm the interpreter profession when they hire incompetent interpreters', as one of the students quoted here observed. Finally, the tendency to ascribe ownership of the problem of communication to the speaker of the minority language in both practice and research indicates an underlying image of the interpreter as the helper of the 'Other'. As argued here, this attitude has consequences of ideology pertaining to the use of 'culture' as an explanatory tool for the communication between 'us' and 'them'. In summary, the delineation of the interpreters' domain for the exercise of discretion has consequences beyond the profession's own integrity, because interpreting quality has impact on the discretion exercised by the high-status professionals that interpreters serve. Therefore, it is necessary to improve the organisational aspect of interpreters' professionalisation through education and research before assuming that there is something wrong with their code of ethics.

Notes

1 Author's translation from Norwegian: 'hva "praksis" i betydningen profesjonell virksomhet betyr' (Molander and Terum 2008: 20).
2 The analysis of the interpreters' 'role' within a general model of professional practice was first presented in Skaaden (2013). Aspects of the approach have since been elaborated on in Skaaden (2016; 2018a; 2018b) and are further elaborated on here.
3 Author's translation from Norwegian: '*anvender* en systematisert *kunnskapsmengde* på enkelttilfeller' (ibid.: 19).
4 'Klienter er avhengig i den forstand at de søker bistand fra fagpersonen for å kunne håndtere forhold som for dem er betydningsfulle' (Molander and Terum 2008:19), author's translation into English.

5 The European Convention on Human Rights of 1950, cf. UN (1948). See also Directives 2010/64/EU and 2012/29/EU.
6 For legal documents pertaining to institutional communication in Norway and Sweden, respectively, see https://lovdata.no/; https://lovdata.no/dokument/LTI/lov/2016-06-10-23 and www.riksdagen.se/sv/dokument-lagar/.
7 The students, two women (f) and two men (m) represent the languages Sorani Kurd and Persian and communicate in their common working language Norwegian that is their second language. For the sake of brevity, only the author's English translation of the chat discourse is rendered here. Note that the translations indicate some L2 features characteristic of the chat postings. Each posting identifies the student by gender (f/m), working language, number of appearances in the excerpt and time of posting.
8 In 2019, Norway has a nationwide shortage of over 2,500 teachers, according to its National Radio and TV channel, NRK: www.nrk.no/rogaland/vil-mangle-2.600-laerere-med-ny-norm-1.13926948 (accessed 22 February 2019). When it comes to practitioners of medicine, the situation in Norway resembles that of other European countries, for instance, the UK and Ireland, but not for the function of teachers (Phelan, personal communication).

References

Agar, M.H. (1985). Institutional discourse. *Text: Interdisciplinary Journal for the Study of Discourse*, 5, 147–168.

Angelelli, C.V. (2004). *Medical Interpreting and Cross-Cultural Communication*. Cambridge: Cambridge University Press.

Baker, M. (1992). *In Other Words*. London: Routledge.

Balogh, K. and Salaets, H. (2016). Videoconference-based interpreting in legal settings: a case study. Paper presented at Linked up with Video in Interpreting Practice and Research. Symposium at KU Leuven. Antwerp, 25–26 February 2016.

Balogh, K. and Salaets, H. (2018) Videoconferencing in legal context: a comparative study of simulated and real-life settings. In J. Napier, R. Skinner, and S. Braun (eds), *Here or There: Research on Interpreting via Video Link* (pp. 264–294). Washington, DC: Gallaudet University Press.

Chesterman, A. (2001). Proposal for a hieronymic oath. *The Translator*, 7(2), 139–154.

Dean, R.K. and Pollard Jr., R.Q. (2013). *The Demand Control Schema: Interpreting as a Practice Profession*. North Charleston, SC: CreateSpace Independent Publishing Platform.

Directive 2010/64/EU of the European Parliament and of the Council of 20 October 2010 on the Right to Interpretation and Translation in Criminal Proceedings. Available at: http://eulita.eu/sites/default/files/directive_en.pdf

Directive 2012/29/EU of the European Parliament and of the Council of 25 October 2012 Establishing Minimum Standards on the Rights, Support and Protection of Victims of Crime, and Replacing Council Framework Decision 2001/220/JHA. Available at: www.gov.uk/government/publications/hmrc-eu-directives-eu-victims-directive-201229eu

Dworkin, R. (1978). *Taking Rights Seriously*. Cambridge, MA: Harvard University Press.

Eriksen, A. (2015). What is professional integrity? *Etikk i prakis. Nordic Journal of Applied Ethics*, 9(2), 3–17.

Fauske, H. (2008). Profesjonsforskningens faser og stridsspørsmål. [Phases and issues in the sociology of professions]. In A. Molander and L. I. Terum (eds), *Profesjonsstudier* (pp. 31–53). Oslo: Universitetsforlaget.

Felberg, T.R. and Šarić, L.J. (2017). Interpreting impoliteness: interpreters' voices. *FLEKS. Scandinavian Journal of Intercultural Theory and Practice*, 4(1), 1–17.

Felberg, T.R. and Skaaden, H. (2012). The (de)construction of culture in interpreter-mediated medical discourse. *Linguistica Antverpiensia, New Series – Themes in Translation Studies*, 11, 67–84.
Finkielkraut, A. (1997 [1984]). *The Wisdom of Love*. Lincoln, NE: University of Nebraska Press.
Flyvbjerg, B. (1993). *Rationalitet og magt. Det konkretes videnskab*. [Rationality and power. Science of the concrete]. Odense: Akademisk Forlag.
Freidson, E. (2001). *Professionalism: The Third Logic*. Cambridge: Polity Press.
Galligan, D.J. (1986). *Discretionary Powers: A Legal Study of Official Discretion*. Oxford: Clarendon.
Garwood, C.J. (2012). The right to an interpreter: the violation of a fundamental right in Italy's courts. *The Interpreters' Newsletter*, 17, 173–189.
Gentile, A. (1995). Translation theory teaching: connecting theory and practice. In C. Dollerup and V. Appel (eds), *Teaching Translation and Interpreting* (pp. 55–63). Amsterdam: John Benjamins Publishing Company.
Gentile, A. (1997). Community interpreting or not? Practices, standards and accreditation. In S. Carr, R. Roberts, A. Dufour and D. Steyn (eds), *The Critical Link: Interpreters in the Community. Papers from the First International Conference on Interpreting in Legal, Health and Social Service Settings* (pp. 109–119). Amsterdam: John Benjamins Publishing Company.
Gentile, A., Ozolins, U., and Vasilakakos, M. (1996). *Liaison Interpreting: A Handbook*. Melbourne: Melbourne University Press.
Giæver, A. (2011). Psyko-ordene han hentet fra nettet, *VG-nett*. [The psycho-words he found on the web] Available at: www.vg.no/vgpluss/article/CKMNG4g
Giambruno, C. (2014). The current state of affairs in the UE: Member State Profiles. In C. Giambruno (ed.), *Assessing Legal Interpreter Quality through Testing and Certification: The Qualitas Project* (pp. 149–191). Alicante: Publicaciones de la Universidad de Alicante.
Gile, D. (2009 [1995]). *Basic Concepts and Models for Interpreter and Translator Training*. Rev. edn. Amsterdam: John Benjamins Publishing Company.
Goffman, E. (1974). *Frame Analysis: An Essay on the Organization of Experience*. Cambridge, MA: Harvard University Press.
Goffman, E. (1981). *Forms of Talk*. Philadelphia, PA: University of Pennsylvania Press.
González, R.D., Vásquez, V.F. and Mikkelson, H. (1991). *Fundamentals of Court Interpretation: Theory, Policy and Practice*. Durham, NC: Carolina Academic Press.
Gooch, G. and Williams, M. (2007). *A Dictionary of Law Enforcement*. Oxford: Oxford University Press.
Grbić, N. (2008). Constructing interpreting quality. *Interpreting*, 10(2), 232–259.
Grimen, H. (2008a). Profesjon og kunnskap. [Profession and knowledge]. In A. Molander and L. I. Terum (eds), *Profesjonsstudier* (pp. 71–87). Oslo: Universitetsforlaget.
Grimen, H. (2008b). Profesjon og tillit. [Profession and trust]. In A. Molander and L. I. Terum (eds), *Profesjonsstudier* (pp. 197–215). Oslo: Universitetsforlaget.
Grimen, H. (2008c). Profesjon og profesjonsmoral. [Professions and professional morals]. In A. Molander and L. I. Terum (eds.), *Profesjonsstudier* (pp. 144–160). Oslo: Universitetsforlaget.
Grimen, H. (2009). *Hva er tillit?* [What is trust?]. Oslo: Universitetesforlaget.
Grimen, H. and Molander, A. (2008). Profesjon og skjønn. [Profession and the exercise of discretion]. In A. Molander and L.I. Terum (eds), *Profesjonsstudier* (pp. 179–196). Oslo: Universitetsforlaget.
Gulbrandsen, P. and Finset, A. (2014). *Skreddersydde samtaler. En veileder i medisinsk kommunikasjon*. [Tailormade Consultations. A guide to medical communication]. Oslo: Gyldendal Akademisk.

Hale, S. (2007). *Community Interpreting*. London: Palgrave Macmillan.
Hale, S. (2008). Controversies over the role of the court interpreter. In C. Valero-Garcés and A. Martin (eds), *Crossing Borders in Community Interpreting: Definitions and Dilemmas* (pp. 99–123). Amsterdam: John Benjamins Publishing Company.
Hibbert, K. (2012). Cultivating capacity: phronesis, learning, and diverisity in professional education. In E.A. Kinsella and A. Pitman (eds), *Phronesis as Professional Knowledge: Practical Wisdom in the Professions* (pp. 61–73). Rotterdam: Sense Publishers.
IMDi. (2007). Fastleger og tolketjenester. [GPs and interpreting services]. *IMDi-rapport*, vol. 6. Oslo: Integrerings-og Mangfoldsdirektoratet.
Jahr, K., Stangvik, G.K., Rachlew, A., Skaaden, H., Karterud, T. and Tuv, E. (2005). *Rett til tolk. Tolking og oversettelse i norsk straffeprosess*. [The right to an interpreter. Interpretation and translation in Norwegian criminal law]. Oslo: Justis- og Politidepartementet.
Jakobson, R. (2000 [1959]). On linguistic aspects of translation. In L. Venuti (ed.), *The Translation Studies Reader* (pp. 138–145). New York: Routledge.
Kale, E. (2006). *"Vi tar det vi har". Om bruk av tolk i helsevesenet i Oslo. En spørreskjemaundersøkelse*. ['We simply use whoever's there': a survey on interpreting in the Oslo health services]. *NAKMIs Skriftserie om Minoriteter og Helse*. vol. 2/2006. Oslo: NAKMI.
Kalina, S. (2002). Quality in interpreting and its prerequisites. A framework for a comprehensive view. In G. Garzone and M. Viezzi (eds), *Interpreting in the 21st Century: Challenges and Opportunities* (pp. 121–130). Amsterdam: John Benjamins Publishing Company.
Kepinska Jakobsen, K., Langballe, Å. and Schultz, J.H. (2017). Trauma-exposed young victims: possibilities and constraints for providing trauma support within the investigative interview. *Psychology, Crime and Law*, 23(5), 427–444. DOI: 10.1080/1068316X.2016.1269903.
Kermit, P. (2002). Hva gjør en tolk og hva gjør en god tolk? Om tolkens yrkesetikk. In D. Mortensen (ed.), *Tolking – Et øvingsopplegg for tolker som skal ta autorisasjonsprøven*. Oslo: Universitetet i Oslo.
Kinsella, E.A. and Pitman, A. (2012a). Engaging phronesis in professional practice and education. In E.A. Kinsella and A. Pitman (eds), *Phronesis as Professional Knowledge: Practical Wisdom in the Professions* (pp. 1–11). Rotterdam: Sense Publishers.
Kinsella, E.A. and Pitman, A. (2012b). Phronesis as professional knowledge: implications for education and practice. In E. A. Kinsella and A. Pitman (eds), *Phronesis as Professional Knowledge: Practical Wisdom in the Professions* (pp. 163–172). Rotterdam: Sense Publishers.
Langacker, R.W. (1987). *Foundations of Cognitive Grammar*, vol. I. *Theoretical Prerequisites*. Stanford, CA: Stanford University Press.
Langacker, R.W. (1991). *Foundations of Cognitive Grammar*, vol. II. *Descriptive Application*. Stanford, CA: Stanford University Press.
Langacker, R.W. (1994). Culture, cognition, and grammar. In M. Pütz (ed.), *Language Contact and Language Conflict* (pp. 25–53). Amsterdam: John Benjamins Publishing Company.
Linell, P. (2009). *Rethinking Language, Mind, and World Dialogically: Interactional and Contextual Theory of Human Sense-Making*. Charlotte, NC: Information Age Publishing.
Lippestad, G. (2013). *Det vi kan stå for* [What we can stand for] Oslo: Aschehoug.
Llewellyn-Jones, P. and Lee, R.G. (2014). *Redefining the Role of the Community Interpreter: The Concept of Role-space*. Lincoln: SLI Press.
Maccallum, E.J. (2002). Othering and psychiatric nursing. *Journal of Psychiatric and Mental Health Nursing*, 9, 87–94.
Mason, I. and Stewart, M. (2001). Interactional pragmatics, face and the dialogue interpreter. In I. Mason (ed.), *Triadic Exchanges: Studies in Dialogue Interpreting* (pp. 51–70). Manchester: St Jerome Publishing.

Merlini, R. (2009). Interpreters in emergency wards. An empirical study of doctor-interpreter-patient interaction. In R. De Pedro Ricoy, I. Perez and C. Wilson (eds), *Interpreting and Translating in Public Service Settings: Policy, Practice, Pedagogy* (pp. 89–115). Manchester: St Jerome Publishing.

Metzger, M. (1999). *Sign Language Interpreting. Deconstructing the Myth of Neutrality*. Washington, DC: Gallaudet University Press.

Meyer, B. (2001). How untrained interpreters handle medical terms. In I. Mason (ed.), *Triadic Exchanges: Studies in Dialogue Interpreting* (pp. 87–107). Manchester: St. Jerome Publishing.

Meyer, B., Apfelbaum, B., Pöchhacker, F., and Bischoff, A. (2003). Analysing interpreted doctor-patient communication from the perspectives of linguistics, interpreting studies and health sciences. In L. Brunette, G. Bastin, I. Hemlin, and H. Clarke (eds), *Critical Link 3: Interpreters in the Community* (pp. 67–79). Amsterdam: John Benjamins Publishing Company.

Mikkelson, H. (1996). Community interpreting: an emerging profession. *Interpreting*, 1(1), 125–131.

Molander, A. (2016). *Discretion in the Welfare State: Social Rights and Professional Judgment*. London: Routledge.

Molander, A. and Grimen, H. (2010). Understanding professional discretion. In L. G. Svensson and J. Evetts (eds), *Sociology of Professions: Continental and Anglo-Saxon Traditions* (pp. 167–187). Gothenburg: Daidalos.

Molander, A. and Terum, L.I. (2008). *Profesjonsstudier*. [The study of professions]. Oslo: Universitetsforlaget.

Morris, R. (2008). Missing stitches: an overview of judicial attitudes to interlingual interpreting in the criminal justice systems of Canada and Israel. *Interpreting*, 10(1), 34–65.

Mortensen, D. (2012). The Norwegian Interpreter Certification Examination. In H. Skaaden and T.R. Felberg (eds), *Nordic Seminar on Interpreter Training and Testing* (vol. 12/2012. pp. 51–60). Oslo: Høgskolen i Oslo og Akershus.

Moser-Mercer, B. (1996). Quality in interpreting: some methodological issues. *The Interpreters' Newsletter*, 7, 43–55.

Munday, J. (2001). *Introducing Translation Studies*. London: Routledge.

Napier, J., Skinner, R. and Braun, S. (2018). *Here or There: Research on Interpreting via Video Link*. Washington, DC: Gallaudet University Press.

Nilsen, A.B., Fylkesnes, S. and Mausethagen, S. (2017). The linguistics in othering: teacher educators' talk about cultural diversity. *Reconceptualizing Educational Research Methodology*, 8(1). DOI:107577/rerm.2556.

NOU. (2014). *Tolking i offentlig sektor: Et spørsmål om rettsikkerhet og likeverd*. [Interpreting in the public sector: a question of legal safeguard and equality]. Oslo: Norges Offentlige Utredninger.

Ozolins, U. (2000). Communication needs and interpreting in multilingual settings: the international spectrum of response. In R. Roberts, S.E. Carr, D. Abraham, and A. Dufour (eds), *The Critical Link 2: Interpreters in the Community. Selected Papers from the Second International Conference on Interpreting in Legal, Health and Social Service Settings* (pp. 21–33). Amsterdam: John Benjamins Publishing Company.

Ozolins, U. (2010). Factors that determine the provision of public service interpreting: comparative perspectives on government motivation and language service implementation. *The Journal of Specialised Translation. JosTrans*, July (14), 194–215.

Parsons, T. (1968). Professions. In D.L. Sills (ed.), *International Encyclopedia of the Social Sciences* (vol. 12, pp. 536–547). New York: The Free Press.

Parsons, T. (1978). *Action Theory and the Human Condition*. New York: The Free Press.
Piller, I. (2011). *Intercultural Communication: A Critical Introduction*. Edinburgh: Edinburgh University Press.
Pöchhacker, F. (1997). Kommunikation mit Nichtdeutschsprachigen in Wiener Gesundheits- und Sozialeinrichtungen. *Dokumentation*, vol. 2. Vienna: Dezernat für Gesundheitsplanung der Stadt Wien.
Pöchhacker, F. (2008). Interpreting as mediation. In C. Valero-Garcés and A. Martin (eds), *Crossing Borders in Community Interpreting: Definitions and Dilemmas* (pp. 9–27). Amsterdam: John Benjamins Publishing Company.
Pöchhacker, F. and Kadrić, M. (1999). The hospital cleaner as healthcare interpreter: a case study. *The Translator*. Special Issue. *Dialogue Interpreting*, 5(2), 161–178.
Riaz, W.K. (2004). Bestikker tolken – jukser seg til førerprøve, [Bribe the interpreter – cheat their way to the driver's licence]. *Aftenposten*, 23 April.2004. Available at: www.aftenposten.no/nyheter/oslo/article779781.ece
Roy, C. (2002 [1993]). The problem with definitions, descriptions, and the role metaphors of interpreters. In F. Pöchhacker and M. Shlesinger (eds), *The Interpreting Studies Reader* (pp. 344–354). London: Routledge.
Rudvin, M. (2009). How neutral is neutral? Issues in interaction and participation in community interpreting. In G. Garzone, P. Mead and M. Viezzi (eds), *Perspectives on Interpreting: Papers from the First Forlì Conference on Interpreting Studies* (pp. 217–233). Bologna: CLUEB.
Schön, D.A. (1987). *Educating the Reflective Practitioner*. San Francisco, CA: Jossey-Bass.
Scollon, R. and Scollon, S.W. (2001). *Intercultural Communication*. Malden, MA: Blackwell Publishing.
Skaaden, H. (1999). Lexical knowledge and interpreter aptitude. *International Journal of Applied Linguistics*, 9(1), 77–99.
Skaaden, H. (2013). *Den topartiske tolken. Lærebok i tolking* [The interpreter's double allegiance: textbook in interpreting]. Oslo: Universitetsforlaget.
Skaaden, H. (2016). Professionalization and trust in public sector interpreting. In E. Dogoriti and T. Vyzas (eds), *Community Interpreting at Greek and International Level: A Step Towards Professional Autonomy*. Special issue of *International Journal of Language, Translation and Intercultural Communication*, 5, 56–66.
Skaaden, H. (2017). "That we all behave like professionals". An experiential–dialogic approach to interpreter education and online learning. In L. Cirillo and N. Niemants (eds), *Teaching Dialogue Interpreting: Research-Based Proposals for Higher Education* (pp. 323–340). Amsterdam: John Benjamins Publishing Company,
Skaaden, H. (2018a). Invisible or invincible? Professional integrity, ethics, and voice in public service interpreting. *Perspectives: Studies in Translation Theory and Practice*. https://doi.org/10.1080/0907676X.2018.1536725
Skaaden, H. (2018b). Profesjonsetikk, skjønn og tillit i tolking. [Professional ethics, discretion and trust]. In H. Haualand, A.L. Nilsson and E. Raanes (eds), *Tolking. Språkarbeid og profesjonsutøvelse* (pp. 279–301). Oslo: Gyldendal.
Skaaden, H. (2018c). Remote interpreting: potential solutions to communication needs in the refugee crisis and beyond. In *The European Legacy. Towards New Paradigms*. 08/2018. Available at: https://doi.org/10.1080/10848770.2018.1499474
Skaaden, H. and Felberg, T.R. (2012). Introduction. In *Nordic Seminar on Interpreter Training and Testing* (vol. 12/2012, pp. 1–7). Oslo: Høgskolen i Oslo og Akershus.
Skaaden, H. and Wadensjö, C. (2014). Some considerations on the testing of interpreting skills. In C. Giambruno (ed.), *Assessing Legal Interpreter Quality through Testing and Certification: The Qualitas Project* (pp. 17–27). Alicante: Publicaciones Universidad de Alicante.

Skaaden, H. and Wattne, M. (2009). Teaching interpreting in cyber space: the answer to all our prayers? In R. de Pedro Ricoy, I. Perez, and C. Wilson (eds), *Interpreting and Translating in Public Service Settings: Policy, Practice, Pedagogy* (pp. 74–88). Manchester: St. Jerome Publishing.

Slagstad, R. (2008). Profesjoner og kunnskapsregimer. [Profession and knowledge regimes] In A. Molander and L.I. Terum (eds), *Profesjonsstudier* (pp. 54–71). Oslo: Universitetsforlaget.

Smeby, J.C. (2008). Profesjon og utdanning. [Profession and education]. In A. Molander and L.I. Terum (eds.), *Profesjonsstudier* (pp. 87–103). Oslo: Universitetsforlaget.

Tipton, R. and Furmanek, O. (2016). *Dialogue Interpreting: A Guide to Interpreting in Public Services and the Community.* London: Routledge.

Toma, E. (2018). The principle of equality of arms – part of the right to a fair trial. *Law Review International Journal of Law and Jurisprudence Online Semiannually Publication.* vol. VIII, Issue 1. e-ISSN 2246-9435.

Toury, G. (1995). *Descriptive Translation Studies – And Beyond.* Amsterdam: John Benjamins Publishing Company.

Venuti, L. (2000). Translation, community, utopia. In L. Venuti (ed.), *The Translation Studies Reader* (pp. 482–502). New York: Routledge.

VG (2002). Kantinemedarbeider måtte tolke [Cafeteria coworker had to do courtroom interpreting]. Available at: ww.vg.no/nyheter/innenriks/trippeldrapet-paa-orderud-gaard/kantinemedarbeider-maatte-tolke/a/5039634/ (accessed 28 July 2016).

Vogler, R. (2014). The principle of immediacy in English criminal procedural law. *Zeitschrift für die gesamte Strafrechtswissenschaft*, 126(1), 239–247. DOI: https://doi.org/10.1515/zstw-2014-0013.

Wadensjö, C. (1992). *Interpreting as Interaction: On Dialogue-Interpreting in Immigration Hearings and Medical Encounters*, vol. 83. Linköping: Linköping University.

Wadensjö, C. (1998a). *Interpreting as Interaction.* London: Longman.

Wadensjö, C. (1998b). *Kontakt genom tolk* [Contact via interpreter]. Stockholm: Dialogos.

Wadensjö, C. (2004). Dialogue interpreting: a monologising practice in a dialogically organized world. *Target: International Journal of Translations Studies*, 16(1), 105–124.

Wadensjö, C. (2009). Telephone interpreting and the synchronization of talk in social interaction. In M. Baker (ed.), *Critical Concepts in Linguistics: Translation Studies* (pp. 301–318). London: Routledge.

Wallace, M. (2013). Rethinking bifurcated testing models in the court interpreter certification process. In D. Tsagari and R. Van Deemter (eds), *Assessment Issues in Language Translation and Interpreting* (pp. 67–85). Frankfurt: Peter Lang.

Wallace, M. (2015). A further call to action: training as a policy issue in court interpreting. In *The Interpreter and Translator Trainer* (pp. 1–15). London: Routledge.

Warren, M.E. (1999). *Democracy and Trust.* Cambridge: Cambridge University Press.

Wikan, U. (2002). *Generous Betrayal: Politics of Culture in the New Europe.* Chicago: University of Chicago Press.

Woloshin, S., Bickell, N.A., Schwartz, L.M., Gany, F. and Welch, G. (1995). Language barriers in medicine in the United States. *Journal of the American Medical Association*, 273, 724–728.

INDEX

Note: Page number followed by 't' indicate tables, by 'f' indicate figures and by 'b' indicate boxes.

accuracy (ethical principle of interpreting) 28, 30, 32, 33; 50, 52, 59, 60, 67, 68, 69b, 72, 73, 75–77 accuracy vs. impartiality/loyalty 59f; accuracy–impartiality/loyalty dilemma 147, 155, 161–162; achieving 76–77n18; code(s) of ethics 93–96, 94t–95t, 97; contractual nature of 68; defining parameter of interpreting 32–33; equivalence and accuracy in translations 60–61; personal ethics as potential obstacle 67; professionally binding character 28; relation to moral philosophy 69b; and relation to virtue/'the Good' in Moral Philosophy 33; in unitarian approach to interpreting 50; relation to societal function 154; *see also* ethics of interpretation
advocacy 111–115, 130–131, 162–164; in code(s) of ethics 111–115; and intercultural mediation 121, 158, 164; in medical interpreting 116–118, 180; Postville raids/Camayad-Freixas case 133–137
Agar, Michael 156
agency, and ethical challenges 25; 162–164
Angelelli, Claudia 110, 115, 116, 132–133, 162, 164
approaches in professional interpretation; *see under own headings:* directly interpreting approach; interactional approach / Wadensjö model; mediating approach

Aquinas, Thomas 41
Arendt, Hannah 17, 20, 32, 43b, 46
Aristotle 39, 43b, 63, 72, 149
associations of translators and interpreters 88–90, 88t–89t; *see also* code(s) of ethics: association codes

Bancroft, Marjory, 90
Betham, Jeremy 9, 10, 15, 43b, 49

Camayd-Freixas, Erik 59, 72, 78, 80, 133–137
Chesterman, Andrew 60, 61, 63–65, 76, 79n46, 149, 179
client 24, 54, 57, 64, 68, 79, 156; and interpreter's double allegiance 157–160
code(s) of ethics 24, 25, 35, 35(b), 49, 51, 52, 54, 56, 64, 65, 71, 73–75, 76, 78; advocacy in 111–115; associations 87–88, 90–93, 91t; company codes for interpreters 119–120; criticism of 108–111; historical examples 85–86; Norwegian example 120–121; principles (core): and coverage in association codes 93–98, 94t–95t; principles (core): role, competence, impartiality, accuracy/completeness, conflict of interest, confidentiality, CPD 93; principles (further): and coverage in association codes 99–105, 99t–100t;